EXPERT RESUMES FOR

SECOND EDITION

CAREER CHANGERS

Wendy S. Enelow and
Louise M. Kursmark

JIST Works
America's Career Publisher

Expert Resumes for Career Changers, Second Edition

© 2010 by Wendy S. Enelow and Louise M. Kursmark

Published by JIST Works, an imprint of JIST Publishing
7321 Shadeland Station, Suite 200
Indianapolis, IN 46256-3923
Phone: 800-648-JIST   Fax: 877-454-7839   E-mail: info@jist.com

Visit our Web site at **www.jist.com** for information on JIST, tables of contents,
sample pages, and how to order our many products!

Quantity discounts are available for JIST books. Please call our Sales Department at
800-648-5478 for a free catalog and more information.

Trade Product Manager: Lori Cates Hand
Cover Designer: Amy Adams
Interior Designer: Trudy Coler
Page Layout: Toi Davis
Proofreader: Jeanne Clark
Indexer: Kelly D. Henthorne

Printed in the United States of America
14 13 12 11 10   9 8 7 6 5 4 3 2

Library of Congress Cataloging-in-Publication Data

Enelow, Wendy S.
  Expert resumes for career changers / Wendy S. Enelow and Louise M.
  Kursmark. – 2nd ed.
      p. cm.
  Includes index.
  ISBN 978-1-59357-781-0 (alk. paper)
  1. Résumés (Employment) 2. Career changes. I. Kursmark, Louise. II. Title.
  HF5383.E47875 2010
  650.14′2–dc22
                              2010001539

ISBN 978-1-59357-781-0

TABLE OF CONTENTS

ABOUT THIS BOOK

If you're reading this book, you're most likely one of tens of thousands of people who are considering a career change—either a change in position or a change in industry. You might have made this decision because of any one of the following reasons:

- Your current industry has been hard hit by the recent economic recession.

- The position that you currently hold has been eliminated in your company and also in many similar companies.

- You're bored in your current position and ready for a change.

- You want to pursue your true passion as your new career.

- Your personal situation has changed and you're now able to pursue a career of real interest to you.

- You're relocating and need to explore new opportunities in your new geographic area.

- You want greater opportunities for increased compensation and advancement.

- You're frustrated and ready for a change.

- You're tired of all the responsibilities of your career and ready to downsize.

These are just a few of the reasons you might be considering a career change. There are many other reasons, and you'll find resumes in this book that are relevant to them all.

Now, here's the good news: You've selected a great time to make a career change! Despite the economic concerns that we have faced, believe it or not, it's a great time to look for a new job or a new career. According to the Bureau of Labor Statistics of the U.S. Department of Labor, the employment outlook is optimistic. Consider these findings for 2006 through 2016:

- Total U.S. employment is projected to increase 10.4 percent.

- Service-producing industries and professional occupations will be the dominant employment generators, each with a gain of 16.7 percent.

- Management, business, and financial occupations are the second-fastest-growing occupational group, with growth projected at 10.4 percent.

In chapter 1, you can read more interesting statistics, all of which will reinforce the fact that you've made the right decision to launch your search campaign today.

To take advantage of all of these opportunities, you must first develop a powerful, performance-based resume. To be a successful job seeker, you must know how to communicate your qualifications in a strong and effective written presentation. Sure, it's important to let employers know essential details, but a resume is more than just your job history and academic credentials. A winning resume is a concise yet comprehensive document that gives you a competitive edge in the job market. Creating such a powerful document is what this book is all about.

We'll explore the changes in resume presentation that have arisen over the past decade. In the past, resumes were almost always printed on paper and mailed. Today, e-mail has become the chosen method for resume distribution in almost every industry and profession. In turn, many of the traditional methods for "typing" and presenting resumes have changed dramatically. This book will instruct you in the methods for preparing resumes for e-mail, scanning, and Web site posting, as well as the traditional printed resume.

By using *Expert Resumes for Career Changers* as your professional guide, you will succeed in developing a powerful and effective resume that opens doors, gets interviews, and helps you land your next great opportunity!

INTRODUCTION

This was one of the most challenging books in the *Expert Resumes* series to write because it covers such a large and diverse audience. There are, however, several common denominators facing every individual who is interested in making a career change, either within their profession or to another industry. In summary, the fact that you are seeking to change careers will dictate almost everything that you write in your resume, how you write it, and where it is positioned. Your goal is to paint a picture of the "new" you and not simply reiterate what you have done in the past, expecting a prospective employer to figure out that you can do the "new" thing just as well. It simply does not work that way!

If you fall into the career-changer category, the critical questions you must ask yourself about your resume and your job search are the following:

- *How* **are you going to paint a picture of the "new" you?** What are you going to highlight about your past experience that ties directly to your current objectives? What accomplishments, skills, and qualifications are you going to "sell" in your resume to support your current career objective?

- *What* **resume format are you going to use?** Is a chronological, functional, or hybrid resume format going to work best for you? Which format will give you the greatest flexibility to highlight the skills you want to bring to the forefront in support of your career change?

- *Where* **are you going to look for a job?** Assuming you know the type of position and industry you want to enter at this point in your career, how are you going to identify and approach those companies?

When you can answer the how, what, and where, you'll be prepared to write your resume and launch your search campaign. Use chapters 1 through 3 to guide you in developing the content for your resume and selecting the appropriate design and layout. Your resume should focus on your skills, achievements, and qualifications, demonstrating the value and benefit you bring to a prospective employer as they relate to your current career goals. The focus is on the "new" you and not necessarily what you have done professionally in the past.

Review the sample resumes in chapters 4 through 12 to see what other people have done—people in similar situations to yours and facing similar challenges. You'll find interesting formats, unique skills presentations, achievement-focused resumes, project-focused resumes, and much more. Most importantly, you'll see samples written by the top resume writers in the U.S., Canada, and Australia. These are real resumes that got interviews and generated job offers. They're the "best of the best" from us to you.

Finally, in chapters 13 and 14 we present a concise yet thorough discussion of cover letters and a sampling of professionally written cover letters that were created specifically for people changing careers. They'll help you create your own winning cover letter for every opportunity you pursue.

What Are Your Career Objectives?

Before you proceed any further with writing your resume, you'll need to begin by defining your career or job objectives—specifically, the types of positions, companies, and industries in which you are interested. This is critical, because a haphazard, unfocused job search will lead you nowhere.

KNOW THE EMPLOYMENT TRENDS

One of the best ways to begin identifying your career objectives is to look at what opportunities are available today, in the immediate future, and in the longer-term future. Two of the most useful tools for this type of research and information collection are the U.S. Department of Labor's Bureau of Labor Statistics Web site (www.bls.gov) and the Bureau's *Occupational Outlook Handbook* (www.bls.gov/oco).

Some of the most interesting findings that you'll discover when investigating potential industry and job targets are these:

- Service-producing industries and professional occupations will continue to be the dominant employment generators, each with a gain of 16.7 percent.

- Management, business, and financial occupations represent the second-fastest-growing occupational group with 10.4 percent projected growth.

- The 10 industries with the largest wage and salary employment growth are

    1. Management, scientific, and technical consulting

    2. Employment services

    3. General medical and surgical hospitals

    4. Elementary and secondary schools

    5. Local government (excluding education and hospitals)

    6. Physician offices

    7. Limited-service eating establishments

    8. Colleges, universities, and professional schools

    9. Computer systems design

    10. Home health care services

- The top 10 occupations with the largest projected employment growth are

    1. Network systems and data communications analysts

    2. Personal and home care aides

3. Home health aides

4. Computer software engineers (applications)

5. Medical assistants

6. Computer systems analysts

7. Food preparation and service workers

8. Registered nurses

9. Postsecondary teachers

10. Management analysts

- Of all goods-producing industries, the only one projected to grow is the construction industry with a 1 percent gain.

- Transportation and material-moving occupations are projected to grow 10.4 percent.

- Office and administrative-support occupations are projected to grow more slowly than average, reflecting the need for fewer personnel as a result of the tremendous gains in office automation and technology.

- Production-related occupations are also projected to grow more slowly as manufacturing automation and technology reduce the need for specific types of employees.

These facts and statistics clearly demonstrate that there are numerous employment opportunities across diverse sectors within our economy, from advanced technology positions to hourly wage jobs in construction and home health care. Although most industries might not be growing at double-digit percentages as in years past, companies continue to expand and new companies emerge every day. The opportunities are out there; your challenge is to find them and position yourself as the "right" candidate.

MANAGE YOUR JOB SEARCH AND YOUR CAREER

To take advantage of these opportunities, you must be an educated job seeker. That means you must know what you want in your career, where the hiring action is, what qualifications and credentials you need to attain your desired career goals, and how best to market your qualifications. It is no longer enough to have a specific talent or set of skills. Whether you're a teacher seeking a position in public relations, a nurse wanting to transfer into pharmaceutical sales, an engineer seeking new opportunities as a financial manager, or a person with any one of hundreds of other career-change goals, you must also be a strategic marketer, able to package and promote your experience to take advantage of this wave of employment opportunity.

There's no doubt that the employment market has changed dramatically from only a few years ago. According to the U.S. Department of Labor, you should expect to hold between 10 and 20 different jobs during your career. No longer is stability the status quo. Today, the norm is movement, onward and upward, in a fast-paced and intense employment market where there are many, many opportunities for career changers. And to take advantage of all of the opportunities, every job seeker—no matter the profession, no matter the industry, no matter the job goal—must proactively control and manage his career.

You are also faced with the additional challenge of positioning yourself for a successful career change. In fact, in many instances, you may be competing against other candidates who have experience within the industry or profession you are attempting to enter. This can make your job search even more difficult than that of the more "traditional" job seeker who moves from one position to another similar position without having to make a career change.

And that is precisely why this book is so important to you. We'll outline the strategies and techniques that you can use to effectively position yourself against other candidates, creating a resume that highlights your skills and qualifications while effectively minimizing the fact that you're seeking a career change.

Job Search Questions and Answers

Before we get to the core of this book—resume writing and design—we'd like to offer some practical job search advice that is valuable to virtually every career changer.

WHAT IS THE MOST IMPORTANT CONSIDERATION FOR A CAREER CHANGER?

As outlined previously, the single most important consideration for any career-change candidate is how you're going to highlight your skills, qualifications, and achievements as they relate to and support your current career objectives. Remember, your career-change resume is not a historical document that simply lists where you've worked and what you've done. Rather, a truly effective career-change resume is one that takes all of the skills and experience you have that are relevant to your new career goal and brings them to the forefront to create a picture of the "new" you.

Sometimes, this can be a relatively easy process. Let's use a nurse transitioning into the field of medical equipment sales as an example. Sheila Barnes already has extensive experience in the medical and health-care fields, has worked closely with physicians and other health-care providers and is comfortable interacting with them, and most likely has a wealth of experience working with a diversity of medical equipment and perhaps with vendors. This is the type of information that will be highlighted in her career-change resume—*not* her daily nursing and patient-care responsibilities.

In other situations, the parallels between past experience and current objectives might not be so closely aligned. Consider John Mackam who, after 20 years in the construction industry, has now decided to seek a position in the field of accounting and finance, an area that has *not* been one of his primary responsibilities. Writing this resume will take more creativity to identify any and all relevant skills he might have (for example, setting project budgets, estimating project costs, writing reports, keeping records, and administering projects). The concept is the same as with the previous nursing example. The stretch to identify transferable skills might be more difficult, but it's certainly not impossible.

Whatever your situation or objectives, when preparing your resume you should keep in mind one critical fact:

Your resume is a marketing tool written to sell YOU!

How Do You Enter a New Career?

Your success in entering a new career field relies on two important factors:

- Highlighting any relevant skills, qualifications, accomplishments, experiences, education, credentials, volunteer work, involvement with professional or civic associations, and more that tie directly into your current career objective.

- Using an integrated job search campaign that will get you in front of decision makers at a wide array of companies in your field of interest. You can read much more about job search strategy in the next few pages of this introduction in the section titled "How Do You Get the Jobs?"

What Is the Best Resume Strategy for Making a Successful Career Change?

The single most important factor in making a career change is to remember that your resume must *sell* what you have to offer:

- If you're a teacher seeking to transition into a position in corporate training and development, *sell* the fact that you created new curricula, designed new instructional programs, acquired innovative teaching materials, and trained new faculty.

- If you're a hands-on computer technician now seeking a position marketing new technology products, *highlight* the wealth of your technical expertise, your success in working with and supporting end-users, your ability to manage projects, and your strong communication skills.

- If you're an accountant pursuing opportunities in general management, *sell* your experience in policy and procedure development, business management, team building and leadership, strategic planning, and organizational development.

When writing your resume, your challenge is to create a picture of knowledge, action, and results. In essence, you're stating "This is what I know, this is how I've used it, and this is how well I've performed." Success sells, so be sure to highlight yours. If you don't, no one else will.

Where Are the Jobs?

The jobs are everywhere—from multinational manufacturing conglomerates to the small retail sales companies in your neighborhood; from high-tech electronics firms in Silicon Valley to 100-year-old farming operations in rural communities; from banks and financial institutions to hospitals and health-care facilities in every city and town. The jobs are everywhere.

How Do You Get the Jobs?

To answer this question, we need to review the basic principle underlying job search:

> Job search is marketing!

You have a product to sell—yourself—and the best way to sell it is to use all appropriate *marketing channels* just as you would for any other product.

Suppose you wanted to sell televisions. What would you do? You'd market your products using newspaper, magazine, and radio advertisements. You might develop a company Web site to build your e-business, and perhaps you'd hire a field sales representative to market to major retail chains. Each of these is a different *marketing channel* through which you're attempting to reach your audience.

The same approach applies to job search. You must use every marketing channel that's right for you. Unfortunately, there is no exact formula that works for everyone. What's right for you depends on your specific career objectives—the type of position you want, the industry you're targeting, your geographic restrictions (if you have any), your salary requirements, and more.

Following are the most valuable marketing channels for a successful job search. These are ordered from most effective to least effective.

1. **Referrals.** There is nothing better than a personal referral to a company, either in general or for a specific position. Referrals can open doors that, in most instances, would never be accessible any other way. If you know anyone who could possibly refer you to a specific organization, contact that person immediately and ask for his or her assistance. This is particularly critical for career changers and will be, by far, your single best marketing strategy to land a new position.

2. **Networking.** Networking is the backbone of every successful job search. Although you might consider it an unpleasant or difficult task, it is essential that you network effectively with your professional colleagues and associates, past employers, past co-workers, suppliers, neighbors, friends, and others who might know of opportunities that are right for you. Another good strategy is to attend meetings of trade or professional associations in your area that are for professions in occupations like those you're seeking to enter. This is a wonderful strategy to make new contacts and start building your network in your new career field. And particularly in today's nomadic job market—where you're likely to change jobs every few years—the best strategy is to keep your network "alive" even when you're *not* searching for a new position.

3. **Responding to newspaper, magazine, and periodical advertisements.** Although the opportunity to post job opportunities online has reduced the overall number of print advertisements, they still abound. Do not forget about this "tried-and-true" marketing strategy. If they've got the job and you have the qualifications—even if you are a career changer, it can be a perfect fit.

4. **Responding to online job postings.** One of the most advantageous results of the technology revolution is an employer's ability to post job announcements online and a job seeker's ability to respond immediately via e-mail. In most (but not all) instances, these are bona fide opportunities, and it's well worth

your while to spend time searching for and responding to appropriate postings. However, don't make the mistake of devoting *too* much time to searching the Internet. It can consume a huge amount of your time that you should spend on other job-search efforts.

To expedite your search, here are the largest and most widely used online job-posting sites—presented alphabetically, not necessarily in order of effectiveness or value:

http://careers.msn.com	www.flipdog.com
http://hotjobs.yahoo.com	www.hirediversity.com
www.americanjobs.com	www.monster.com
www.careerbuilder.com	www.net-temps.com
www.employmentguide.com	www.netshare.com
www.execunet.com	www.theladders.com
www.dice.com	

5. **Posting your resume online.** The Net is swarming with reasonably priced (if not free) Web sites where you can post your resume. It's quick, easy, and the only *passive* thing you can do in your search. All of the other marketing channels require action on your part. With online resume postings, once you've posted, you're done. You then just wait (and hope!) for some response. Again, it's important not to invest too much time, energy, or anticipation in this approach. Your chances of landing a job this way are slim. But because it is quick, easy, and low- or no-cost, it is certainly a worthwhile activity.

6. **Targeted e-mail campaigns (resumes and cover letters) to recruiters.** Recruiters have jobs, and you want one. It's pretty straightforward. The only catch is to find the "right" recruiters who have the "right" jobs. Therefore, you must devote the time and effort to preparing the "right" list of recruiters. There are many resources on the Internet where you can access information about recruiters (for a fee), sort that information by industry (such as banking, sales, manufacturing, purchasing, transportation, finance, public relations, or telecommunications), and then cross-reference it with position specialization (such as management, technical, or administration). This allows you to identify the recruiters who would be interested in a candidate with your qualifications. Because these campaigns are transmitted electronically, they are easy and inexpensive to produce. Here are some sites to help with this activity:

www.profileresearch.com

www.kennedyinfo.com

When working with recruiters, it's important to realize that they *do not* work for you! Their clients are the hiring companies that pay their fees. They are not in business to "find a job" for you, but rather to fill a specific position with a qualified candidate, either you or someone else. To maximize your chances of finding a position through a recruiter or agency, don't rely on just one or two, but distribute your resume to many that meet your specific criteria.

A word of caution: Most recruiters are looking to fill specific positions with individuals with very specific qualifications. As a career changer, you are likely to find that recruiters are not your best source of job opportunities because they are not paid to "think outside the box." If their client (the hiring company) has requested a candidate with experience in x, y, and z, recruiters are going to present only those job seekers with precisely that experience. Knowing that you're attempting to change careers and might not have precisely the background that the company is looking for, recruiters might simply pass you by. Don't be alarmed; it's their job! But what this means for you as a career changer is that you should invest minimal effort toward recruiter searches and certainly shouldn't think that it will be "the" approach for you. Quite likely, it will not.

7. **Targeted e-mail and print resume-mailing campaigns to employers.** Just as with campaigns to recruiters (see item 6), you must be extremely careful to select just the right employers that would be interested in a candidate with your qualifications. The closer you stick to "where you belong" in relation to your specific experience, the better your response rate will be. Just as with recruiters, human resources professionals and hiring managers might have difficulty appreciating the unique set of skills and qualifications career changers bring to a position.

If you are targeting companies in a technology industry, we recommend that you use e-mail as your preferred method for resume submission. However, if the companies you are contacting are not in the technology industry, we believe that print campaigns (paper and envelopes mailed the old-fashioned way) are a more suitable and effective presentation—particularly if you are a management or executive candidate.

8. **In-person "cold calls" to companies and recruiters.** We consider this the least effective and most time-consuming marketing strategy. It is extremely difficult to just walk in the door and get in front of the right person—or any person who can take hiring action. You'll be much better off focusing your time and energy on other, more productive channels.

Conclusion

Career opportunities abound today, even for the career changer. It has never been easier to learn about and apply for jobs than it is now with all the Internet resources available to us. Your challenge is to arm yourself with a powerful resume and cover letter, identify the best ways to get yourself and your resume into the market, and shine during every interview. If you're committed and focused, we can almost guarantee that you'll make a smooth transition into your new career field and find yourself happily employed.

PART I

Resume Writing, Strategy, and Formats

CHAPTER 1

Resume-Writing Strategies for Career Changers

If you're reading this book, chances are you have decided to change your career direction; enter a new industry; or pursue a new, more fulfilling profession. Regardless of the underlying reasons for your career change, you are faced with some unique challenges in your job search and, more specifically, in how you write your resume. What can you do to capture employers' attention, impress them with your qualifications and achievements, and not be put "out of the running" because you do not have experience in a particular industry or profession?

Before we answer those questions and many others, let's talk about who this book was written for—people representing just about every profession and industry imaginable. The *only* thing that our readers have in common is that each one has decided to make a career change for any one of a host of personal or professional reasons. Consider this book an excellent resource for tips, strategies, and techniques on resume writing if you are making a career change because of any of the following reasons:

- Your original industry or profession has been extremely hard hit by economic recession or fundamental changes in our global economy and opportunities have virtually dried up.

- You have always wanted to pursue a different career track but were unable to do so because of family, financial, or other personal obligations.

- You fell into a position right out of college and pursued that career for years, and then woke up one day and realized it was time to do what you wanted to do and not what you were "supposed" to do.

- You are now in a position to pursue the lifelong dream or hobby that has been burning inside of you since your early days.

- You are relocating to a new area where opportunities for individuals with your experience are quite limited and you need to open yourself to new opportunities and career challenges.

- You have decided you want to pursue a career that will offer greater opportunities for career progression.

- You are driven to make more money, and the best strategy to achieve this goal is to leave your current, low-paying industry or profession.

- Your volunteer work has become increasingly important and you want to pursue professional opportunities with an association, a not-for-profit organization, or a similar entity.

- You are frustrated by the lack of opportunities and the tremendous volatility in the corporate marketplace and have decided to pursue a career with federal, state, or local government where you believe your job will be more stable.

- You retired from your original career and have now decided to return to work in a different, yet more personally rewarding, position.

- You are tired of the tremendous responsibilities associated with your position and want to downsize your career into a less-stressful job.

For every job seeker—those currently employed and those not currently working—a powerful resume is an essential component of the job search campaign. In fact, it is virtually impossible to conduct a search without a resume. It is your calling card that briefly, yet powerfully, communicates the skills, qualifications, experience, and value you bring to a prospective employer. It is the document that will open doors and generate interviews. It is the first thing people will learn about you when you forward it in response to an advertisement, and it is the last thing they'll remember when they're reviewing your qualifications after an interview.

Your resume is a sales document, and you are the product! You must identify the *features (what you know* and *what you can do)* and *benefits (how you can help an employer)* of that product and then communicate them in a concise and hard-hitting written presentation. Remind yourself over and over, as you work your way through the resume process, that you are writing marketing literature designed to sell a new product—YOU—into a new position.

Your resume can have tremendous power and a phenomenal impact on your job search. So don't take it lightly. Rather, devote the time, energy, and resources that are essential to developing a resume that is well written, visually attractive, and effective in communicating *who* you are and *how* you want to be perceived.

The Top Nine Strategies for an Effective Resume

Following are the nine core strategies for writing effective and successful resumes.

RESUME STRATEGY #1: WHO ARE YOU AND HOW DO YOU WANT TO BE PERCEIVED?

Now that you've decided to change your career direction, the very first step is to identify your career interests, goals, and objectives. *This task is critical* because it is the underlying foundation for *what* you include in your resume, *how* you include it, and *where* you include it. Knowing that you want to make a career change is not enough. To write a powerful and effective resume, you must know—to some degree of certainty—the type or types of position you will be seeking.

There are two concepts to consider here:

- **Who you are:** This relates to what you have done professionally and/or academically. Are you a sales representative, contract administrator, training professional, engineer, banker, scientist, technologist, or management executive? What is it that you have done for a living all these years? Who are you?

- **How you want to be perceived:** This is critical and relates to your current career objectives. Consider the following scenario: You're a customer service representative in the telecommunications industry and you've decided to pursue opportunities in personnel training and development, where you believe you will be more personally rewarded. Rather than focus your resume on your customer service career, focus it on the skills you've acquired in that career track that relate to a position in training and development. Specifically, you'll want to include information about employee training programs that you've helped to create and deliver, one-on-one training that you've provided, consultations with management about internal training needs, any experience you have in developing and designing training materials, any other personnel experience you may have (for example, hiring, orientation, employee development planning), your public-speaking experience, and, of course, your outstanding communication skills.

    Here's another example: You're a successful insurance sales associate, but you've had enough of that career: You're bored, you're unfulfilled, and you're ready for new challenges. You're somewhat uncertain as to your specific career objective at this point, but you do know you want an "inside" job that will use your strong planning, analytical, financial-reporting, and related skills. Rather than focus on your chronological work experience that will put tremendous emphasis on your insurance experience, prepare a resume that highlights all the relevant skills you bring to the position—the skills we outlined previously, along with any relevant achievements. Allow the beginning of your resume to focus on all that you've accomplished and the value you bring to a new employer as you want them to perceive it; then, just briefly list your work history at the end.

The strategy is to connect these two concepts by using the *who you are* information that ties directly to the *how you want to be perceived* message to determine what information to include in your resume. By following this strategy, you're painting a picture that allows a prospective employer to see you as you want to be seen—as an individual with the qualifications for the type of position you are pursuing.

WARNING: If you prepare a resume without first clearly identifying what your objectives are and how you want to be perceived, your resume will have no focus and no direction. Without the underlying knowledge of "This is what I want to be," you do not know what to highlight in your resume. As a result, the document becomes a historical overview of your career and not the sales document you need to facilitate your successful career change.

RESUME STRATEGY #2: SELL IT TO ME...DON'T TELL IT TO ME

We've already established the fact that resume writing is sales. You are the product, and you must create a document that powerfully communicates the value of that product. One particularly effective strategy for accomplishing this is the "Sell It to Me...Don't Tell It to Me" strategy, which impacts virtually every word you write on your resume.

If you "tell it," you are simply stating facts. If you "sell it," you promote it, advertise it, and draw attention to it. Look at the difference in impact between these examples:

> **Tell It Strategy:** Managed start-up of a new 100-employee teleclass center.

> **Sell It Strategy:** Directed team of 12 in the successful start-up, staffing, policy/procedure development, budgeting, and operations design for a new $1.4 million teleclass center.

> **Tell It Strategy:** Coordinated all secretarial, clerical, and administrative functions for large commodities export company.

> **Sell It Strategy:** Implemented a series of process improvements that reduced staffing requirements 20%, increased daily productivity 30%, and reduced billing errors 14% for a large commodities export company. Full responsibility for all secretarial, clerical, and administrative functions.

> **Tell It Strategy:** Set up PCs for newly hired sales and service staff.

> **Sell It Strategy:** Installed more than 100 PCs and implemented customized applications to support nationwide network of sales and service staff for one of the world's largest insurance companies. Provided ongoing troubleshooting and technical support that reduced PC downtime by 38% over a 6-month period.

What's the difference between "telling it" and "selling it"? In a nutshell...

Telling It	Selling It
Describes features.	Describes benefits.
Tells what and how.	Sells why the "what" and "how" are important.
Details activities.	Includes results.
Focuses on what you did.	Details how what you did benefited your employer, department, team members, students, and so on.

RESUME STRATEGY #3: USE KEYWORDS

No matter what you read or who you talk to about searching for jobs, the concept of keywords is sure to come up. Keywords (or, as they were previously known, buzz words) are words and phrases that are specific to a particular industry or profession. For example, keywords for the manufacturing industry include *production-line operations, production planning and scheduling, materials management, inventory control, quality, process engineering, robotics, systems automation, integrated logistics, product specifications, project management,* and many, many more.

When you use these words and phrases—in your resume, in your cover letter, or during an interview—you are communicating a very specific message. For example, when you include the word "merchandising" in your resume, your reader will most likely assume that you have experience in the retail industry—in product selection, vendor/manufacturing relations, in-store product display, inventory management, mark-downs, product promotions, and more. As you can see, people will make inferences about your skills based on the use of just one or two specific words.

Here are a few other examples:

- When you use the words **investment finance,** people will assume you have experience with risk management, mergers, acquisitions, initial public offerings, debt/equity management, asset allocation, portfolio management, and more.

- When you mention **sales,** readers and listeners will infer that you have experience in product presentations, pricing, contract negotiations, customer relationship management, new product introduction, competitive product positioning, and more.

- By referencing **Web technologies** in your resume, you convey that you most likely have experience with Web site design, Web site marketing, metatags, HTML, search-engine registration, e-learning, and more.

- When you use the words **human resources,** most people will assume that you are familiar with recruitment, hiring, placement, compensation, benefits, training and development, employee relations, human resources information systems (HRIS), and more.

Keywords are also an integral component of the resume-scanning process, whereby employers and recruiters electronically search resumes for specific terms to find candidates with the skills, qualifications, and credentials for their particular hiring needs. Over the past several years, keyword scanning has dramatically increased in its popularity because of its ease of use and efficiency in identifying prime candidates. Every job seeker today must stay on top of the latest trends in technology-based hiring and employment to ensure that their resumes and other job-search materials contain the "right" keywords to capture the interest of prospective employers.

In organizations where it has been implemented, electronic scanning has replaced the more traditional method of an actual person reading your resume (at least initially). Therefore, to some degree, the *only* thing that matters in this instance is that you have included the "right" keywords to match the company's or the recruiter's needs. Without them, you will most certainly be passed over.

Of course, in virtually every instance your resume will be read at some point by human eyes, so it's not enough just to throw together a list of keywords and leave it at that. In fact, it's not even necessary to include a separate "keyword summary" on your resume. A better strategy is to incorporate keywords naturally into the text within the appropriate sections of your resume.

For career changers, keywords are particularly relevant and require a good deal of thought, because you do not necessarily want to include keywords that are descriptive of your past experiences. Rather, you want to include keywords that reflect your current career goals so that those words are the ones that will get your resume noticed and not passed over. There are basically two ways to accomplish this:

- **In sections throughout your resume, integrate keywords from your past experiences that directly relate to your current career goals.** Referring back to the example we gave of a customer service representative seeking to transition into a position in personnel training and development, that individual did have experience in personnel training, new employee orientation, training program design, and the like. Those are the keywords that should be highlighted on the resume. Even though these tasks might have been a minor part of the career changer's experience, they are relevant to his current goals and, therefore, should be highlighted on the resume.

- **Include an "Objective" section on your resume that states the type of position that you are seeking and the associated responsibilities.** For example, "Seeking a position in purchasing management where I can utilize my strong skills in research, analysis, negotiations, and product management." This is the recommended strategy if you do *not* have the appropriate experience (keywords) in your background to include in the career summary and experience sections on your resume that will support your current career goals.

Keep in mind, too, that keywords are arbitrary; there is no defined set of keywords for a secretary, production laborer, police officer, teacher, electrical engineer, construction superintendent, finance officer, sales manager, or chief executive officer. Employers searching to fill these positions develop a list of terms that reflect the specifics they desire in a qualified candidate. These might be a combination of professional qualifications, skills, education, length of experience, and other easily defined criteria, along with "soft skills," such as organization, time management, team building, leadership, problem-solving, and communication.

> **NOTE:** Because of the complex and arbitrary nature of keyword selection, we cannot overemphasize how vital it is to be certain that you include in your resume *all* of the keywords that summarize your skills *as they relate to your current career-change objectives.*

How can you be sure that you are including all the keywords, and the *right* keywords? Just by describing your work experience, achievements, educational credentials, technical qualifications, objective, and the like, you might naturally include most of the terms that are important in your new career field. To cross-check what you've written, review online or newspaper job postings for positions that are of interest to you. Look at the precise terms used in the ads and be sure you have included them in your resume (as appropriate to your skills and qualifications).

Another great benefit of today's technology revolution is our ability to find instant information, even information as specific as keywords for hundreds of different industries and professions. Refer to the appendix for a listing of Web sites that list thousands of keywords, complete with descriptions. These are outstanding resources.

RESUME STRATEGY #4: USE THE "BIG" AND SAVE THE "LITTLE"

When deciding what to include in your resume, try to focus on the "big" things—new programs, special projects, cost savings, productivity and efficiency improvements, new products, technology implementations, and more. Give a good, broad-based picture of what you were responsible for and how well you did it. Here's an example:

> Supervised daily sales, customer service, and maintenance-shop operations for a privately owned automotive repair facility. Managed a crew of 12 and an annual operating budget of $300,000 for supplies and materials. Consistently achieved/surpassed all revenue, profit, quality, and production objectives.

Then, save the "little" stuff—the details—for the interview. With this strategy, you will accomplish two things:

- You'll keep your resume readable and of a reasonable length (while still selling your achievements).

- You'll have new and interesting information to share during the interview, instead of merely repeating what is already on your resume.

Using the preceding example, when discussing this experience during an interview you could elaborate on your specific achievements—namely, improving productivity and efficiency ratings, reducing annual operating and material costs, improving employee training, strengthening customer relations, increasing sales volume, and managing facility upgrades.

RESUME STRATEGY #5: MAKE YOUR RESUME "INTERVIEWABLE"

One of your greatest challenges is to make your resume a useful interview tool. Once the employer has determined that you meet the primary qualifications for a position (you've passed the keyword scanning test or initial review) and you are contacted for a telephone or in-person interview, your resume becomes all-important in leading and prompting your interviewer during your conversation.

Your job, then, is to make sure the resume leads the reader where you want to go and presents just the right organization, content, and appearance to stimulate a productive discussion. To improve the "interviewability" of your resume, consider these tactics:

- Make good use of Resume Strategy #4 (Use the "Big" and Save the "Little") to invite further discussion about your experiences.

- Be sure your greatest "selling points" are featured prominently, not buried within the resume.

- Conversely, don't devote lots of space and attention to areas of your background that are irrelevant or about which you feel less than positive; you'll only invite questions about things you really don't want to discuss. This is particularly true for career changers who want their resumes to focus on the skills that will be needed in their new profession and not necessarily on skills they acquired in past positions.

- Make sure your resume is highly readable—this means plenty of white space, an adequate font size, and a logical flow from start to finish.

RESUME STRATEGY #6: ELIMINATE CONFUSION WITH STRUCTURE AND CONTEXT

Keep in mind that your resume will be read *very quickly* by hiring authorities! You might agonize over every word and spend hours working on content and design, but the average reader will skim quickly through your masterpiece and expect to pick up important facts in just a few seconds. Try to make it as easy as possible for readers to grasp the essential facts:

- **Be consistent.** For example, put job titles, company names, and dates in the same place for each position.

- **Make information easy to find** by clearly defining different sections of your resume with large, highly visible headings.

- If relevant to your new career path, **define the context in which you worked** (for example, the organization, your department, and the specific challenges you faced) before you start describing your activities and accomplishments.

RESUME STRATEGY #7: Use Function to Demonstrate Achievement

When you write a resume that focuses only on your job functions, it can be dry and uninteresting, and it will say very little about your unique activities and contributions. Consider the following example:

> Responsible for all aspects of consumer lending at the branch level.

Now, consider using that same function to demonstrate achievement and see what happens to the tone and energy of the sentence. It becomes alive and clearly communicates that you deliver results:

> Processed and approved more than $30 million in secured and unsecured consumer loans for Wachovia's largest branch operation in Memphis, Tennessee. Achieved and maintained a less-than-2% write-off for unrecoverable loans (18% less than the industry average).

Try to translate your functions into achievements and you'll create a more powerful resume presentation.

RESUME STRATEGY #8: Remain in the Realm of Reality

We've already established that resume writing is sales. And, as any good salesperson does, one feels somewhat inclined to stretch the truth, just a bit. However, be forewarned that you must stay within the realm of reality. Do not push your skills and qualifications outside the bounds of what is truthful. You never want to be in a position where you have to defend something that you've written on your resume. If that's the case, you'll lose the job opportunity before you ever get the offer.

RESUME STRATEGY #9: Be Confident

You are unique. There is only one individual with the specific combination of employment experience, qualifications, achievements, education, and special skills that you have. In turn, this positions you as a unique commodity within the competitive job search market. To succeed, you must prepare a resume that is written to sell *you* and highlight *your* qualifications and *your* successes as they relate to your current career-change goals. If you can accomplish this, you will have won the job search game by generating interest, interviews, and offers.

There Are No Resume Writing Rules

One of the greatest challenges in resume writing is that there are no rules to the game. There are certain expectations about information that you will include: principally, your primary skills, employment history, and educational qualifications. Beyond that, what you include is entirely up to you and what you have done in your career. You have tremendous flexibility in determining how to include the information you have selected. In chapter 2, you'll find a wealth of information on each possible category you might include in your resume, the type of information to be placed in each category, preferred formats for presentation, and lots of other information and samples that will help you formulate *your* best resume.

Although there are no rules, there are a few standards to live by as you write your resume. The following sections discuss these standards in detail.

CONTENT STANDARDS

Content is, of course, the text that goes into your resume. Content standards cover the writing style you should use, items you should be sure to include, items you should avoid including, and the order and format in which you list your qualifications.

Writing Style

Always write in the first person, dropping the word "I" from the front of each sentence. This style gives your resume a more aggressive and more professional tone than the passive third-person voice. Here are some examples:

First Person

> Manage 22-person team responsible for design and market commercialization of a new portfolio of PC-based applications for Marley's $100 million consumer-sales division.

Third Person

> Mr. Reynolds manages a 22-person team responsible for the design and market commercialization of a new portfolio of PC-based applications for Marley's $100 million consumer-sales division.

By using the first-person voice, you are assuming "ownership" of that statement. You did such-and-such. When you use the third-person voice, "someone else" did it. Can you see the difference?

Phrases to Stay Away From

Try *not* to use phrases such as "responsible for" and "duties included." These words create a passive tone and style. Instead, use active verbs to describe what you did.

Compare these two ways of conveying the same information:

> Responsible for all marketing and special events for the store, including direct mailing, in-store fashion shows, and new-product introductions and promotions.

OR

Orchestrated a series of marketing and special-event programs for Macy's Reston, one of the company's largest and most profitable operating locations. Managed direct-mail campaigns, in-store fashion shows, and new-product introductions and promotions.

Resume Style

The traditional **chronological** resume lists your work experience in reverse-chronological order (starting with your current or most recent position). The **functional** style deemphasizes the "where" and "when" of your career and instead groups similar experience, talents, and qualifications regardless of when they occurred.

Today, however, most resumes follow neither a strictly chronological nor strictly functional format; rather, they are an effective mixture of the two styles usually known as a "combination" or "hybrid" format.

Like the chronological style, the hybrid includes specifics about where you worked, when you worked there, and what your job titles were. Like a functional resume, a hybrid emphasizes your most relevant qualifications—perhaps within chronological job descriptions, in an expanded summary section, in several "career highlights" bullet points at the top of your resume, or in project summaries. Most of the examples in this book are hybrids and show a wide diversity of organizational formats that you can use as inspiration for designing your own resume.

We strongly recommend hybrid-style resumes for career changers. They allow you to begin your resume with an intense focus on skills, competencies, experience, accomplishments, and more that are directly related to your new career objective. Then, to substantiate a solid work experience, employment history is briefly listed with a focus on specific achievements, responsibilities, and projects that again relate to that individual's current career goals.

Although a functional style might seem the best choice because it allows you to downplay work history that is unrelated to your current goals, most employers dislike the functional style and prefer to see a chronological structure so that they can get a better grasp of where you have been and what you have done. Thus, we recommend that you use the functional style *only* if it is the very best way to present your qualifications. Look through the sample resumes in this book to find effective functional resumes and an even larger number of hybrid/chronological resumes that worked exceptionally well for a diverse range of career changers.

Resume Formats

Resumes, which are principally career summaries and job descriptions, are most often written in a paragraph format, a bulleted format, or a combination of both. Following are three job descriptions, all very similar in content, yet presented in each of the three different writing formats. The advantages and disadvantages of each format are also addressed.

Paragraph Format

> **Business Manager**   2000 to 2010
>
> **Smith Ag Production Company,** Garnerville, Arkansas
>
> Purchased run-down, debt-ridden farming operation and transformed it into a near showplace, honored as one of the best commercial Angus operations in southern Arkansas. Developed a far-reaching network throughout the agricultural industry and with leaders in state government, banking, and commercial lending.
>
> Held full management authority for cattle and alfalfa production generating 2,500+ tons of hay per year and running up to 500 stock cows. Hired, trained, and supervised all employees. Managed budgets of $750,000 annually and more than $2 million in operating lines of credit. Directed the sale/purchase of all commodities to support business operations. Gained an in-depth knowledge of the commercial agricultural industry and its unique financial, economic, and operating challenges.

Advantages

Requires the least amount of space on the page. Brief, succinct, and to the point.

Disadvantages

Achievements get lost in the text of the paragraphs. They are not visually distinctive, nor do they stand alone to draw attention to them.

Bulleted Format

> **Business Manager**   2000 to 2010
>
> **Smith Ag Production Company,** Garnerville, Arkansas
>
> - Purchased run-down, debt-ridden farming operation and transformed it into a near showplace, honored as one of the best commercial Angus operations in southern Arkansas.
>
> - Developed a far-reaching network throughout the agricultural industry and with leaders in state government, banking, and commercial lending.
>
> - Held full management authority for cattle and alfalfa production generating 2,500+ tons of hay per year and running up to 500 stock cows.

- Hired, trained, and supervised all employees.

- Managed budgets of $750,000 annually and more than $2 million in operating lines of credit.

- Directed the sale/purchase of all commodities to support business operations.

- Gained an in-depth knowledge of the commercial agricultural industry and its unique financial, economic, and operating challenges.

Advantages

Quick and easy to peruse.

Disadvantages

Responsibilities and achievements are lumped together, with everything given equal value. In turn, the achievements get lost and are not immediately recognizable.

Combination Format

Business Manager   2000 to 2010

Smith Ag Production Company, Garnerville, Arkansas

Held full management authority for cattle and alfalfa production generating 2,500+ tons of hay per year and running up to 500 stock cows. Hired, trained, and supervised all employees. Managed budgets of $750,000 annually and more than $2 million in operating lines of credit. Directed the sale/purchase of all commodities to support business operations.

- Purchased run-down, debt-ridden farming operation and transformed it into a near showplace, honored as one of the best commercial Angus operations in southern Arkansas.

- Developed a far-reaching network throughout the agricultural industry and with leaders in state government, banking, and commercial lending.

- Gained an in-depth knowledge of the commercial agricultural industry and its unique financial, economic, and operating challenges.

Advantages

Our recommended format. Clearly presents overall responsibilities in the introductory paragraph and then accentuates each achievement as a separate bullet.

Disadvantages

If you don't have clearly identifiable accomplishments, this format is not effective. It also may shine a glaring light on the positions where your accomplishments were less notable. For career changers, past accomplishments might not be relevant to current career objectives, and therefore this format might be less appropriate.

You'll find numerous other examples of how to best present your employment experience in the resume samples that follow in chapters 4 through 12. Chapter 2 discusses formats you can use to highlight your skills and achievements more prominently than your work history. In many career-change situations, this approach is critical to get yourself noticed and not passed over.

E-mail Address and URL

Be sure to include your e-mail address prominently at the top of your resume. As we all know, e-mail has become one of the most preferred methods of communication between employers and job seekers. If you don't yet have an e-mail address, visit www.yahoo.com, www.hotmail.com, or www.gmail.com, where you can get a free e-mail address that you can access through the Web on any computer with an Internet connection.

In addition to your e-mail address, if you have a URL (Web site address) where you have posted your Web resume, be sure to also display that prominently at the top of your resume. For more information on Web resumes, refer to chapter 3.

PRESENTATION STANDARDS

Presentation focuses on the way your resume looks. It relates to the fonts you use, the paper you print it on, any graphics you might include, and how many pages your resume should be.

Typestyle

Use a typestyle (font) that is clean, conservative, and easy to read. Stay away from anything that is too fancy, glitzy, curly, and the like. Here are a few recommended typestyles:

Tahoma	Times New Roman
Arial	Bookman
Krone	Book Antiqua
Soutane	Garamond
CG Omega	Century Schoolbook
Century Gothic	Lucida Sans
Gill Sans	Verdana

Although it is extremely popular, Times New Roman is our least preferred typestyle simply because it is overused. More than 90 percent of the resumes we see are printed in Times New Roman. Your goal is to create a competitive-distinctive document, and, to achieve that, we recommend an alternative typestyle.

Your choice of typestyle should be dictated by the content, format, and length of your resume. Some fonts look better than others at smaller or larger sizes; some have "bolder" boldface type; some require more white space to make them readable. Once you've written your resume, experiment with a few different typestyles to see which one best enhances your document.

Type Size

Readability is everything! If the type size is too small, your resume will be difficult to read and difficult to skim for essential information. Interestingly, a too-large type size, particularly for senior-level professionals, can also give a negative impression by conveying a juvenile or unprofessional image.

As a general rule, select type from 10 to 12 points in size. However, there's no hard-and-fast rule, and a lot depends on the typestyle you choose. Take a look at the following examples:

Very readable in 9-point Verdana:

Won the 2009 "Employee of the Year" award at Chrysler's Indianapolis plant. Honored for innovative contributions to the design and manufacturability of the Zodiac product line.

Difficult to read in too-small 9-point Gill Sans MT:

Won the 2009 "Employee of the Year" award at Chrysler's Indianapolis plant. Honored for innovative contributions to the design and manufacturability of the Zodiac product line.

Concise and readable in 12-point Times New Roman:

Training & Development Consultant specializing in the design, development, and presentation of multimedia training programs for hourly workers, skilled labor, and craftsmen.

A bit overwhelming in too-large 12-point Bookman Old Style:

Training & Development Consultant specializing in the design, development, and presentation of multimedia training programs for hourly workers, skilled labor, and craftsmen.

Type Enhancements

Bold, *italics*, <u>underlining</u>, and CAPITALIZATION are ideal to highlight certain words, phrases, achievements, projects, numbers, and other information to which you want to draw special attention. However, do not overuse these enhancements. If your resume becomes too cluttered with special formatting, nothing stands out.

> **NOTE:** Resumes intended for electronic transmission and computer scanning have specific restrictions on typestyle, type size, and type enhancements. We discuss these details in chapter 3.

Page Length

For most industries and professions, the "one- to two-page rule" for resume writing still holds true. Keep it short and succinct, giving just enough information to pique your readers' interest. However, there are many instances when a resume can be longer than two pages. For example:

- **You have an extensive list of technical qualifications that are relevant to the position for which you are applying.** You might consider including these on a separate page as an addendum to your resume.

- **You have extensive educational training and numerous credentials/certifications, all of which are important to include.** You might consider including these on a separate page as an addendum to your resume.

- **You have an extensive list of special projects, task forces, and committees to include that are important to your current career objectives.** You might consider including these on a separate page as an addendum to your resume.

- **You have an extensive list of professional honors, awards, and commendations.** This list is tremendously valuable in validating your credibility and distinguishing you from the competition, and deleting it from your resume would be a disadvantage. It might be best to let your resume run to three, four, or even five pages to include this information. Just be sure that what you are including is relevant to your new career direction.

If you create a resume that's longer than two pages, make it more reader-friendly by carefully segmenting the information into separate sections. Your sections might include a career summary, work experience, education, professional or industry credentials, honors and awards, technology and equipment skills, publications, public-speaking engagements, professional affiliations, civic affiliations, volunteer experience, foreign-language skills, and other relevant information you want to include. Put each into a separate category so that your resume is easy to peruse and your reader can quickly see the highlights. You'll read more about each of these sections in chapter 2.

Paper Color

Be conservative. White, ivory, and light gray are ideal. Other "flashier" colors are inappropriate for most individuals unless you are in a highly creative industry and your paper choice is part of the overall design and presentation of a creative resume.

Graphics

An attractive, relevant graphic can really enhance your resume. When you look through the sample resumes in chapters 4 through 12, you'll see some excellent examples of the effective use of graphics to enhance the visual presentation of a resume. Just be sure not to get carried away; be tasteful and relatively conservative.

Color

Because many resumes are viewed onscreen and can easily be printed on color printers, the use of color has crept into resume design. We think this is a wonderful idea, provided that you use color tastefully and it does not interfere with the readability of your resume. Be particularly careful about using color for any text in your resume—it might not print as clearly as black type—and make sure that your resume is equally readable whether printed on a color printer or a black-and-white/grayscale printer. Our preferred style is to use color for borders, shadings, and graphic accents and to keep text in solid black.

White Space

We'll say it again—readability is everything! If people have to struggle to read your resume, they simply won't make the effort. Therefore, be sure to leave plenty of white space. It really does make a difference.

ACCURACY AND PERFECTION

The very final step, and one of the most critical in resume writing, is the proofreading stage. It is essential that your resume be well written; visually pleasing; and free of any errors, typographical mistakes, misspellings, and the like. We recommend that you carefully proofread your resume a minimum of three times, and then have two or three other people also proofread it. Consider your resume an example of the quality of work you will produce on a company's behalf. Is your work product going to have errors and inconsistencies? If your resume does, it communicates to a prospective employer that you are careless, and this is the "kiss of death" in job search.

Take the time to make sure that your resume is perfect in all the little details that do, in fact, make a big difference to those who read it.

CHAPTER 2

Writing Your Resume

For many job seekers, resume writing is *not* at the top of the list of fun and exciting activities! How can it compare to landing a new account, cutting costs, introducing new technology, streamlining operations, or starting a new production plant? In your perception, we're sure that it cannot.

However, resume writing can be an enjoyable and rewarding task. When your resume is complete, you can look at it proudly, reminding yourself of all that you have achieved. It is a snapshot of your career and your success. When it's complete, we guarantee you'll look back with tremendous self-satisfaction as you launch and successfully manage your job search.

As the very first step in finding a new position or advancing your career, resume writing can be the most daunting of all tasks in your job search. If writing is not one of your primary skills or a past job function, it might have been years since you've actually sat down and written anything other than e-mail or notes to yourself. Even for those of you who write on a regular basis, resume writing is unique. It has its own style and a number of peculiarities, as with any specialty document.

Recommended Resume-Writing Strategy and Formats for Career Changers

Writing career-change resumes is a unique challenge, and many of the strategies and formats that the more "typical" job seeker uses are generally not applicable for career changers. Standard formats most often put an emphasis on past work experience, along with the responsibilities and achievements of each of those positions. If you're a career changer, most likely your goal is to downplay your specific work experience and job titles on your resume while highlighting your skills and core competencies as they relate to your current objectives.

CAREER-CHANGER STRATEGIES

In chapter 1 we provided an overview of strategies; here we get down to the nuts and bolts of deciding what to include in your resume (the strategies) and how to organize and present it (the format). As with every good resume, it's important to start out with a clear understanding of your ultimate target so that your resume is a clear and sharply focused presentation of qualifications for that target.

Know Your Career Goal

Before you even begin to start writing your career-change resume, you must know the specific type(s) of position(s) you are going after. This will give your resume a "theme" around which you can build the entire document. Your "theme" (or objective) should dictate everything that you include in your resume, how you include it, and where. Writing a career-change resume is all about creating a picture of how you want to be perceived by a prospective employer—a picture that closely mirrors the types of people who are hired in that career field.

From researching the type of career you want to pursue, you will have collected a great deal of information about the duties and responsibilities for positions in that field. You should then carefully review your past employment experience, educational background, volunteer work, professional affiliations, civic affiliations, and more to identify skills you've acquired that are transferable to your new career. These, then, are the items that become the foundation of your resume.

> **WARNING:** If you don't know what your objective is—you only know that you want to change careers—we strongly urge that you spend some time investigating potential career tracks to determine your overall areas of interest. Without this knowledge, you cannot focus your resume in any one particular direction and, as a result, it simply becomes a recitation of your past work experience. To effectively position you for new career opportunities, your resume must have a theme and a focus. If you're having difficulty determining your objective, you might want to consider hiring a career coach who can help you critically evaluate your skills and qualifications, match them to potential career opportunities, explore new professions, and guide you in setting your direction.

Identify Your Transferable Skills

Transferable skills are the foundation for every successful career-change resume. If you're not sure how to identify your transferable skills, here's an easy way to do just that. First, review advertisements for positions that are of interest. You can get this information from newspapers, professional journals, and hundreds of online resources. You can also talk to and network with people who are already working in your new career field and ask them about their specific responsibilities, the challenges they face, the opportunities that are available, how to get into the field, and so much more.

Once you've collected this information, make a detailed list of the specific requirements for these jobs (for example, budgeting, staff training, staff supervision, project management, statistical analysis, and customer relationship management). Be as comprehensive as possible, even if the list goes on and on for pages. Then, go through the list and highlight each of the skills in which you have some experience from your work, education, or outside activities. Finally, take some time to think of specific examples of how you've used those skills. Used in your resume, these "success stories" will be powerful proof that you already possess the very skills and competencies you want to use in your new job.

> **NOTE:** There is no need to describe these skills as "transferable" in your resume, cover letter, or conversations during your job search. Why highlight the fact that your skills are not directly related to the field you want to pursue? Quite simply, these are skills you possess, experience you own, and activities you have accomplished. They are the foundation of your performance in past experiences and in your new role.

It is important to remember that your *entire* background counts—everything that you've ever done—from your 10-year sales career to your 6-year volunteer position coordinating your local Special Olympics. Just think of the great skills you acquired in event planning, logistics, volunteer training, fund raising, media affairs, and contract negotiations. Those skills are just as important to include in your career-change resume as any other skills you acquired in a paid position.

SAMPLE FORMATS AND SITUATIONS FOR CAREER-CHANGE RESUMES

Following are three excellent examples of career-change resumes, all of which focus on transferable skills, but each of which uses a different format and structure to highlight those skills. Think about which of these formats and styles is most appropriate for you, based on your particular situation and career objectives. It is very unlikely that you will find a format that exactly "matches" your life, experience, and educational credentials. Use the following examples as the foundation for your resume, customizing and reformatting as necessary to create your own winning resume.

Charles: A New Career After Additional Education

Charles was a most interesting job seeker. After a successful career in building maintenance, he returned to college to earn a graduate degree in Counseling Psychology in preparation for changing his career track. He had always had a passion for counseling and knew that to successfully change careers, he would have to get the requisite academic training.

Charles's resume begins with a brief, yet hard-hitting listing of his core skills and competencies as they relate to the field of counseling. The headline format that was used ("COUNSELING/HUMAN RELATIONS") clearly identifies "who" Charles is and "what" he wants. Then, at the top of the list, is his master's degree—a necessity for anyone pursuing a professional career in counseling. The other items highlight his core skills, the types of clients he has worked with, and professional credentials. This format is particularly effective because the reader can simply glance and "get it all," rather than having to read through paragraphs of text.

Immediately following his summary is detailed information about Charles's educational qualifications. Note that specific coursework is included as a great strategy to highlight his particular areas of training while being sure to include all the buzz words (or keywords) that are relevant to a career in counseling. Although Charles cannot say that he necessarily has "hands-on" experience in each of these areas, he can include them as areas of training. Not only will these catch a reader's attention, but they will also get Charles's resume selected if it is run through scanning technology that is searching for those specific terms.

The next section is detailed information about Charles's eight-month counseling internship. The job description is comprehensive and clearly creates the perception that Charles is an experienced counseling professional, despite the fact that this job was an internship.

Most important to note about this resume is that all of page 1 focuses on counseling and relevant skills. You never realize that Charles is a maintenance supervisor until you turn to page 2.

The writer was also very clever in how she formulated Charles's job description. Of course, it is obvious that he's a maintenance supervisor—we can't change the facts. However, much of the job description focuses on skills, responsibilities, projects, and more that required strong counseling, communication, and interpersonal skills. All of a sudden the maintenance man begins to disappear and the counselor begins to emerge.

CHARLES M. SUGARMANN

608 Covington Lane
Newtown, PA 18940

(267) 291-4866
csugarmann@dotresume.com

COUNSELING / HUMAN RELATIONS

Master's Degree
Adolescents & Adults
Drug & Alcohol Abuse
EAP & HMO Precertification
Assessments & Treatment Plans
Group, Individual, and Family Counseling
Supervision, Administration, Coordination

EDUCATION

M.A., Counseling Psychology, Immaculata University, Immaculata, PA, 2009
Maintained **3.7 GPA** while working full-time and taking an average of 6 credits per semester.

Courses: Adolescent Counseling, Appraisal in Counseling, Brief Strategic Therapy, Counseling Theory & Practice, Crisis Interventions, Ethical & Legal Issues in Counseling, Family Interventions, Gestalt Approach—Counseling, Group Counseling Theory & Practice, Human Growth & Development, Lifestyle & Career Development, Psychopathology, Research & Evaluation, Strategies for "At-Risk" Students, Substance Abuse Counseling

Labs: Counseling Diverse Populations, Counseling Skills, Group Dynamics

B.B.A., Temple University, Philadelphia, PA, 1999

EXPERIENCE

REHAB CENTER AT ARDMORE, PA, 5/2008–12/2008
A drug and alcohol outpatient rehabilitation facility for adults, adolescents, and families

Counselor Intern

Counseled adult and adolescent substance abusers in group, individual, and family sessions using education, psychodrama, psychotherapy, solution-focused counseling, cognitive-behavioral therapy, and person-centered counseling. Performed psychosocial assessments, developed treatment plans, and documented case activity. Precertified clients for HMO and EAP coverage. Recruited AA (Alcoholics Anonymous) and NA (Narcotics Anonymous) members to chair 12-step meetings for adolescents.

- Helped family members move from a state of powerlessness to active participation in client's therapy and life through education and awareness of family dynamics.

- Achieved numerous individual successes; for example, helped client gain acceptance by peers upon return to work, enabled counseling to proceed smoothly by helping to resolve medication problem of dual MH/D&A client, and counseled former drug dealer who is now a scholarship student.

- Commended by supervisor for relating well with clients and establishing an excellent rapport.

continued

Resume for Charles M. Sugarmann (written and designed by Jan Holliday, MA, NCRW, of Arbridge Communications).

CHARLES M. SUGARMANN

page 2

EXPERIENCE
continued

ST. MARK'S ACADEMY, Norristown, PA, 3/2001–present
A Catholic high school with 950 students and 100 staff members

Maintenance Supervisor, 2/2003–present
Head Groundskeeper, 1/2002–2/2003
Maintenance Man, 3/2001–1/2002

As maintenance supervisor, oversee staff of 10 to maintain school building and grounds. Serve as liaison to organizations that rent school facilities and to archdiocesan headquarters for special capital projects. Work with Delaware County Community Service to coordinate tasks for adolescents and adults performing work at the school in lieu of jail time—teach skills, where necessary, and apply counseling principles to make program run smoothly and to the benefit of all. Review grant proposals to advise on jobs that can be delegated to community-service workers.

- Praised by school president for success of community-service program.

- Sought out by students and maintenance staff for help with daily problems.

- Served as junior varsity softball coach for 5 years and as freshman basketball coach for 1 year.

- Ensured completion of work in all classrooms and restored amicable relationship between teachers and maintenance department by reinstituting use of service request form.

- Averted building fire through quick response; placed on list of national fire heroes by Curt Weldon, a member of the United States House of Representatives.

PRIOR EXPERIENCE in construction/home improvement, real estate sales, and tourism.

COMPUTER SKILLS

Experience with Microsoft Word and specialized spreadsheet applications.

Peter: From Attorney to Educator

Peter was a practicing attorney with more than 20 years of experience. Now he wanted to make a change. Because teaching had always been his passion, he decided to pursue that career on a full-time basis. His primary objective was a position teaching legal studies to junior and senior high school students, but he would also look at other related teaching opportunities.

Peter's resume begins with a comprehensive career summary that clearly identifies his two areas of expertise—teaching and the law. The resume then follows with a strong summary of his relevant teaching, program-development, classroom-management, and public-speaking skills, with concurrent emphasis on his areas of teaching specialization (for example, accounting, business law, and professional legal liability). The summary creates the perception of an individual with a wealth of teaching experience in a variety of professional settings.

The second section is Peter's education. As you can see, this section clearly demonstrates that he has the academic credentials to support his teaching specializations.

The next and most substantial section is Peter's employment history. Rather than focus on his actual legal practice, however, the resume highlights Peter's teaching, mentoring, and public-speaking experience—his transferable skills related to his current objective. People will review this resume and see someone who was an attorney but devoted a tremendous amount of his professional time to teaching. As such, he has positioned himself as a well-qualified candidate for an appropriate teaching position. When reviewing this resume, the reader does not "see" an attorney, but rather "sees" a teacher.

The writer used a highly effective strategy of creating a new hierarchy of skills, where teaching became the primary emphasis in the resume and Peter's law career became secondary.

PETER JONES, JR.

98 Ben Franklin Drive
Unit 5B, The Esplanade
Pensacola Beach, FL 32561

peterjones@midway.net

Home (850) 222-3333
Work: (850) 222-4444
Home Fax: (850) 222-7777

EDUCATOR/ATTORNEY AT LAW

Accomplished trainer and facilitator, experienced in the design and implementation of dynamic, state-of-the-art education and training programs for colleges, public educational organizations, small businesses, and large corporations. Encourage active student participation and engagement in learning, instilling in students a sense of self-direction by extending and enhancing the learning process. Creative and intuitive problem solver, cheerfully meeting challenges. *Core Competencies include*

- ☑ Training & Development
- ☑ Classroom Motivation Techniques
- ☑ Instructional Design & Development
- ☑ Adult Education Training & Facilitation
- ☑ College & Corporate Educational Course Design

- ☑ Accounting
- ☑ Business Law
- ☑ Professional Legal Liability
- ☑ Corporate & Individual Income Tax
- ☑ Mediation/Alternative Dispute Resolution

EDUCATION

J.D., Juris Doctor
FLORIDA STATE UNIVERSITY COLLEGE OF LAW, Tallahassee, FL

B.S., Accounting
FLORIDA STATE UNIVERSITY, Tallahassee, FL

CERTIFICATIONS: Supreme Court of Florida Certified Family Law Mediator

PROFESSIONAL LICENSES: Attorney At Law—Florida
Certified Public Accountant—Florida

PROFESSIONAL EXPERIENCE

PETER JONES, ATTORNEY AT LAW — Pensacola, FL   JAN 1995–PRESENT

Attorney At Law

Direct operations with full responsibility for P&L, business development, client relationship management, case management, staff recruitment, and training.

Key Achievements:

➢ Professional presenter/spokesperson at numerous continuing-education seminars in Tampa, Miami, and Pensacola, Florida. Areas of discussion included taxation, qualified retirement plans, accountants' legal liability, family law, mediation/alternative dispute resolution, and estate planning.

➢ Outstanding mentor and coach: Educated, trained, mentored, and motivated employees, stimulating them to higher levels of performance.

➢ Successfully created Peter Jones, Attorney At Law, as a financially viable start-up business, demonstrating decisive, proactive, and action-driven entrepreneurial leadership.

Resume for Peter Jones, Jr. (written and designed by Jennifer Rushton, CERW, CARW, CEIC, CWPP, of Keraijen).

PETER JONES, JR.

Professional Experience, Continued

➤ Established and maintained excellent business relationships with clients from diverse backgrounds through consistent demonstration of professionalism, preparedness, and good business ethics.

STEWARTS, BROOKS, MATTHEWS & TRENT — Pensacola, FL   OCT 1982–DEC 1995

Attorney/ Shareholder

Key Achievements:

➤ Facilitated continuing-education seminars, conducting instructor-led training to 25–100 attorney and CPA participants.
➤ Pioneered the development of numerous educational training programs in income tax and accounting for non-business majors as an adjunct professor at the University of West Florida.
➤ Initiated efforts to continually improve operations by developing the first legal assistant (paralegal) pool for use by the firm members.
➤ Key player in the development of a "structured settlement" approach to financial settlements in personal injury and wrongful death cases, resulting in favorable tax treatments for plaintiffs.

SMITH, WALLACE & COLLINS— Pensacola, FL   JUN 1980–OCT 1982

Associate Attorney

Key Achievements:

➤ Collaborated with associates in developing the condominium ownership concept in Florida; contributed to the taxation issues concerning the evolving concept of condominium ownership.

COOPERS & LYBRAND— Pensacola, FL   MAR 1978–JUN 1980

Taxation Specialist

Key Achievements:

➤ Designed and taught educational lessons to enhance student knowledge in taxation and accounting as an adjunct professor at the University of West Florida.
➤ Instrumental in developing and presenting continuing-education courses on tax law changes to members and guests of the firm.

PROFESSIONAL AFFILIATIONS

Member, Estate Planning Councils of Tampa
Member, Florida State & Local Bar Associations
Member, Florida Institute of Certified Public Accountants

COMMUNITY ACTIVITIES

Legal Member, Ombudsman Committee
Speaker, High School Life Sciences classes

Mike: A Functional Resume to Support His Transition from Educator to Top Business Executive

Although, as we discussed in chapter 1, combination or hybrid resume formats are preferred style, there are instances when a functional resume can be the best presentation of skills. As you review Mike Burns's resume, you will see that is certainly the case. After 13 years as a teacher and elementary school principal, Mike wanted to transfer his skills and qualifications into a corporate career track where he felt greater opportunities would exist for career growth and compensation.

Just like Charles's resume, Mike's begins with a headline format ("SEASONED MANAGER AND ADMINISTRATOR...Developing Strategic Plans/Managing Projects/Leading Operations and People"). This is one of our favorite formats because it allows the reader to quickly identify "who" the job seeker is.

Mike's Executive Profile is just that—a profile of an accomplished executive who has experience in virtually all key management disciplines. As you'll note, this section highlights finance, critical thinking, leadership, decision making, process management, relationship building, and many other skills, all of which are essential characteristics of a senior-level business manager. This section creates just the right perception of Mike without mentioning that he's an elementary school principal.

The third section of this resume is exceptionally strong and is the bulk of the remaining information that Mike shares about his background. Although Mike's actual employment experience is very briefly listed at the bottom of page 2, it is not the focus on this document. Rather, the third section highlights his particular areas of expertise and related projects, accomplishments, and responsibilities. Again, it's not until you get halfway through page 2 that you are aware that Mike is an elementary school principal.

Note that in the short section that lists Mike's employment, no job descriptions are used. The only information included in that section, beyond employers and job titles, is his list of professional honors and awards. This clearly communicates that Mike is a producer who delivers results and wins recognition from his employer.

Mike's education is included at the end of this resume because it is related to education and, therefore, the writer did not want to draw attention to it. And, finally, the resume ends with a great quote that highlights his management competencies and not his teaching competency.

MIKE BURNS

77002 Borgert Avenue
Anoka, MN 55304

Home: (763) 555-3789
Office: (763) 555-0562

mikeburns@anok.net

SEASONED MANAGER AND ADMINISTRATOR

Developing Strategic Plans / Managing Projects / Leading Operations and People

EXECUTIVE PROFILE

➢ More than seven years of senior-level experience in the administration of fiscally challenged organizations. Organized, take-charge professional with exceptional follow-through abilities and excellent management skills; able to plan and oversee projects/programs from concept to successful conclusion.

➢ A hands-on manager and critical thinker who can learn quickly, develop expertise, and produce immediate contributions in systems, analysis, business operations, and motivational team management. Possess a valuable blending of leadership, creative, and analytical abilities that combine efficiency with imagination to produce bottom-line results.

Core Strengths & Capabilities

Shared Decision Making ▪ Budget Development & Administration ▪ Staff / Team Training & Development
Operations Management ▪ Goal Setting & Strategic Planning ▪ Human Resources Leadership
Customer Care ▪ Cross-Functional Relationship Building ▪ Process Management ▪ Ideas & Opportunities
Consensus Building ▪ Productivity & Efficiency Improvement ▪ Service Design & Delivery Systems
Analysis & Assessment ▪ Organizational Communications ▪ Grant Writing ▪ Public Speaking ▪ "Can-Do" Mindset

RELEVANT CAREER SUCCESSES

STAFF TRAINING & DEVELOPMENT / HUMAN RESOURCES MANAGEMENT
➢ Directed human resource activities for two facilities with yearly budgets of $2 million and $4 million, respectively.
  ▪ Established successful Staff Mentoring Program in Plymouth. Collaborated with tenured staff to develop a 3-year plan toward easing new staff's transitions into the field. Paired tenured and new staff one-to-one.
  ▪ Led staff training opportunities with an average yearly budget of $40,000, providing much of the training myself.
  ▪ Hired professional, support, and all other staff. Directly supervised more than 70 employees.
  ▪ Proactively hired and teamed 20 new staff members within budget, accommodating Anoka's 300-student increase.

BUDGET & FISCAL MANAGEMENT / CAPITAL DEVELOPMENT
➢ Individually managed an average annual building budget of $4 million. Served on an administrative team managing a yearly $25 million budget (faced with an average $1 million in cuts each year).
  ▪ Weathered student population **increase from 550 to 850 in three years** by streamlining operations, cutting costs, and creatively raising funds, including co-authoring a successful $30,000 grant to hire a Behavior Planning Specialist.
  ▪ Played a key leadership and support role under the acting superintendent to lead a successful Building Bond Referendum Campaign. Results included a balanced budget and $6 million in new building construction. Also served on a team that successfully passed a $4 million referendum.

OPERATIONS MANAGEMENT
➢ Directed food service, custodial and maintenance, computer and media services, front office, and bussing operations as well as teaching/non-teaching staff activities for two community schools.
  ▪ Scheduled and coordinated facility utilization.
  ▪ Supervised maintenance and custodial staff; redefined performance standards to streamline operations.
  ▪ Handled all repair and maintenance requests, and supervised staff in their implementation.
  ▪ Headed the integration and upkeep of technology applications including voice mail, computer, and Internet.

Resume for Mike Burns (written and designed by Barbara Poole, CCMC, CLTMC, CERW, CPRW, CPHR, of Hire Imaging).

MIKE BURNS / RELEVANT CAREER SUCCESSES, CONTINUED

RELATIONSHIP BUILDING & COMMUNICATIONS
➤ Excelled at establishing and nurturing collaborative relationships with staff, parents, administrators, students, and other community members to clarify goals and communicate progress.
- Rallied community and parental support in school districts by sharing with them a vision based on the belief that all children are gifted and talented in their own way.
- Frequently served as public speaker to small and large groups: Graduation Emcee, Banquet Emcee, and University of Minnesota Educational Administration Class Presenter.
- Led monthly "Fun Night" recognition for volunteers, increasing attendance by 300+ per event.
- Acted as liaison with staff, families, and the school board. Commended for leading unified decision-making efforts.
- Directed the production of a school newsletter to foster school/community communications and connections.

EVENT MANAGEMENT
➤ Initiated and/or coordinated numerous programs and events.
- Initiated Spanish, science, and language-arts curriculum; a knowledge bowl; and a goal-setting conference.
- Spearheaded and coordinated career events, holiday events, school-wide enrichment themes, and other activities.

LEADERSHIP & TEAM ROLES
Graduation Standards ▪ Leadership Team ▪ District Strategic Planning ▪ Building President ▪ Advisory Board
Co-Op Mentor Board ▪ Title I Coordinator ▪ Student Council Advisor ▪ Parent Involvement Council
Curriculum Committees ▪ Staff Development Coordinator ▪ Construction Leadership

CAREER PATH

ANOKA PUBLIC SCHOOLS—Anoka, MN   2004–present
Elementary Principal
➤ Honored in 2005 as "Outstanding Service Award" recipient, a distinguished award given to only 5 out of 450 statewide employees annually.
- First administrator to ever receive the award.
- Second first-year employee to be honored with this award.

PLYMOUTH PUBLIC SCHOOLS—Plymouth, MN   1996–2004
Elementary Principal (2001–2004)
Superintendent Intern (Superintendent) (2003)
Fifth-Grade Teacher (1997–2001)
➤ At the age of 29, based on my performance, was hired in 2001 as the youngest principal in the state of Minnesota.

EDUCATION

UNIVERSITY OF MINNESOTA—Minneapolis, MN
Specialist's Degree, Educational Leadership and Administration   2005
Master's Degree, Educational Leadership and Administration   2001
Bachelor's Degree, Elementary Education   1997

> *"I was immensely impressed with Mike's performance from my very first contact with him … He has strong communication skills, an excellent background, and intelligence that provides him with a quick perception of most situations … He was quickly recognized for his sincerity, genuine interest in others, and leadership qualities … He has enriched the entire community."*
> **—Sam Johnson, Superintendent, Plymouth Public Schools**

WHY FORMAT IS SO IMPORTANT

To see how important the right format is to the success of your resume and job search, carefully review the following two resumes. They are prime examples of how critical it is for career changers to bring their transferable skills to the forefront of the resume and let other, non-related experience become secondary (even if that experience is where they've spent the majority of their careers).

Both resumes are for the same job seeker but use a different format and strategy. When you read the first resume, which follows the traditional chronological format, you're instantly drawn to the fact that Mary is a classroom teacher. Her teaching career has been solid but is certainly not supportive of her current objective to transition into an outside sales position.

Now look at Mary's second resume. What you see is a talented sales professional with experience in sales, relationship building, customer service, communications, organization, planning, and follow-through. Two-thirds of this resume is devoted to her sales skills, accomplishments, and experience, while the remainder briefly summarizes her teaching background. This format instantly changes the perception of who Mary is. She's no longer "just a classroom teacher." Rather, she's an experienced sales professional who will bring value to any sales position. The writer (Louise Garver, MA, JCTC, CMP, CPRW, MCDP, CEIP, of Career Directions in Connecticut) did an excellent job of changing the perception of "who" Mary is to closely align with her current career objectives.

MARY A. DANVERS

466 Forester Drive
Baltimore, MD 21099

Tel: (415) 877-9976
E-mail: danvers@earthlink.net

CAREER FOCUS: SALES

PROFILE

Outgoing, energetic professional with a successful record in challenging positions. Currently employed as a full-time classroom teacher with previous experience in sales, customer relationship management, customer service, and fund raising. Excellent communication and interpersonal relationship skills. Proven ability to establish and achieve professional and business objectives. Experienced presenter/trainer with excellent listening skills and a positive demeanor. Adept at identifying customer needs and creatively solving problems. Seeking new professional challenges and opportunities.

Computer proficient with MS Office suite and Internet research.
Foreign-language fluency in Spanish.

EMPLOYMENT EXPERIENCE

ARLINGTON PUBLIC SCHOOLS, Baltimore, MD • 2003 to present
Spanish Teacher

- Design and present curriculum in level-1 and -2 Spanish-language courses at a middle school and high school; effectively manage classes comprised of 30 students.
- Develop and implement innovative lesson plans that stimulate students' interest in the learning process.
- Combine lecture and demonstration with audiovisuals and other materials to enhance presentations.
- Demonstrate effective leadership and encourage team concepts to accomplish organizational goals.
- Initiated, created, and provide guidance to the Spanish Club.

HARRINGTON STORES, Baltimore, MD • 1997 to 2003
Sales Associate

WALLACE UNIVERSITY 2000 CAMPAIGN, Baltimore, MD • 1994 to 1996
Fund Raiser

LANCER ESTATES, Baltimore, MD • 1995
Sales Assistant

MARRIETTA & ASSOCIATES, Baltimore, MD • 1992 to 1995
Staff Accountant & Auditor

EDUCATION

B.S., Business Administration
Major in Accounting and Minor in Spanish
WALLACE UNIVERSITY, Baltimore, MD, 1998

Mary's resume in chronological format.

MARY A. DANVERS

466 Forester Drive
Baltimore, MD 21099

Tel: (415) 877-9976
E-mail: danvers@earthlink.net

CAREER FOCUS: SALES

Contributing to a company's success through application of key skills: Sales, Relationship Building, Customer Service, Persuasive Communications, Organization, Planning, and Follow-Through.

PROFILE

Outgoing, energetic professional with a successful record in challenging positions involving extensive communications with management, the general public, and peers. Proven ability to establish and achieve professional and business objectives. Experienced presenter/trainer with excellent listening skills and a positive demeanor. Adept in identifying customer needs and creatively solving problems. Computer proficient with MS Office (including Word and Excel) and Internet research. Foreign-language fluency in Spanish.

SELECTED ACCOMPLISHMENTS

- **Consistently ranked among the top 3 sales producers at Harrington Stores, exceeding weekly quotas. Effective in promoting products and creating displays that attracted customer attention.**
- **Cultivated long-term customer relationships that resulted in 80% referral/repeat business, contributing to business growth at Harrington Stores.**
- **Recognized as one of the top 3 fund raisers in generating $75,000 for Wallace University's 2000 Campaign. Contacted and persuaded physicians and other professionals to contribute.**
- **Generated prospective buyers' interest by effectively describing property features; provided referrals to real estate agents at Lancer Estates.**
- **Contributed to successful fund-raising activities for the Special Olympics and Variety Club that benefited handicapped children.**

SALES EXPERIENCE

Sales Associate • HARRINGTON STORES, Baltimore, MD • 1997 to 2003
Fund Raiser • WALLACE UNIVERSITY 2000 CAMPAIGN, Baltimore, MD • 1994 to 1996
Sales Assistant • LANCER ESTATES, Baltimore, MD • 1995

CURRENT EMPLOYMENT

ARLINGTON PUBLIC SCHOOLS, Baltimore, MD • 2003 to present
Spanish Teacher

Design and present curriculum in level-1 and -2 Spanish-language courses at a middle school and high school; effectively manage 30-student classes. Develop and implement innovative lesson plans that stimulate students' interest in the learning process. Combine lecture and demonstration with audiovisuals and other materials to enhance presentations. Demonstrate effective leadership and encourage team concepts to accomplish organizational goals. Initiated, created, and provide guidance to the Spanish Club.

Prior Experience: Staff Accountant and Auditor, MARRIETTA & ASSOCIATES, Baltimore, MD

EDUCATION

B.S., Business Administration
Major in Accounting and Minor in Spanish
WALLACE UNIVERSITY, Baltimore, MD, 1998

Mary's new resume, which emphasizes her sales and customer relationship management skills while effectively downplaying her teaching background.

Step-by-Step: Writing the Perfect Resume

What follows is a detailed discussion of the various sections that you might include in your resume (for example, Career Summary, Professional Experience, Education, Technical Qualifications, Professional Memberships, Public Speaking, Publications, Honors and Awards, and Volunteer Experience), what each section should include, and where to include it.

CONTACT INFORMATION

Before we get into the major sections of the resume, let's briefly address the very top section: your name and contact information.

Name

You'd think writing your name would be the easiest part of writing your resume! But there are several factors you might want to consider:

- Although most people choose to use their full, formal name at the top of a resume, it has become increasingly more acceptable to use the name by which you prefer to be called.

- Bear in mind that it's to your advantage when readers feel comfortable calling you for an interview. Their comfort level may decrease if your name is gender-neutral, difficult to pronounce, or very unusual; they don't know how to ask for you. You can make it easier for them by following these examples:

> Lynn T. Cowles (Mr.)
>
> (Ms.) Michael Murray
>
> Tzirina (Irene) Kahn
>
> Ndege "Nick" Vernon

Address

You should always include your home address on your resume. If you use a post-office box for mail, include both your mailing address and your physical residence address if possible.

An exception to this guideline is when you are posting your resume on the Internet. For security purposes, it is a good idea to include just your phone and e-mail contact as well as possibly your city and state with no street address.

Telephone Number(s)

Include one or at most two telephone numbers where people can reliably reach you. For many people this is a cell number, and it's perfectly fine to include only your cell number on your resume. Of course, if you are more easily reached at home, you can include your home number instead of or in addition to your cell phone. Do not include a business phone number unless you answer it directly and it is the only way for people to reach you during business hours. For any number that you publish on your resume, be certain that you have a brief, professional voice-mail greeting, frequently check for messages, and return calls promptly.

E-mail Address

You must include an e-mail address on your resume. E-mail is now often the preferred method of communication in job search, particularly in the early stages of each contact. If you do not have an e-mail account, you can obtain a free, accessible-anywhere address from a provider such as www.yahoo.com, www.hotmail.com, or www.gmail.com.

As you look through the samples in this book, you'll see how resume writers have arranged the many bits of contact information at the top of a resume. You can use these as models for presenting your own information. The point is to make it as easy as possible for employers to contact you!

Page Two

We strongly recommend that you include your name, phone number, and e-mail address at the top of the second page of your resume and any additional pages. If, by chance, the pages get separated, you want to be sure that people can still contact you, even if they have only page 2 of your resume.

Now, let's get into the nitty-gritty of the core content sections of your resume.

CAREER SUMMARY

The Career Summary is the section at the top of your resume that summarizes and highlights your knowledge and expertise. You might be thinking, "But shouldn't my resume start with an Objective?" Although many job seekers still use Objective statements, we believe that a Career Summary is a much more powerful introduction. The problem with Objectives is that they are either too specific (limiting you to an "Electrical Engineering position") or too vague (doesn't everyone want "a challenging opportunity with a progressive organization offering the opportunity for growth and advancement"?). In addition, objective statements can be read as self-serving because they describe what *you* want rather than suggesting what you have to offer an employer.

In contrast, an effective Career Summary allows you to position yourself as you want to be perceived, and this is particularly important for people changing careers. A Career Summary allows you to immediately "paint a picture" of yourself that directly supports your current career objective.

It is critical that this section focus on the specific skills, qualifications, and achievements of your career that are related to your objectives. Your summary is *not* a historical overview of your career. Rather, it is a concise, well-written, and sharp presentation of information designed to *sell* you into your next position.

This section can have various titles, such as the following:

Career Summary	**Management Profile**
Career Achievements	**Professional Qualifications**
Career Highlights	**Professional Summary**
Career Synopsis	**Profile**
Executive Profile	**Summary**
Expertise	**Summary of Achievement**
Highlights of Experience	**Summary of Qualifications**

Or, as you will see in the Headline Format example shown later, your summary does not have to have any title at all.

The Career Summary section can be the single most important section on any career changer's resume because of its content—the skills, qualifications, achievements, technical competencies, and other facts that you offer that are in line with your current career objectives. Your goal is to capture your reader's attention and immediately communicate the value you bring to their organization. If you are able to bring your relevant skills to the forefront, you will have favorably positioned yourself before a prospective employer; the fact that your prior work experience is in a different profession or industry becomes much less significant.

A Career Summary is a great thing because it allows you to include skills and competencies that you've acquired through volunteer work, training, internships, sabbaticals, association memberships, and other activities. The skills you include in your Summary *do not* have to be as a direct result of paid work experience. This is wonderful news for career changers! Remember, a summary is just that—a summary of the things that you do best—and it doesn't matter where you learned to do them.

The Career Summary probably will be the focal point of your career-changer resume. Be sure to package and sell all of your qualifications as they relate to your current career goals. Don't be concerned if your Career Summary is longer than normal. This section is the foundation for your entire resume, so be thorough so you're sure to sell yourself into your next job.

Here are five sample Career Summaries. Consider using one of these as the template for developing your Career Summary, or use them as the foundation to create your own presentation. You will also find some type of Career Summary in just about every resume included in chapters 4 through 12. Closely review them as well to find a format and style that's in line with your specific needs.

Bullet Format

Career Change: Government employee with diverse work experience seeking new career as manager of administrative affairs in "corporate" America.

HIGHLIGHTS

- 15 years of increasingly responsible experience at various administrative levels.
- Numerous college-level business courses and in-house training programs.
- Outstanding follow-up skills; goal-driven; always seek to bring projects to completion on time and within budget.
- Self-starter who sees what has to be done and then does it.
- Recipient of many Outstanding Service Awards.

RELEVANT SKILLS AND EXPERIENCE

Office Technology

- Mastery of MS Office suite (Word, Excel, Access) and Windows and Mac operating systems.
- Expertise in other software packages (SAS, SPSS, PROFS, Dreamweaver).
- Keyboarding skills of 50 wpm.

Administration

- Developed and managed operating budgets.
- Scheduled and taught training classes.
- Served on personnel screening and selection panels.
- Organized nationwide management conferences.

Leadership

- Supervised 7 to 9 employees as Team Leader for the Special Projects Task Force.
- Coordinated development, implementation, and operation of an advanced information systems application supporting employees worldwide.
- Honored with an Outstanding Leadership Award—Administrative Division.

Writing

- Wrote policy statements, procedures manuals, and programs of instruction.
- Wrote user manuals for 6 new system implementations.
- Wrote comprehensive personnel, asset, and resource analysis reports.

This career changer had a wealth of experience working for the federal government in a variety of administrative, training, and project support positions. Knowing that she wanted to transition out of the government, her core skills and qualifications were presented in a "skills-based" format with no mention of her government background. In turn, her skills are precisely the skills one would need for a position in corporate administration.

Headline Format

Career Change: Telecommunications engineering manager seeking new career in international telecommunications sales.

> # INTERNATIONAL BUSINESS PROFESSIONAL
> ### Telecommunications Products, Solutions & Technologies
> ### MBA, Executive Management, Harvard University
> ### Cornell University Executive Sales Leadership

Although this individual's background was principally in managing the design and development of telecommunications products and technologies, the summary was written to downplay his technical expertise while highlighting his strong general management, international, and industry-related experience.

Paragraph Format

Career Change: Corporate sales and service manager seeking new career in corporate training and development.

> ### CAREER SUMMARY
>
> **TRAINING & DEVELOPMENT PROFESSIONAL** with proven expertise in the design and implementation of cost-effective staff training, e-learning, customer service, sales management, and marketing programs. Recognized for innovation and creativity in designing real-world training programs that focus on the development of core skills and competencies. Talented speaker, motivator, and group facilitator. Skilled in seminar and conference planning/logistics.

Although this individual's primary job responsibilities have been in sales and service, he also had years of experience in training his own staff. As such, and based on his current career goal, the summary was used to highlight his relevant training and development experience.

Core Competencies Summary Format

Career Change: Entrepreneur/owner of a small retail business now seeking a career in corporate finance and accounting.

> ### PROFESSIONAL QUALIFICATIONS SUMMARY
> #### CORPORATE FINANCE & ACCOUNTING
> #### Manufacturing / Retail / Food Service
>
> - Budget Development & Administration
> - Profit & Loss Reporting
> - Cash Flow Planning & Control
> - Capital Expenditures
> - Benefits Administration
> - Revenue & Expense Forecasting
> - Long-Range Fiscal Planning
> - ROI, ROA & ROE Analysis
> - Contract Negotiations
> - Policy & Procedure Development

After 20 years as a self-employed business owner, this individual had acquired a wealth of experience in finance and accounting. Rather than focus his resume on the diversity of his management and entrepreneurial experience, all of the skills and qualifications listed focus on his current career goals and clearly position him as a well-qualified financial executive.

Project Format

Career Change: Business manager of a small bookkeeping-supply company now seeking a career as a computer programmer and applications developer.

PROFESSIONAL QUALIFICATIONS

Programmer / Technologist with 5+ years of experience with C/C++, Java, Visual Basic, Oracle (SQL, SQL*Plus, PL/SQL), DataEase, Windows, and UNIX. Major projects have included

▶ ▶ **Point-of-Sale (POS) System** for The Tech Corner, Inc. Created a normalized relational database (using DataEase on a Windows network) to provide complete invoicing, billing, accounts receivable, and accounts payable management for a $2 million company with 200 active accounts.

▶ ▶ **Client-Service Sales Module in Java** for Sounds Systems LLC. Using TCP/IP sockets, connected GUI front end to console application, allowing user to query server for price, availability, and credit status.

▶ ▶ **Sales Module in Visual Basic** for class project. Created GUI front end to Access database, allowing input of customer information, parts numbers, and quantities and automatically generating orders, invoices, and sales summaries.

▶ ▶ **Billing System in Oracle** for class project. Generated users, tables, views, sequences, and triggers using SQL, SQL*Plus, and PL/SQL to create Oracle database. Imported data and used Developer to create forms.

During this job seeker's 12-year career, he had risen through the ranks to hold a relatively senior-level management position directing daily business, sales, and personnel operations. During the past five years, he had also spearheaded all technology development and implementation projects for the company (as well as several projects at a technical school he was attending). These projects became the cornerstone of his new career-change resume to create the perception that he is a skilled programmer and technologist.

PROFESSIONAL EXPERIENCE

As a career changer, how much information you include in your Professional Experience section will depend entirely on how relevant that experience is to your current career objectives. If relevant (or if just parts of it are relevant), you'll want to be sure to highlight that information—in detail—on your resume. If irrelevant, you'll want to be very brief with your job descriptions, if you include them at all. As discussed previously, the best strategy for a career changer might be a functional or hybrid format focusing on skills and qualifications while downplaying work experience. Read further and you'll understand why.

Writing your Professional Experience section might take you the longest of any section of your resume. Suppose, for example, that you had the same position for 10 years. How can you consolidate all that you have done into one short section? If, on the opposite end of the spectrum, you've had several short-term jobs over the past several years, how can you make your experience seem substantial, noteworthy, and relevant? And, for all of you whose experience is in between, what do you include, how, where, and why?

These are not easy questions to answer. In fact, the most truthful response to each question is, "it depends." It depends on you, your experience, your achievements and successes, your current career objectives, and how closely your past experience ties into and supports those objectives.

Here are five samples of Professional Experience sections. Review how each individual's unique background is organized and emphasized, and consider your own background when using one of these as the template or foundation for developing your Professional Experience section. And be sure to review the resume samples in chapters 4 through 12 to get even more ideas.

Achievement Format

Career Change: Director of emergency medical services seeking a new career as a college instructor. Format emphasizes rapid promotion through each position, overall scope of responsibility, and resulting achievements particularly relevant to his new career objective.

PROFESSIONAL EXPERIENCE

ALBANY COUNTY FIRE DEPARTMENT, Colonie, NY   1995 to 2009

DIRECTOR OF EMERGENCY MEDICAL SERVICES (2003 to 2009)
SHIFT COMMANDER—CAPTAIN (1999 to 2003)
ENGINE COMPANY OFFICER—LIEUTENANT (1997 to 1999)
EMERGENCY MEDICAL TECHNICIAN—ENGINEER (1995 to 1997)

Supervised Emergency Medical Services comprising 45 EMTs and paramedics at 3 fire stations. Participated in the direction of all aspects of personnel relations, including training, hiring, new-employee orientation, staff development, and performance evaluations. Served as Incident Commander at medical emergencies and structure fires. Coordinated all phases of EMS and served as Chairman of EMS Operations Committee. Wrote and implemented EMS protocols.

Achievements:

- Served as Emergency Medical Services Training Officer with responsibility for planning, organizing, and delivering EMS training, testing, and recertification for 63 EMTs.

- Catalyst in the conceptualization of an innovative paramedic training program for Albany County Fire Department.

- Created the model for state licensure for other fire departments based on stringent training and performance requirements.

- Established and launched Fire Cadet Program (paid internship) to allow 17- to 21-year-olds to participate in fire service through a comprehensive training and mentoring opportunity.

- Reduced annual material costs by 50% through more efficient vendor sourcing and purchasing processes.

Challenge, Action, and Results (CAR) Format

Career Change: Corporate sales manager seeking a career change to a position as a general manager, division vice president, or other senior-level operating management position. Format emphasizes the challenge of each position, the action taken, and the results delivered.

EXPERIENCE AND ACHIEVEMENTS————————————————————

Corporate Sales Manager   2006 to Present
DOLINVEST CORPORATION   Chicago, Illinois

Challenge: Plan and execute a complete turnaround, revitalization, and return to profitability of the nonperforming Chicago metro region for $20M specialty gift products manufacturer.

Action: Revitalized relationships with more than 300 accounts, negotiated credit line to support corporate cash requirements, recruited talented staff and management teams, and launched a massive cost-reduction initiative. Rewrote corporate policies and procedures, introduced advanced technologies, and eliminated reliance on third-party consultants.

Results: ➤ Achieved/surpassed all turnaround objectives and returned operation to profitability in first year. Delivered strong and sustainable gains:
- 128% increase in sales revenues over 12 months.
- 8.5% increase in bottom-line profitability.
- $1.8M in sales from new products.
- 100% on-time customer delivery.

➤ Won the company's 2008 Leadership Achievement Award.

➤ Quoted in the National Management Association's annual publication as one of 2007's *"Turnaround Specialists."*

➤ Developed and taught the corporation's flagship Leadership Development program.

➤ Eliminated more than $2.8M in excess spending and reduced annual contractor fees by more than 30%.

➤ Invested $800K in new technology to automate and streamline all core business functions. Delivered an additional 4% to bottom-line profit contribution.

Functional Format

Career Change: Director of day-care center seeking a new career in outside sales in the toy, pharmaceutical, consumer products, or cosmetics industries. Format emphasizes the functional areas of responsibility within her job and her associated achievements.

EMPLOYMENT EXPERIENCE

Center Director   ARNOLD'S LEARNING CENTER, Minneapolis, MN   2002–Present

Member of three-person management team directing the operations of a large-scale day-care facility with more than 200 children and more than 40 full-time and part-time staff. Scope of responsibility is extensive and includes the following:

SALES/MARKETING

- ☑ Attracted potential customers through print advertising, tours, referrals, open houses, and outreach to area schools. Utilized guest registration forms to grow prospect list, and conducted follow-up mail and callback campaigns.

- ☑ Personally credited with delivering 25%+ annual growth, year-over-year, for 7 consecutive years.

- ☑ Wrote, designed, and directed production of the first-ever brochure and accompanying marketing literature.

- ☑ Positioned center as the fastest growing and most profitable operation of its kind in a 200-mile radius.

CUSTOMER RELATIONSHIP MANAGEMENT & CUSTOMER SERVICE

- ☑ Introduced the center's first formal customer service program to ensure that parents had easy access to information and to decision makers.

- ☑ Created a customer satisfaction survey and administered it annually. Utilized collected data to expand and strengthen existing service operations.

- ☑ Trained newly hired staff in effective communication and service strategies.

FUND RAISING & SPECIAL EVENTS MANAGEMENT

- ☑ Planned, staffed, and coordinated an average of 10 special events each year (for example, open houses, talent shows, orientations, competitive sporting events).

- ☑ Managed all event promotions, publicity, media relations, and marketing. Demonstrated excellent oral and written communication skills.

- ☑ Acted as emcee at numerous events, speaking to groups of more than 200 at a time.

Project Highlights Format

Career Change: An experienced media sales representative seeking a new career as a graphic designer and illustrator. This format highlights her special projects and activities as they relate to graphic design although this was a very small component of her overall position.

Sales Representative, December 2005 to September 2009

THE DALLAS CENTURION NEWS, Dallas, Texas

High-profile position working with companies throughout the Dallas metro region to provide expert leadership in the creative design, development, and execution of media advertising campaigns. Expanded scope of client relationships to include a portfolio of graphic design and illustration services.

- ◆ **Dallas County Arts Commission.** Commissioned by DCAC to design artwork for mural and footpath for the Buck Henry Theater.

- ◆ **Oodles & Oodles.** Designed and painted mural for one of Dallas's hottest night spots.

- ◆ **Transventure Insurance.** Created graphics for a 200-page investor report.

- ◆ **Dallas Regional Broadcasting Company.** Guided design of 3-D animation, characters, and designs for new television series.

- ◆ **Toy Crazy.** Designed corporate logo, letterhead, brochure, and sales documentation.

- ◆ **National Speakers Association.** Illustrated 252-page book written and published by NSA.

Experience Summary Format

Career Change: Site remediation superintendent seeking new career working in environmental regulatory affairs. Format briefly emphasizes relevant highlights of each position because the bulk of this individual's experience in remediation will have been summarized—at length—in the Career Summary.

EXPERIENCE SUMMARY

Site Superintendent, ABX REMEDIATION SERVICES, Cincinnati, OH—2004 to 2009

- Investigated, analyzed, and identified objectives for remedial actions/cleanups throughout the Midwest.
- Negotiated with state and federal regulators to establish plans for the remediation of specific sites nationwide.
- Independently handled the filing of all regulatory documents, reports, and other submissions mandated by local, state, and federal officials.
- Coordinated remediation of 50,000 tons of lead-contaminated soil from 150 residential sites 2 weeks ahead of schedule and $56,000 under budget.

Senior Electrician, ABX ELECTRICAL SERVICES, Cincinnati, OH—1999 to 2004

- Installed electrical, plumbing, and gas systems in decontamination, office, lab trailers, and project sites. Often worked at hazardous/EPA-controlled sites.
- Researched relevant regulations and trained other employees to meet regulatory standards.
- Filed regulatory documentation and met with regulators to resolve any potential field issues.

Electrician, MYERS ELECTRIC, Covington, KY—1997 to 1999

- Installed, maintained, and repaired residential electrical systems and service.

EDUCATION, CREDENTIALS, AND CERTIFICATIONS

Your Education section should include college, certifications, credentials, licenses, registrations, and continuing education. For career changers whose greatest selling point for their new career is education, this section is extremely important and will, most likely, be placed on your resume immediately following your Career Summary. Be sure to display your educational qualifications prominently if they are a key selling point in your transition into a new career track.

Here are five sample Education sections that illustrate a variety of ways to organize and format this information.

Academic Credentials Format

EDUCATION

M.S., Counseling Psychology, University of Akron, 2001
B.S., Psychology, University of Miami, 1999

Highlights of Continuing Professional Education:
- Organizational Management & Leadership, Ohio Leadership Association, 2008
- Industrial Relations, Purdue University, 2007
- Conflict Resolution & Violence Management in the Workplace, Institute for Workplace Safety, 2005

Licensed Clinical Psychologist, State of Ohio, 2001 to Present
Licensed Recreational Therapist, National Recreation Association, 2003 to Present

Executive Education Format

EDUCATION

Executive Leadership Program	STANFORD UNIVERSITY
Executive Development Program	NORTHWESTERN UNIVERSITY
Master of Business Administration (MBA)	HARVARD UNIVERSITY GRADUATE SCHOOL
Bachelor of Science	UNIVERSITY OF PENNSYLVANIA

Certifications Format

TECHNICAL CERTIFICATIONS & DEGREES

Registered Nurse, University of Maryland, 1994

Bachelor of Science in Nursing (BSN), University of Maryland, 1994

Certified Nursing Assistant, University of Maryland, 1992

Associate of Arts in General Studies, Byerstown Community College, Byerstown, Delaware, 1992

Certified Nursing Aide, State of Maryland, 1988

Specialized Training Format

Technical Licenses & Certifications

- Rhode Island Journeyman License #67382
- Vermont Journeyman License #LK3223839
- Licensed Electrician #8737262
- Construction Supervisor #99089
- Impact Training, Motor Control Seminar, 2009
- CAT-5 Certification, 2008
- Variable Speed Drive Certification, 2007
- Soars Grounding of Electrical Systems for Safety Certification, 2006
- Graduate, Jefferson Forest High School, Lynchburg, VA, 2003

Non-Degree Format

TRAINING & EDUCATION

UNIVERSITY OF FLORIDA, Tampa, Florida
B.S. Candidate—Business Administration (senior class status)

UNIVERSITY OF OREGON, Portland, Oregon
Dual Majors in Business Administration & Computer Science (2 years)

Completed 100+ hours of continuing professional education through the
University of Miami, University of Georgia, and University of Phoenix.
Topics included business administration, finance, strategic planning,
organizational development, team building, and communications.

THE "EXTRAS"

The primary focus of your resume should be on information that is directly related to your career goals, whether from your paid work experience, volunteer experience, education and training, affiliations, or elsewhere. However, you also should include things that will distinguish you from other candidates and clearly demonstrate your value to a prospective employer. And, not too surprisingly, it is often the "extras" that get the interviews.

Following is a list of the other categories you might or might not include on your resume depending on your particular experience and your current career objectives. If one of these categories is pertinent to you, use the samples for formatting your own data. Remember, however, that if something is truly impressive, you might want to draw even more attention to it by including it in your Career Summary at the beginning of your resume. If this is the case, it's not necessary to repeat the information at the end of your resume.

Technology Skills and Qualifications

Many technology professionals will have a separate section on their resumes for technology skills and qualifications. It is here that you will summarize all the hardware, software, operating systems, applications, networks, and more that you know and that are relevant to your current career objectives.

You'll also have to consider placement of this section in your resume. If the positions for which you are applying require strong technical skills, we would recommend you insert this section immediately after your Career Summary (or as a part thereof). If, on the other hand, your technical skills are more of a plus than a specific requirement, the preferred placement is further down on your resume.

Either way, these skills are vital in virtually any technology-related position. As such, this is extremely important information to a prospective employer, so be sure to display it prominently.

Here are two different ways to format and present your technical qualifications:

TECHNOLOGY PROFILE

Operating Systems	Windows 7/Vista/XP/Server 2008; Novell NetWare
Protocols/Networks	TCP/IP, NetBEUI, IPX/SPX, Gigabit Ethernet
Hardware	Hard drives, printers, scanners, fax/modems, CD-ROMs, Cat5 cables, hubs, NIC cards
Software	Microsoft Office Modules, FileMaker Pro, pcAnywhere, MS Exchange, ARCserve, Project Manager

TECHNOLOGY SKILLS SUMMARY

Windows 7/Vista/XP	SAP	TCP/IP
Windows Server 2008	MRP	Gigabit Ethernet
Novell NetWare 6.x	DRP	IPX/SPX
Microsoft Office	MS Exchange	ARCserve
Project Manager	pcAnywhere	FileMaker Pro

If your goal is to simply mention the fact that you are proficient with specific PC software, a quick line at the end of your Career Summary should cover this information. For example:

PC proficient with Word, Excel, and Access.

Equipment Skills and Qualifications

People employed in manufacturing, construction, engineering, and related industries will have a unique portfolio of equipment skills and knowledge. If this information is relevant to your current career goals, it is critical that you communicate it in your resume, highlighting all the equipment with which you are proficient or familiar. Consider this format for an individual with extensive experience in pharmaceutical product packaging:

Trained in and worked on a diversity of packaging equipment and technology, including R.A. Jones, Hoppmann, Syntron, Lakso, Scandia, Westbrook, Wexxar, and Edson:

Leaflet Inserters	Cappers	Bottle Cleaners & Elevators
Fillers	Desiccants	Neckbanders
Heat Tunnels	Labelers	Cartoners
Case Packers & Sealers	Hoppers	Bundlers
Sorters	Carousels	Cottoners

Honors and Awards

If you have won honors and awards, you can either include them in a separate section near the end of your resume, or integrate them into the Education or Professional Experience section if they are particularly noteworthy or related to your current career objectives. If you choose to include them in a separate section, consider this format:

- Winner, 2009 **"Sales Performance"** award from the Bechtel Mortgage Company, Inc.

- Winner, 2006 **"Customer Service"** award for outstanding contributions to customer service and retention from Kraft Foods, Inc.

- Named **"Employee of the Year,"** Kraft Foods, Inc., 2005

- **Cum Laude Graduate,** Southern Illinois University, 1997

Public Speaking

Experts are the ones who are invited to give public presentations at conferences, seminars, workshops, training programs, symposia, and other events. So if you have public-speaking experience, others must consider you an expert. Be sure to include this very complimentary information in your resume. Here's one way to present it:

- Keynote Speaker, "Architectural Engineering & Design," AAI National Conference, New York City, 2009

- Panel Presenter, "Maximizing Space Design & Utilization," AAI National Conference, Dallas, 2007

- Session Leader, "Ergonomic Design," Ohio Society of Architects, Cleveland, 2005

Publications

If you're published, you must be an expert (or at least most people will think so). Just as with your public-speaking engagements, be sure to include your publications. They validate your knowledge, qualifications, and credibility. Publications can include books, articles, online Web site content, manuals, and other written documents. Here's an example:

- Co-author, *Computer-Aided Design of Hybrid Microcircuits*, National Electronic Packaging Conference, 2008.

- Author, *Subtle Aspects of Micro-Packaging*, Product Assurance Conference, 2006.

- Author, *Micro-Packaging Practices, Policies, and Processes*, IBM Training Manual, 2004.

Teaching and Training Experience

Many professionals, regardless of their industry or profession, also teach or train at colleges, universities, technical schools, and other organizations, in addition to training that they may do "on the job." If this is applicable to you and your current objectives, you will want to include that experience on your resume. If someone hires you (paid or unpaid) to speak to an audience, it communicates a strong message about your skills, qualifications, knowledge, and expertise. Here's a format you might use to present that information:

- **Adjunct Faculty,** Department of Chemical Engineering, Texas A&M University, 2004–2008. Taught Introductory and Advanced Chemical Engineering.

- **Guest Lecturer,** Department of Statistics, Reynolds Community College, 2003–2007. Provided semiannual, day-long lecture series on the applications of statistics and statistical theory in the workplace.

- **Trainer,** Macmillan School of Engineering, 2000–2002. Taught Chemical Engineering 101 and Chemical Lab Analysis to first-year students.

Committees and Task Forces

Many professionals serve on committees, task forces, and other special project teams either as part of, or in addition to, their full-time job responsibilities. Again, this type of information further strengthens your credibility, qualifications, and perceived value to a prospective employer when it is related to your current objectives. Consider a format such as this:

- Member, 2009–2010 Corporate Planning & Reorganization Task Force

- Member, 2007 Study Team on "Redesigning Corporate Training Systems to Maximize Employee Productivity"

- Chairperson, 2006–2007 Committee on "Safety & Regulatory Compliance in the Workplace"

Professional Affiliations

If you are a member of any educational, professional, or leadership associations, be sure to include that information on your resume. It communicates a message of professionalism, a desire to stay current with the industry, and a strong professional network. If you have held leadership positions within these organizations, be sure to include them. Here's an example:

NATIONAL EDUCATION ASSOCIATION (NEA)

Professional Member (2000 to Present)

Fundraising Committee Member (2007 to 2009)

Curriculum Committee Member (2005 to 2007)

NATIONAL TEACHERS ASSOCIATION (NTA)

Professional Member (2003 to Present)

Instructional Materials Design Committee Member (2006 to 2009)

Technology Task Force Member (2004 to 2006)

LAFAYETTE TEACHERS ASSOCIATION (LTA)

President (2007 to 2009)

Vice President (2005 to 2007)

Member (1997 to Present)

Civic Affiliations

Civic affiliations are fine to include if they fit one of the following criteria:

- Are with a notable organization
- Demonstrate leadership experience
- May be of interest to a prospective employer

However, things such as treasurer of your local condo association and singer with your church choir are not generally of value in marketing your qualifications unless, of course, that experience is directly relevant to your current career objectives. Here's an example of what to include and how:

- Volunteer Chairperson, United Way of America—Detroit Chapter, 2008 to Present

- President, Greenwood Environmental District, 2006 to Present

- Treasurer, Habitat for Humanity—Memphis Chapter, 2005 to 2008

Personal Information

We do not recommend that you include such personal information as birth date, marital status, number of children, and related data. However, there may be instances when personal information is appropriate. If this information will give you a competitive advantage or answer unspoken questions about your background, by all means include it. Here's an example:

- Born in Belgium. U.S. Permanent Residency Status since 1997.

- Fluent in English, French, German, Flemish, and Dutch.

- Competitive Triathlete. Top-5 finish, 2000 Midwest Triathlon and 2004 Des Moines Triathlon.

Note in the preceding example that the job seeker is multilingual. This is a particularly critical selling point. Although it's listed under Personal Information in this example, it is more appropriately highlighted in your Career Summary.

Consolidating the Extras

Sometimes you have so many extra categories at the end of your resume, each with only a handful of lines, that spacing becomes a problem. You certainly don't want to have to make your resume a page longer to accommodate five lines, nor do you want the "extras" to overwhelm the primary sections of your resume. Yet you believe the information is important and should be included. Or perhaps you have a few small bits of information that you think are important but don't merit an entire section. In these situations, consider consolidating the information using one of the following formats. You'll save space, avoid overemphasizing individual items, and present a professional, distinguished appearance. Here are two examples of how to consolidate and format your "extras":

PROFESSIONAL PROFILE

Technology Qualifications	IBM & HP Platforms Microsoft Office Suite, SAP, ProjectPlanner, MRP, DRP, LAN, WAN, Lotus Notes, Novell NetWare
Affiliations	Association of Quality Control Institute of Electrical & Electronic Engineers American Electrical Association
Public Speaking	Speaker, IEEE Conference, Chicago, 2009 Presenter, AEA National Conference, Miami, 2006 Panelist, IEEE Conference, Detroit, 2004
Languages	Fluent in English, Spanish, and German

ADDITIONAL INFORMATION

- Co-chair, Education Committee, Detroit Technology Association.
- PC literate with MRP, DRP, SAP, and Kaizen technologies.
- Available for relocation worldwide.
- Eagle Scout ... Boy Scout Troop Leader.

Writing Tips, Techniques, and Important Lessons

At this point, you've done a lot of reading, probably taken some notes, highlighted samples that appeal to you, and are ready to plunge into writing your resume. To make this task as easy as possible, we've compiled some "insider" techniques that we've used in our professional resume-writing practices. These techniques were learned the hard way through years of experience! We know they work; they will make the writing process easier, faster, and more enjoyable for you.

GET IT DOWN—THEN POLISH AND PERFECT IT

Don't be too concerned with making your resume "perfect" the first time around. It's far better to move fairly swiftly through the process, getting the basic information organized and on paper (or on screen), rather than agonizing about the perfect phrase or ideal formatting. When you've completed a draft, we think you'll be surprised at how close to "final" it is, and you'll be able to edit, tighten, and improve formatting fairly quickly.

WRITE YOUR RESUME FROM THE BOTTOM UP

Here's the system:

1. **Start with the easy things**—Education, Technology, Professional Affiliations, Public Speaking, Publications, and any other extras you want to include. These items require little thought and can be completed in just a few minutes.

2. **Write short job descriptions for your older positions.** Be very brief and focus on highlights such as rapid promotion; achievements; innovations; professional honors; or employment with well-respected, well-known companies.

NOTE: Even if you plan to create a functional resume that combines job achievements in one "front-and-center" location, we recommend that you first draft these descriptions in a chronological format. It will be easier to remember what you did if you take each of your jobs in turn. Later you can regroup your statements to emphasize related skills and abilities, and leave your employment history as a simple list or brief description to support your career-change objectives.

Once you've completed this, look at how much you've written in a short period of time! Then move on to the next step.

3. **Write the job descriptions for your most recent positions.** This will take a bit longer than the other sections you have written. Remember to focus on the overall scope of your responsibility, major projects and initiatives, and significant achievements as they relate directly to your current objectives. Tell your reader what you did and how well you did it. You can use any of the formats recommended earlier in this chapter, or you can create something that is unique to you and your career.

   Now, see how far along you are? Your resume is 90 percent complete with only one section left to do.

4. **Write your career summary.** Before you start writing, remember your objective for this section. The summary should not simply rehash your previous experience. Rather, it is designed to highlight the skills and qualifications you have that are most closely related to your current career objective(s). The summary is intended to capture the reader's attention and "sell" your expertise and is the *most important* section for any career-change resume.

That's it. You're done. We guarantee that the process of writing your resume will be much, much easier if you follow the "bottom-up" strategy. Now, on to the next tip.

INCLUDE NOTABLE OR PROMINENT "EXTRA" STUFF IN YOUR CAREER SUMMARY

Remember the "extra-credit sections" that are normally at the bottom of your resume? If this information is particularly significant or prominent—you won a notable award, spoke at an international conference, developed a new teaching methodology, designed a new product that generated tens of millions of dollars in new revenues, or slashed 60 percent from operating costs—you might want to include it at the top in your Career Summary. Remember, the summary section is written to distinguish you from the crowd of other qualified candidates. As such, if you've accomplished anything that clearly demonstrates your knowledge, expertise, and credibility, consider moving it to your Career Summary for added attention. Refer to the sample career summaries earlier in the chapter for examples.

Use Resume Samples to Get Ideas for Content, Format, and Organization

This book is just one of many resources where you can review sample resumes to help you in formulating your strategy, writing the text, and formatting your resume. You don't have to struggle alone. Rather, use all the available resources at your disposal.

Be forewarned, however, that it's unlikely you will find a resume that fits your life and career to a "t." It's more likely that you will use "some of this sample" and "some of that sample" to create a resume that is uniquely "you."

Include Dates or Not?

Unless you are over age 50, we recommend that you date your work experience and your education. Without dates, your resume becomes vague and difficult for the typical hiring manager or recruiter to interpret. It often communicates the message that you are trying to hide something. By including the dates of your education and your experience, you create a clean and concise picture that one can easily follow to track your career progression.

If you want the dates to be prominent, consider putting them at the right margin. Conversely, if you want to downplay the dates, put them in small type immediately after the name of your company or the title of your position, or even at the end of the descriptive paragraph for each position.

An Individual Decision

If you are over age 50, dating your early positions must be an individual decision. On the one hand, you do not want to "date" yourself out of consideration by including dates from the 1960s and 1970s. On the other hand, those positions might be worth including for any of a number of reasons. Further, if you omit those early dates, you might feel as though you are misrepresenting yourself (or lying) to a prospective employer.

Here is a strategy to overcome those concerns while still including your early experience: Create a separate category titled "Previous Professional Experience," in which you summarize your earliest employment. You can tailor this statement to emphasize just what is most important about that experience.

If you want to capitalize on the good reputation of your past employers, include a statement such as this:

- Previous experience includes supervisory positions with IBM, Dell, and Xerox.

If you want to focus on the rapid progression of your career, consider this example:

- Promoted rapidly through a series of increasingly responsible sales and marketing management positions with Hilton Hotels.

If you want to focus on your early career achievements, include a statement such as this:

> • Member of 6-person task force credited with the design and rollout of Davidson's first-generation videoconferencing technology.

By including any one of the preceding paragraphs, under the heading "Previous Professional Experience," you are clearly communicating to your reader that your employment history dates further back than the dates you have indicated on your resume. In turn, you are being 100 percent aboveboard and not misrepresenting yourself or your career. You're also focusing on the success, achievement, and prominence of your earliest assignments.

Include Dates in the Education Section?

If you are over age 50, we generally do not recommend that you date your education or college degrees. Simply include the degree and the university with no date. Why exclude yourself from consideration by immediately presenting the fact that you earned your college degree in 1968, 1972, or 1976—about the time the hiring manager was probably being born? Remember, the goal of your resume is to share the highlights of your career and open doors for interviews. It is *not* to give your entire life story. As such, it is not mandatory to date your college degree.

However, if you use this strategy, be aware that the reader is likely to assume there is *some* gap between when your education ended and your work experience started. Therefore, if you choose to begin your chronological work history with your first job out of college, omitting your graduation date could actually backfire, because the reader might assume that you have experience that predates your first job. In this case, it's best either to *include your graduation date* or *omit dates of earliest experience,* using the summary strategy discussed earlier.

Always Send a Cover Letter When You Forward Your Resume

Sending a cover letter every time you send a resume is expected and is appropriate job search etiquette. As a career changer, your cover letter is *vital* to the success of your job search campaign.

Consider the following: When you write a resume, you are writing a document that you can use for every position you apply for, assuming that the requirements for all of those positions will be similar. You invest a great deal of time and effort in crafting just the "right" resume for you, but once it's done, it's done.

Your cover letter, however, is a document that is constantly changing to meet the needs of each individual situation for which you apply. In essence, it is the tool that allows you to customize your presentation to each company or recruiter, addressing their specific hiring requirements. Use your cover letter to highlight the most important qualifications, experiences, and achievements you bring to that specific company so that a prospective employer doesn't have to search through your resume to find what is most important. It is also the appropriate place to include any specific information that has been requested, such as salary history or salary requirements.

Your cover letter will allow you to briefly address why you're making a career change. Some examples might include the following:

> After years of success in the health care industry, I have decided to transition my skills to the pharmaceutical sales industry, where I can continue to apply my medical and nursing knowledge while achieving new career milestones.

> Although my career with CBS News has been exceptional and presented me with opportunities I never imagined possible, my real passion has always been public relations. As such, I have given my notice to CBS and am now interviewing with PR firms throughout New York to identify professional opportunities where I can begin to learn the business and establish my new career track.

> When I graduated from college in 1995, I was immediately recruited by Federal Express, where I have continued to work since that date. Now, 15 years later, I wonder what happened to my dreams of being a commercial photographer. Somehow, between career and family, they were sidetracked. Well, no more! I've committed myself to making a career change and am approaching it with energy, enthusiasm, and a real commitment to success.

> My 14-year career with Autos International was an extraordinary experience, highlighted by rapid promotions and numerous corporate commendations. However, the company fell on hard times and my position was subsequently eliminated this past month. Knowing that the auto industry is undergoing remarkable change and reorganization, I have decided to now concentrate my purchasing career in the more stable software industry—thus, my interest in your company.

Be sure to review part III of this book for an extensive discussion of cover letters and numerous excellent examples of cover letters that worked well for career changers.

Always Remember That You Are Selling

As we have discussed over and over throughout this book, resume writing is sales. Understand and appreciate the value you bring to a prospective employer, and then communicate that value by focusing on your achievements. Companies don't want to hire just anyone; they want to hire "the" someone who will make a difference. Show them that you are that candidate.

CHAPTER 3

Printed, Scannable, Electronic, and Web Resumes

After you've worked so tirelessly to write a winning resume, your next challenge is the resume's design, layout, and presentation. It's not enough for it to read well; your resume must also have just the right look for the right audience.

The Four Types of Resumes

In today's employment market, job seekers use four types of resume presentations:

- Printed

- Scannable

- Electronic (e-mail attachments and ASCII text files)

- Web

The following sections give details on when you would need each type, as well as how to prepare these types of resumes.

THE PRINTED RESUME

We know the printed resume as the "traditional resume," the one that you mail to a recruiter, take to an interview, and forward by mail or fax in response to an advertisement. When preparing a printed resume, you want to create a sharp, professional, and visually attractive presentation. Remember, that piece of paper conveys the very first impression of you to a potential employer, and that first impression goes a long, long way. Never be fooled into thinking that just because you have the best qualifications in your industry, the visual presentation of your resume does not matter. It does, a great deal.

THE SCANNABLE RESUME

The scannable resume can be referred to as the "plain-Jane" or "plain-vanilla" resume. All of the things that you would normally do to make your printed resume look attractive—bold print, italic, multiple columns, sharp-looking typestyle, and more—are stripped away in a scannable resume. You want to present a document that can be easily read and interpreted by scanning technology.

Although the technology continues to improve—and many scanning systems in fact can read a wide variety of type enhancements—it's sensible to appeal to the "lowest common denominator" when creating your scannable resume. Follow these formatting guidelines:

- Choose a commonly used, easily read font such as Arial or Times New Roman.

- Don't use bold, italic, or underlined type.

- Use a minimum of 11-point type size.

- Position your name, and nothing else, on the top line of the resume.

- Keep text left-justified, with a "ragged" right margin.

- It's okay to use common abbreviations (for instance, scanning software will recognize "B.S." as a Bachelor of Science degree). But, when in doubt, spell it out.

- Eliminate graphics, borders, and horizontal lines.

- Use plain, round bullets or asterisks.

- Avoid columns and tables, although a simple two-column listing can be read without difficulty.

- Spell out symbols such as % and &.

- If you divide words with slashes, add a space before and after the slash to be certain the scanner doesn't misread the letters.

- Print using a laser printer on smooth white paper.

- If your resume is longer than one page, be sure to print on only one side of the paper; put your name, telephone number, and e-mail address on the top of page two; and don't staple the pages together.

- For best possible results, mail your resume (don't fax it), and send it flat in a 9 × 12 envelope so that you won't have to fold it.

Scannable resumes are becoming less common and less in demand as the majority of career documents are transmitted by e-mail or pasted into online applications. It is only when your resume pages need to physically pass through a scanner that you will need a scannable resume. We recommend that you not worry about this format until and unless you are required to produce one for a specific company. For electronic resume guidelines, see the next section.

THE ELECTRONIC RESUME

Your electronic resume can take two forms: e-mail attachments and ASCII text files.

E-mail Attachments

When including your resume with an e-mail, simply attach the word-processing file of your printed resume. Because a vast majority of businesses use Microsoft Word, it is the most acceptable format and will present the fewest difficulties. However, given the tremendous variety in versions of software and operating systems, not to mention printer drivers, it's quite possible that your beautifully formatted resume will look quite different when viewed and printed at the other end. To minimize these glitches, use generous margins (at least 0.75 inch all around). Don't use unusual typefaces, and minimize fancy formatting effects.

Test your resume by e-mailing it to several friends or colleagues, and then having them view and print it on their systems. If you use WordPerfect, Microsoft Works, or another word-processing program, consider saving your resume in a more universally accepted format such as RTF or PDF. Again, try it out on friends before sending it to a potential employer.

Although employers can easily open, view, and print a PDF (Portable Document Format) file, we do not recommend this as your primary electronic format. A PDF file is viewed as a graphic rather than an editable file, and therefore the data from your resume cannot be read into a company's resume-storage system unless it is printed and physically scanned. PDF is an excellent option if your resume has an unusual design, and especially if design skills are an important part of your qualifications. But for the most part, the PDF format will be less useful than a word-processing file format (such as .doc) for the companies receiving your resume.

ASCII Text Files

You'll find many uses for an ASCII text version of your resume:

- To avoid formatting problems, you can paste the text into the body of an e-mail message rather than send an attachment. Many employers actually prefer this method. Pasting text into an e-mail message lets you send your resume without the possibility of also sending a virus.

- You can readily copy and paste the text version into online job application and resume bank forms, with no worries that formatting glitches will cause confusion.

- Although it's unattractive, the text version is 100 percent scannable.

To create a text version of your resume, follow these simple steps:

1. Create a new version of your resume using the Save As feature of your word-processing program. Select "text only" or "ASCII" in the Save As option box.

2. Close the new file.

3. Reopen the file, and you'll find that your word processor has automatically reformatted your resume into Courier font, removed all formatting, and left-justified the text.

4. To promote maximum readability when sending your resume electronically, reset the margins to 2 inches left and right, so that you have a narrow column of text rather than a full-page width. (This margin setting will not be retained when you close the file, but in the meantime you can adjust the text formatting for best screen appearance. For instance, if you choose to include a horizontal line to separate sections of the resume, by working with the narrow

margins you won't make the mistake of creating a line that extends past the normal screen width. Plus, you won't add hard line breaks that create odd-length lines when seen at normal screen width.)

5. Review the resume and fix any "glitches" such as odd characters that may have been inserted to take the place of "curly" quotes, dashes, accents, or other nonstandard symbols.

6. Remove any tabs and adjust spacing as necessary. You might add a few extra blank lines or move text down to the next line.

7. If necessary, add extra blank lines to improve readability.

8. Consider adding horizontal dividers to break the resume into sections for improved skimmability. You can use any standard typewriter symbols such as *, -, (,), =, +, ^, or #.

To illustrate what you can expect when creating these versions of your resume, on the following pages are some examples of the same resume in traditional printed format, scannable version, and electronic (text) format.

THE WEB RESUME

This newest evolution in resumes combines the visually pleasing quality of the printed resume with the technological ease of the electronic resume. You host your Web resume on your own Web site (with your own URL), to which you refer prospective employers and recruiters. Now instead of seeing just a "plain-Jane" version of your e-mail resumes, with just one click an employer can view, download, and print your Web resume—an attractive, nicely formatted presentation of your qualifications.

What's more, because the Web resume is such an efficient and easy-to-manage tool, you can choose to include more information than you would in a printed, scannable, or electronic resume. Consider separate pages for project highlights, achievements, technology qualifications, equipment skills, honors and awards, management skills, volunteer contributions, professional memberships, civic memberships, publications, public speaking, international travel and foreign languages, and anything else you believe will improve your market position. Remember, you're working to sell yourself into your next job!

If you are in a technology-related position, you can take it a step further and create a virtual multimedia presentation that not only tells someone how talented you are, but also visually and technologically demonstrates it. Web resumes are an outstanding tool for people seeking jobs in technologically or visually related professions.

Your Web resume can also include all of the items that you would include in a professional portfolio, such as photographs of your work, writing samples, designs, or job evaluations. Testimonials and letters of reference can be another powerful part of your Web resume.

Depending on your technology skills, you might decide to create and manage your own Web resume/portfolio. We suggest visiting www.visualcv.com, where you can enhance your traditional resume with a full selection of add-ons. This service is free to individuals and is a versatile tool for job search and lifelong career management. Another option is to outsource this project to a firm that specializes in career portfolios. We like Blue Sky Portfolios (www.blueskyportfolios.com).

An online version of your Microsoft Word resume can also serve as a simple Web resume. Instead of attaching a file to an e-mail that you send to an employer, you can include a link to the online version. This format is not as graphically dynamic as a full-fledged Web resume, but it can be a very useful tool for your job search. For instance, you can offer the simplicity of text in your e-mail, plus the instant availability of a printable, formatted word-processing document for the interested recruiter or hiring manager.

T. RICHARD POLAWSKI

5252 Memory Lane — Shuffletown, NC 28217 — 704-365-1818 — trpolawski@carolina.rr.com

CAREER GOAL

Position as Instructor in an environment focused on education, enlightenment, and encouragement.

KEY BENEFITS

- Exceptional ability to communicate technical information to end users. Have provided end-user training and ongoing support in network, Internet/Web, and various Microsoft applications (Windows, Outlook, Exchange).
- Offer a unique, valuable perspective gained from longevity in the field (11 years with Microsoft Corporation), complemented by a passion for technology, an enjoyment of training delivery, and an inner drive to remain on the cutting edge.
- Expertise in systematically troubleshooting network messaging problems, upgrading hardware/software, and performing service work; received superlative grades in courses in Pascal, Advanced Pascal, Fortran, COBOL, and C languages.

INFORMATION TECHNOLOGY COMPETENCIES

- *Microsoft Certified Systems Engineer (MCSE),* 2003; *Microsoft Certified Professional (MCP),* 2000: Design, install, maintain, troubleshoot, test, and repair computer systems. Experienced in building and rebuilding computers and related peripherals.
- Strong background in developing and evaluating new products and implementing "best practices." Extensive experience in writing technical (including user-training) procedures.

RECENT EMPLOYMENT HISTORY

MICROSOFT CORPORATION — Charlotte, NC 1999–Present
Product Support Engineer

Currently provide product support for MS Exchange: Troubleshoot message-flow problems across various networks and the Internet, to include interfacing with Lotus Domino and Novell GroupWise servers. Previously provided support for MS Word for Windows and Macintosh. **Wrote technical procedures for user functions,** including repair, optimization, and other customer requirements.

A section of the print version of the resume.

T. Richard Polawski
5252 Memory Lane, Shuffletown, NC 28217
704-365-1818 — trpolawski@carolina.com

CAREER GOAL
Position as Instructor in an environment focused on education, enlightenment, and encouragement.

KEY BENEFITS
- Exceptional ability to communicate technical information to end users. Have provided end-user training and ongoing support in network, Internet / Web, and various Microsoft applications (Windows, Outlook, Exchange).
- Offer a unique, valuable perspective gained from longevity in the field (11 years with Microsoft Corporation), complemented by a passion for technology, an enjoyment of training delivery, and an inner drive to remain on the cutting edge.
- Expertise in systematically troubleshooting network messaging problems, upgrading hardware / software, and performing service work; received superlative grades in courses in Pascal, Advanced Pascal, FORTRAN, COBOL, and C languages.

INFORMATION TECHNOLOGY COMPETENCIES
- Microsoft Certified Systems Engineer (MCSE), Microsoft Certified Professional (MCP): Design, install, maintain, troubleshoot, test, and repair computer systems. Experienced in building and rebuilding computers and related peripherals.
- Strong background in developing and evaluating new products and implementing best practices. Extensive experience in writing technical (including user-training) procedures.

RECENT EMPLOYMENT HISTORY
MICROSOFT CORPORATION, Charlotte, NC, 1999–Present
Product Support Engineer
Currently provide product support for MS Exchange: Troubleshoot message-flow problems across various networks and the Internet, to include interfacing with Lotus Domino and Novell GroupWise servers. Previously provided support for MS Word for Windows and Macintosh. Wrote technical procedures for user functions, including repair, optimization, and other customer requirements.

A section of the scannable version of the resume.

```
T. Richard Polawski
5252 Memory Lane, Shuffletown, NC 28217
704-365-1818 — trpolawski@carolina.rr.com

==========================================
CAREER GOAL

Position as Instructor in an environment focused on education, enlightenment, and
encouragement.

==========================================
KEY BENEFITS

* Exceptional ability to communicate technical information to end users. Have
provided end-user training and ongoing support in network, Internet/Web, and various
Microsoft applications (Windows, Outlook, Exchange).
* Offer a unique, valuable perspective gained from longevity in the field (11 years
with Microsoft Corporation), complemented by a passion for technology, an enjoyment
of training delivery, and an inner drive to remain on the cutting edge.
* Expertise in systematically troubleshooting network messaging problems, upgrading
hardware/software, and performing service work; received superlative grades in
computer programming courses.

==========================================
INFORMATION TECHNOLOGY COMPETENCIES

* Microsoft Certified Systems Engineer (MCSE), Microsoft Certified
Professional (MCP): Design, install, maintain, troubleshoot, test, and repair
computer systems. Experienced in building and rebuilding computers and related
peripherals.
* Strong background in developing and evaluating new products and implementing
''best practices.'' Extensive experience in writing technical (including user-
training) procedures.

==========================================
RECENT EMPLOYMENT HISTORY

MICROSOFT CORPORATION, Charlotte, NC, 1999-Present
----------------------------
Product Support Engineer
----------------------------
Currently provide product support for MS Exchange: Troubleshoot message-flow
problems across various networks and the Internet, to include interfacing with Lotus
Domino and Novell GroupWise servers. Previously provided support for MS Word for
Windows and Macintosh. Wrote technical procedures for user functions, including
repair, optimization, and other customer requirements.
```

A section of the electronic version of the resume.

The Four Resume Types Compared

This chart quickly compares the similarities and differences between the four types of resumes we've discussed in this chapter.

	PRINTED RESUMES	SCANNABLE RESUMES
TYPESTYLE/ FONT	Sharp, conservative, and distinctive (see our recommendations in chapter 1).	Clean, concise, and machine-readable: Times New Roman, Arial, Helvetica.
TYPESTYLE ENHANCEMENTS	**Bold,** *italic,* and <u>underlining</u> for emphasis.	CAPITALIZATION is the only type enhancement you can be certain will transmit.
TYPE SIZE	10-, 11-, or 12-point preferred; larger type sizes (14, 18, 20, 22, and even larger, depending on typestyle) will effectively enhance your name and section headers.	11- or 12-point or larger.
TEXT FORMAT	Use centering and indentations to optimize the visual presentation.	Type all information flush left.
PREFERRED LENGTH	1 to 2 pages; 3 if essential.	1 to 2 pages preferred, although length is not as much of a concern as with printed resumes.
PREFERRED PAPER COLOR	White, ivory, light gray, light blue, or other conservative background.	White or very light with no prints, flecks, or other shading that might affect scannability.
WHITE SPACE	Use appropriately for best readability.	Use generously to maximize scannability.

ELECTRONIC RESUMES	**WEB RESUMES**
Courier.	Sharp, conservative, and distinctive… attractive onscreen and when printed from an online document.
CAPITALIZATION is the only enhancement available to you.	**Bold,** *italic,* and <u>underlining</u>, and color for emphasis.
12-point.	10-, 11-, or 12-point preferred; larger type sizes (14, 18, 20, 22, and even larger, depending on typestyle) will effectively enhance your name and section headers.
Type all information flush left.	Use centering and indentations to optimize the visual presentation.
Length is immaterial; almost definitely, converting your resume to text will make it longer.	Length is immaterial; just be sure your site is well organized so viewers can quickly find the material of greatest interest to them.
N/A.	Paper is not used, but do select your background carefully to maximize readability.
Use white space to break up dense text sections.	Use appropriately for best readability, both onscreen and when printed.

Are You Ready to Write Your Resume?

To be sure that you're ready to write your resume, go through the following checklist. Each item is a critical step that you must take in the process of writing and designing your own winning resume.

- ❏ Clearly define "who you are" and how you want to be perceived.

- ❏ Document your key skills, qualifications, and knowledge.

- ❏ Document your notable career achievements and successes.

- ❏ Identify one or more specific job targets or positions.

- ❏ Identify one or more industries that you are targeting.

- ❏ Research and compile keywords for your profession, industry, and specific job targets.

- ❏ Determine which resume format suits you and your career best.

- ❏ Select an attractive font.

- ❏ Determine whether you need a print resume, a scannable resume, an electronic resume, a Web resume, or all four.

- ❏ Secure a private e-mail address.

- ❏ Review resume samples for up-to-date ideas on resume styles, formats, organization, and language.

PART II

Sample Resumes for Career Changers

CHAPTER 4

Resumes for Career Changers Seeking Accounting, Finance, Banking, Administrative, Office Management, Business Management, and Insurance Positions

Resumes in this chapter represent a wide array of functions, but they share a focus on relevant skills, recent training, and pertinent experiences that qualify each individual for a new career goal.

- Contract analyst to administrative assistant
- Real estate agent to business support specialist
- Sales to administrative support
- Truck driver to insurance claims
- Researcher and fitness trainer to banking/finance professional
- Retail sales associate to bank teller
- Law enforcement professional to actuary
- Nurse to medical insurance professional
- Retail manager to accountant
- Physician to accounting/finance professional
- Retail manager to accountant/auditor/tax specialist
- Auto service manager to corporate transportation manager
- Military to corporate supervisor or manager
- Elementary school teacher to business project manager
- Attorney to sports industry executive
- Nightclub general manager to building/facilities manager
- Call-center manager to finance executive
- Research scientist to management consultant

JESSICA MANSFIELD

203 Willow Lane
Costa Mesa, CA 92627

949-646-8149
jmansfield@hotmail.com

ADMINISTRATIVE ASSISTANT

Energetic and competent office professional with more than 10 years of administrative assistant/secretarial experience, recognized for dependable and detail-oriented work in support of top management. Excellent computer, communication, and office support skills. Well known by management as someone who gets things done. Proven skills in

Database Management	Meeting/Travel Arrangements	Customer Relations
PowerPoint Presentations	Appointment Scheduling	Problem Solving
Computer Programs	Contract Analysis	Editing
Correspondence	Office Machines	Billing

Promoted to Administrative Assistant and Executive Secretary to President as a result of excellent and consistently dependable performance.

PROFESSIONAL EXPERIENCE

Administrative Assistant and Executive Secretary

- Managed calendar and daily schedule for President, coordinating multiple activities in a fast-paced environment. Scheduled appointments and recorded them on electronic calendar.

- Liaised with COO, corporate executives, management, and clients to coordinate meetings and confirm information for presentations and documents. Edited documents for COO and management.

- Maximized corporate information storage and retrieval systems by reorganizing and maintaining all major company files, contracts, patents, and secrecy agreements.

- Organized executive and client meetings/luncheons (in-house and off-site), planning all amenities.

- Arranged domestic and international travel itineraries for Chief Operating Officer, President, Vice Presidents, and Management.

Secretary

- Maintained and coordinated calendar, set appointments, screened telephone calls, sorted mail, and made travel arrangements for the President.

- Assisted in PowerPoint presentations—editing, coordinating, and integrating multiple facets to facilitate a smooth corporate presentation.

- Communicated directly with all clients by writing routine correspondence and responding to telephone requests. Transcribed correspondence as requested.

- Edited reports, company proposals, government proposals, and contracts for clients and management.

- Monitored corporate website and wrote a monthly report on website activity, outlining and consolidating information about e-mail content, trends, and geographic activity.

(continued)

Career Change: *From contract analyst in a technology industry to administrative assistant in the health care field.*

Jessica Mansfield   page 2   949-646-8149

Contract Analyst

- Managed the entire process of recording and receipting all incoming signed contracts, purchase orders, credits, and cancellations and entered contract information into database.

- Reorganized billing department by implementing new billing protocol and filing procedures. Results: Expedited billing process and increased employee effectiveness.

- Monitored accounts and billing process, generating 300–500 invoices and credit memos per week for client base of 2,000 transportation, 300 media, and 100 energy customers.

- Consistently updated and maintained customer and product database, providing corporate personnel with accurate and compatible information at all times.

- Interfaced with internal members of operations and customer support staff, as well as clients, and oversaw all inquiries relating to the administration of contract terms and agreements.

- Researched billing problems with clients and sales department and determined appropriate corrective actions while continually optimizing customer satisfaction.

EMPLOYMENT HISTORY

Satellite Media Corporation, Costa Mesa, CA   2004–Present
    Contract Analyst, Finance Department
    Administrative Assistant to Chief Operating Officer

TransNational Engineering Corporation, Fullerton, CA   1993–2004
    Executive Secretary to President
    Secretary to Technical Director

EDUCATION

Mesa West Community College, Orange, CA   2006
Business Administration Courses

Fullerton Community College, Fullerton, CA   Graduated 1993
Secretarial Program

COMPUTER SKILLS

Microsoft Word, Excel, PowerPoint; PeopleSoft Billing; data entry

Strategy: *Use functional format to highlight relevant experience from prior career in health care administration.*

RESUME 2: BY CAROL ALTOMARE, MRW, ACRW, CPRW, CCMC, CJSS

DEIDRE CHEVALIER

1027 Harbor View Road ◆ Baltimore, MD 21220 ◆ (410) 559-9862 ◆ dchevalier@gmail.com

BUSINESS SUPPORT SPECIALIST

*Recognized go-to resource with strong problem-solving skills
and a flair for client relations*

Well-regarded support professional with a proven record of success in overseeing administrative processes and coordinating programs in support of business goals. Organized, effective multi-tasker known for persistent approach, thorough follow-through, and calmness under pressure. Persuasive communicator who is effective in developing rapport with others while building trust and respect. Disciplined self-starter who can be relied on to get the job done no matter what the challenge.

Key Strengths:

▷ Project Coordination	▷ Research/Reporting	▷ Recordkeeping
▷ Process Management	▷ Problem-Solving	▷ Billing/Invoicing
▷ Relationship Building	▷ Customer Service	▷ General Accounting

SELECT ACCOMPLISHMENTS

➤ **Established record of success in coordinating projects, managing all administrative details of as many as 15 property listings at a time.**
  - ▷ Processed files and coordinated preparation of marketing materials to get new listings into system.
  - ▷ Worked closely with attorney offices, mortgage companies, home inspectors, and clients, serving as liaison to expedite transactions and facilitate the sales process.
  - ▷ Earned praise from manager and clients for success in maintaining open lines of communication and keeping projects on track, hastening sales.

➤ **Leveraging on-target customer service instincts and keen attention to detail, earned reputation for consistency in delivering service excellence.**
  - ▷ Implemented communication plan to keep clients informed of sale progress and alert them to next steps, building sense of confidence and trust that cemented relationships and promoted loyalty.
  - ▷ Included special touches in communications, earning praise from clients for providing service levels that went above and beyond industry standards.
  - ▷ Diligently followed up on all details, providing advice and insights to smooth process for clients.

➤ **Quick to master new processes and procedures, served as resource to others to improve overall office effectiveness.**
  - ▷ Provided computer training to new office personnel to help them get up to speed on new systems.
  - ▷ Updated and maintained office listing that compiled contact information for business resources (mortgage companies, attorneys, home inspectors, etc.) for recommendation to clients.
  - ▷ Reviewed, edited, and approved content for brochures and website.

➤ **Oversaw office operations for small business, setting up and implementing all administrative processes and procedures.**
  - ▷ Implemented QuickBooks to improve ease and accuracy of recordkeeping and accounting.
  - ▷ Cultivated and maintained strong relationships with supply companies, leveraging interpersonal skills to gain top-level service.
  - ▷ Provided timely, accurate invoicing and bill-paying services.

Career Change: *From real estate agent to business support specialist.*

Strategy: *Use a headline and branding statement to immediately establish expertise. Then highlight specific accomplishments and areas of expertise using a functional format.*

Deidre Chevalier ◆ Page 2   (410) 559-9862 ◆ dchevalier@gmail.com

PROFESSIONAL EXPERIENCE

LORD CALVERT REALTY   2000 to 2009
Administrative Assistant/Sales Agent
Serving as right-hand assistant to company's top producer, handled all administrative aspects related to listing and marketing of properties as well as negotiation and closing of sales.

PIMLICO REALTY   1995 to 2000
Sales Agent
Marketed and sold properties, specializing in Baltimore and Prince George's counties.

Earlier Experience:
Background also includes experience as office manager for small, family-run construction company.

EDUCATION & LICENSURE

A.S., Secretarial Science, Prince George's County Community College

Licensed Real Estate Agent (Maryland)

TECHNOLOGY SKILLS

Word; QuickBooks; Realtor Manager; Internet and e-mail applications

VOLUNTEER ACTIVITIES

Fund-Raising Volunteer, Girls on the Run of Baltimore (supporting girls in athletics)
Corporate Volunteer, Crab Festival (representing Lord Calvert Realty)
Vice President, Towson High School Football Booster Club
Fund-Raising and Event Volunteer, Riverview Mill
Volunteer, Silver Springs Community Day

Annette Alstad
1775 Greene Avenue, Rockaway, NJ 07866
(973) 957-5555 ▪ annalstad@yahoo.com

Administrative Support/Customer Service—Medical/Clinical Setting

Dedicated, experienced professional with strong organizational, communications, and project management skills. Calm demeanor under stress; cooperative team leader. Recent training in medical billing, medical terminology, and ICD-9-CM coding. Proven multitasking/operations support skills. Adept in

☑ Client Relationship Management   ☑ Medical Records Terminology   ☑ Budget Controls
☑ Account/Territory Management   ☑ Customer Needs Assessment   ☑ Program Management

KEY SUPPORTING SKILLS

- **Administration:** Diverse administrative expertise includes directing nationwide SHARE (State Hospital Association Review & Evaluation) program for American Hospital Association; managing four-county sales territory in central California; and maintaining large, upscale apartment complexes.

- **Time Management:** Demonstrate top-notch organizational skills, with ability to prioritize and multitask. Developed records management systems to expedite back-office operations for sales generation, residential and retail property management, and meeting and event planning.

- **Communications:** Employ proactive problem-solving communications skills to generate "win-win" scenarios. Effectively communicated special situations and potential problem areas to management.

- **Personal Strengths:** Conscientious in following through on commitments and deadlines. Mature, discreet team player with experience interfacing with high-level executives and corporate clients.

EDUCATION

Medical Records Technician Program, Samuel Morris College, Morristown, NJ—2009
Courses: Medical Terminology, Advanced Medical Terminology, Medical Billing, ICD-9-CM Coding
Associate of Arts Degree, Fullerton Community College, Fullerton, CA

PROFESSIONAL EXPERIENCE

Estate and Health Care Management   2006–2009
✓ **Administrative Management.** Acted as prime interface with physicians, nurses, hospice, attorneys, CPA, stockbroker, and insurance companies for elderly parents with progressive, debilitating illnesses. Managed health care appointments and treatment as well as daily living arrangements on-site.

✓ **Records Management.** Submitted insurance claims and tracked insurance reimbursements. Oversaw distribution of $1 million estate. Arranged sale of house and distribution of all household goods.

Manufacturer's Representative   2000–2006
Kimball Associates, San Francisco, CA, and The Paper & Gift Center, Los Angeles, CA
Independent contractor representing fine gift, paper/stationery, and greeting-card lines for two businesses.

✓ **Account Management.** Grew accounts by 45% (from 175 to 250) and increased sales by 10% in four-county central California territory. Generated 20 new key accounts (such as Yosemite Park gift shops) through thorough market research, competitive market analysis, and persuasive prospect interaction.

✓ **Customer Relationship Management.** Developed strong client communications networks, building relationships with 250 buyers for retail stores, museums, hospital gift shops, and nurseries. Educated buyers in 60+ lines of merchandise, updating them on retail trends and demographics-driven marketing.

Career Change: *From sales to administrative support.*

Strategy: *Create a strong profile that presents just the right skill set for an administrative professional. Support desire to enter health care field by citing relevant recent training.*

Annette Alstad
(973) 957-5555 ▪ annalstad@yahoo.com   Page 2

PROFESSIONAL EXPERIENCE (continued)

Residential Property Management   1997–2000
Treadwell Properties, Inc., San Diego, CA (1999–2000), and Harmony Place, San Diego, CA (1997–1999)

✓ **Administrative Management.** Managed two upscale apartment communities (up to 516 units), with monthly rent collections of $432,000. Supervised on-site leasing as well as maintenance and grounds staff. Controlled expense budget, closely monitoring five vendor services. Oversaw renovation of 35 apartment units, coordinating workflow and scheduling of carpet, flooring, paint, and fixture vendors.

✓ **Customer Service.** Maintained 92% residency rate and achieved 98% on-time rent collection by developing proactive tenant relationship programs. Initiated educational newsletter for tenants and open-door policy for tenant complaints. Credited with stabilizing the tenant community through lawful evictions of known drug dealers.

Retail Property Management   1994–1997
The Andrus Company, Somerset, NJ; Highlands, Inc., Los Angeles, CA; Boltman & Graves, Boston, MA

✓ **Administrative Management.** Initiated and developed specialty leasing programs for three major developers (12 regional shopping centers) in high-profile metropolitan areas. Maintained high occupancy rates by actively recruiting retailers for year-round common area as well as developing long-term, favorable leases for in-line sales operations.

✓ **Program Management.** Supervised design projects for kiosks, store decor, and marketing communications (brochures, print advertising, and directories). Developed and met program budgets, generating in excess of $500,000 for each shopping center annually.

Meeting and Event Management   1991–1994
American Hospital Association, Highland Park, IL

✓ **Program Management.** Served as Director of SHARE (State Hospital Association Review & Evaluation) program. Traveled nationwide conducting peer-review meetings for 8 to 10 state hospital associations. Wrote comprehensive reports and recommendations based on participant feedback and critical observations and analysis of policies and procedures in place.

✓ **Customer Service.** Facilitated in-house discussions on-site of hospital personnel and management at all levels to increase quality assurance, strengthen employee relations, improve customer service, and streamline processes and procedures.

COMPUTER SKILLS

▪ Experienced in composing and editing letters, memos, marketing communications, and reports. Utilize Windows and Mac OS, Microsoft Word, Internet Explorer, and e-mail.

Richard G. Scanlon

129 Northgate ➤ Clear Spring, MD 21722

Residence: 301.555.0567   rgscanlon@aol.com   Cell: 240.555.2426

Career Target: Insurance Claims Representative

Offering 15+ Years of Transferable Experience

Logistics Management ➤ Motor Vehicle Maintenance ➤ Repair ➤ Military Leadership

Specialized Skills and Experience

Class "A CDL"/TPM Endorsements	Logistics Management
Qualified Road Tester Certification	Federal Contracts Management
Safety Inspections	Foreign Car Repair and Restoration
Petroleum Supply	Computer Literacy

Relevant Experience

Tractor Trailer Operator   2001–present
Sealy Mattress   Williamsport, MD

Established a reputation for reliability and efficiency in delivering company merchandise to warehouses and distribution centers throughout metro DC/Baltimore and surrounding areas. Work independently in planning and executing daily delivery routes while interfacing with warehouse supervisors, dispatchers, store managers, scale-house personnel, and state highway police. Accurately complete and record maintenance and safety inspections of the vehicle, adhering to all DOT standards.

Transportation Manager/Supervisor   1996–2000
Government Contracting Services   Alexandria, VA

Managed a three-year, $1.5M contract supplying comprehensive transportation services to the personnel and programs housed in Fort Ritchie, MD. Provided leadership and direction to a staff of 15–20 full- and part-time personnel; maintained oversight for a fleet of 125 motor vehicles. Established a vital link between the contractor and the federal government, earning high marks for efficiency and flexibility. Directed and controlled project resources to produce optimum results within the financial constraints of the contract. Held a federal security clearance.

> Collaborated with contract consultants in defining bid specifications regarding estimated man-hours and vehicle/machinery requirements.

> Hired and supervised military and non-military personnel, ensuring sufficient staffing levels for 24/7 operation coverage.

> Maintained a 95% vehicle readiness rate by establishing and maintaining effective maintenance schedules and seamless working relationships with numerous auto body and maintenance shops.

> Coordinated the logistics of transporting military and civilian personnel in and out of high-security sites.

> Collaborated with Military Police in motor accident follow-up, including review of accident reports; arranged for transport of accident vehicles for disposal or repair.

> Orchestrated the scheduling and instruction of driver safety and licensing training for personnel; made final recommendations for motor vehicle operators' license approval.

> Created and maintained an electronic spreadsheet to track employee hours for payroll.

Career Change: *From truck driver to insurance claims.*

Strategy: *Leverage prior experience as a transportation manager as well as knowledge of vehicles and maintenance to position him as a knowledgeable claims adjuster.*

Richard G. Scanlon	301.555.0567	**Page 2**

United States Army   1989-1996

Honorably Discharged Sergeant, with a diverse military career characterized by a record of "exceptionally meritorious service, dedication, and determination." Served in Germany, Korea, and Washington State. Scope of responsibility included supply and equipment records and parts; material storage and handling; vehicle repair and maintenance; and petroleum distribution.

➤ Earned leadership command of six subordinate personnel (Motor Sergeant) and 12 subordinate soldiers (Squad Leader); recognized for providing "superb guidance and leadership, which ensured optimum efficiency in the completion of tasks."

➤ Oversaw maintenance and use of 250 motor vehicles, consistently rendering outstanding achievement in procuring high-priority repair parts.

➤ Demonstrated technical expertise in repairing and replacing unserviceable parts on gas and diesel cars and trucks; interpreted work orders and determined intermediate maintenance operations for extending vehicle use.

➤ Completed military training in Defensive Driving, Small Engine Repair, Quality Management, and Quality Improvement Through Defect Prevention.

➤ Managed $20K building supply inventory, including procurement, storage, and distribution.

Additional Employment Experience

Correctional Officer   2000-2001
Cumberland Federal Correctional Institution   Cumberland, MD

Completed an eight-week training, prior to assuming responsibility for the supervision and security of 100 inmates in a newly opened maximum-security facility.

Carpenter/Mason   1988-1989
R F Kline   Frederick, MD

Interpreted drawings, blueprints, and plans to determine layout and material specifications for the construction of trestles, bridges, piers, and wharfs. Operated various hand tools and pieces of power equipment, including loaders, backhoes, mixers, and forklifts.

Education

Graduate, Williamsport High School, Williamsport, MD

College credits earned through Central Texas College and Big Bend Community College,
Wiesbaden, Germany; Central Texas College, Korea

RESUME 5: BY MYRIAM-ROSE KOHN, CPRW, CEIP, JCTC, CCM, CCMC

WILLIAM NEVADA

8917 Central Avenue
Agoura, California 91301

818-753-2548
w_nevada@aol.com

Mature, proactive, results-oriented young professional seeking to apply extensive research and data experience to the **loan** and **investment** industries. Resourceful, efficient, honest, and highly ethical, with a strong work ethic. Quick problem solver while dealing with new concepts, systems, and procedures. Decisive and self-starting in implementation. Conscientious application of policies and procedures. Professional and articulate; qualified for client / customer interaction at all levels. Committed. Recognized for

- Competency and thoroughness
- Going above and beyond requirements
- Analytical aptitude
- Organizational skills
- Being meticulous and detail oriented

- Strong communication skills
- Outstanding customer service skills
- Patience and composure
- Upbeat and positive attitude
- Working well under pressure

SKILLS

Computer   Microsoft Office Applications (Word, Excel, PowerPoint, Access)
SPSS
Extensive Internet research experience

Personal   Excellent one-on-one communication
Consistently exceed expectations
Basic conversational Spanish

EDUCATION

Bachelor of Science, Kinesiology, Exercise Science. California State University, Northridge, California, 2008 (Dean's List; GPA: 3.45)

EMPLOYMENT HISTORY

Forensic Biomechanics Assistant   2009
Gary Villareal ▪ Pacific Palisades, CA
    Perform research on various cars relating to auto accident investigations. Prepare presentations using various Microsoft Office applications.

Personal Trainer   2007–Present
Training Center ▪ Flintridge, CA   (concurrently)
    Create personal and effective exercise programs for clients. Develop good professional relationships with clients.

Spinal Cord Injury Research Assistant   2008
Robert Sephears ▪ CSUN, Northridge, CA
    Conducted literature reviews of prior related studies. Composed compilation reviews of research. Organized and entered collected data.

Career Change: *From researcher and fitness trainer to banking/finance professional.*

Strategy: *Emphasize background in research, data analysis, and working with numbers.*

WILLIAM NEVADA • 818-753-2548   Page 2

Research Assistant   2008
Richard Spencer • CSUN, Northridge, CA
> Conducted independent research regarding aquatic exercise for adapted populations through various sources: Internet, library, medical reports, and peer-review journals. Selected relevant material.

Physical Therapy Aide   2006–2007
Providence Saint Joseph Medical Center • Burbank, CA
> Supervised workout regimen for recovering surgery patients. Instructed patients in specific use of major muscle groups of lower extremities.

Day Camp Counselor   2006–2007
The Village Schools • Sherman Oaks, CA
> Instructed and cared for middle-school students in various settings. Directed and supervised group and water games with aerobic benefit. Taught group lessons and led discussions.

COMMUNITY INVOLVEMENT
Middle and High School Youth Group Leader, Sun Valley, CA
Camp Counselor, Redlands, CA
Guitar Instructor, Sylmar, CA

CERTIFICATIONS
Red Cross Adult CPR Certification
Red Cross Water Safety Instructor Certification
Aerobics and Fitness Association of America: Personal Trainer Certification

CAROLINE SMITH

29 River Street, Norwalk, CT 06854
(203) 838-3052 • carolinesmith@snet.net

BANK TELLER

Superb customer-service skills honed by 15 years of retail experience to develop and maintain customer loyalty. Highly organized; keep all records with accuracy and thoroughness.

- Customer service
- Cashier transactions
- Strong communications skills
- Patience and humor

- Long-term customer relationships
- Team member
- Membership services, marketing
- Problem solving

PC proficiency in business applications, including MS Word, Excel, and Outlook.

PROFESSIONAL EXPERIENCE

Costless, Norwalk, CT
CASHIER / CUSTOMER SERVICE / MEMBERSHIP / MARKETING   2006–Present
- Control cash flow while ringing out customers. Keep lines of shoppers moving smoothly with courtesy and humor. Receive and direct patrons at the door.
- Work with security and loss-prevention issues.
- Develop customer relationships for long-term loyalty. Known for treating shoppers like family.
- Care for all client concerns: Sign up customers for Costless and American Express charge cards; communicate with main office; update membership accounts; offer general information and product availability by telephone and in person.
- Sell memberships to businesses and individuals in local-area towns. Upgrade current members to Executive Membership for increased cash flow and customer loyalty.

PetPals, Norwalk, CT
JUNIOR MANAGER ON DUTY   2004–2006
- All aspects of opening and closing facility, including arming/disarming system, booting up computers, communicating with corporate office, counting store safe and register cash, and setting up the store.
- Created computer reports on sales, returns, and loss prevention for the corporate office.
- Motivated employees, developed customers, and oversaw animal care from ordering to sale.

Burger King, Norwalk, CT
JUNIOR MANAGER / SHIFT LEADER   1997–2004
- Opened kitchen and registers for breakfast. Observed strict food-service regulations. Met temperature and sanitizing standards.
- Supervised and motivated crew. Built solid relationships with patrons.

HealthDeli, Norwalk, CT
CASHIER   1994–1997
- Operated registers; assisted in deli; performed light stock work.
- Became knowledgeable about vitamins/supplements to advise shoppers. Worked to create trust with customers for lasting relationships.

Entrepreneurial Businesses, Norwalk, CT   Prior to 1997
HOUSE CLEANING SERVICE
OFFICE TEMPORARY WORK

EDUCATION

Psychology, Norwalk Community College, Norwalk, CT

Career Change: *From retail sales associate to bank teller.*

Strategy: *Highlight relevant skills in customer service, cash handling, and computer use; clearly show how her current position, though seemingly unrelated, requires extensive use of these skills.*

1854 Country Trail
Rochester, MN 55904

ROBERTA T. ELLIOTT

507-555-1166
bobbye@comcast.com

PROFILE

☒ Committed to excellence as an Actuary; pursued course work and exams while working full time.
☒ Recognized for assessment, analytical, problem-solving, and creative thinking skills.
☒ Effectively "read" and communicate with wide range of personalities in unusually stressful situations.
☒ Exemplify strong work ethic; goal-driven and self-motivated. Abide by principles of integrity.
☒ Long-standing interest and natural ability in personal investing, mathematics, and the sciences.
☒ Technology: Microsoft Office, Windows, Linux OS.

RELEVANT QUALIFICATIONS

☒ Passed Exam 1/P–Probability exam (2008)
☒ Currently studying for Exam 2/FM–Financial Mathematics
☒ Earned VEE credits for Economics and Corporate Finance
☒ Former member, University of Minnesota Actuarial Club

EDUCATION

UNIVERSITY OF MINNESOTA • Minneapolis, Minnesota
Actuarial Science Specialization (2009)
GPA: 3.7 | *Courses included:*

- Actuarial Models
- Probability & Statistics I: Probability
- Direct Study of Statistical Probability
- Introduction to Micro- and Macro-Economics

- Financial Management
- Theory of Investments
- Theory of Mathematical Interest
- Principles of Financial Accounting

B.A. – Chemistry (2001)

MACALISTER COLLEGE • St. Paul, Minnesota
Completed course work toward **Ph.D.** in Organic Chemistry (2002)

EMPLOYMENT HISTORY

OLMSTED COUNTY SHERIFF'S OFFICE • Rochester, Minnesota (2002–Present)
Deputy Sheriff/Patrol Officer (POST-Certified Police Officer)

- Respond to emergency and non-emergency calls including traffic accidents, personal injury accidents, property crimes, and medical assistance. Evaluate and coordinate scene while developing appropriate action plan. Conduct initial investigation and share information with detectives.
- Conduct patrols of county encompassing 653 sq miles with population of more than 124,000.
- Participate in community policing. Interact with neighborhood watch organizations. Represent the department and maintain presence within the community. Present informational programs.
- Collaborate with representatives from neighboring jurisdictions as well as county, state, and federal law enforcement agencies.
- Awarded multiple Unit Citations and Letters of Merit for professionalism, command presence, diligence, teamwork, and initiative.

Certified Motor Carrier Officer (2005–2008)

- Filled this special assignment simultaneously with patrol responsibilities.
- Inspected commercial vehicles to ensure compliance with state and federal laws with special attention to mechanical/safety issues and permits.
- Completed training through Minnesota State Patrol under auspices of the Federal Motor Carrier Act.

Career Change: *From law enforcement professional to actuary.*

Strategy: *Emphasize recent relevant training and strong academic credentials. List coursework to show expertise and include keywords in the resume.*

Maureen Welland

22398 Fox Lane • Little Rock, AR 72202 • (501) 380.6011 • moewelland@msn.com

PROFESSIONAL PROFILE

Medical Terminology • Medical Procedures • Healthcare Services • Medical Care • Insurance • Inventory/Ordering

Highly qualified medical professional with experience dealing with a multitude of medical-related administration procedures, products, and services.

- Empathetic and intuitive in client interactions; committed to providing quality care as an essential link in healing processes and pain management.
- Poised and confident contributing member of the healthcare team.
- Flexible in quickly mastering new terms, technologies, and systems.
- Demonstrated flexibility and resourcefulness in adapting to ever-changing complexity in the healthcare industry.

EXPERIENCE

HURON VALLEY OUTPATIENT SURGERY CENTER; Comanche, AR
Multi-specialty medical center providing expertise in orthopedic, plastic surgery, and ENT
Staff RN • 2003–2009

- Promoted patient health through a comprehensive range of healthcare services.
- Identified patient care requirements; established a compassionate environment; assured quality of care; resolved patient problems and needs; protected patient and employee rights; documented patient care services; maintained continuity among nursing/physician/therapist teams; maintained medical supply inventory.
- Kept updated on professional and technical knowledge; managed a cooperative relationship among healthcare teams and contributed to the team effort.

SOUTHERN MEDICAL CENTER; Landsdale, AR
Multi-specialty trauma center
Staff RN • 1996–2003

- Managed duties in both scrubbing and circulating for multi-specialty cases, including general, orthopedic, cardiovascular, ophthalmic, gynecologic, plastic, and urologic.
- Member of Trauma Team; dealt with life-threatening surgical conditions and critical medical conditions requiring surgical intervention.
- Managed orthopedic department (equipment, supplies); oversaw orthopedic cases throughout medical procedures.

EDUCATION & TRAINING

VATTEROTT COLLEGE; Joplin, MO
Bachelor of Science Degree in Nursing • 1996

Numerous in-service classes and medical-related courses

Basic understanding of MS Word and Excel

OTHER INFORMATION

Active in:

- School activities—room parent, lunch aide, member of several committees.
- Church committees—involved with various special events and programs.

Career Change: *From nurse to medical insurance professional (claims and administration).*

Strategy: *Create a strong Professional Profile that combines hard skills and medical knowledge with the attributes she will bring to her next position.*

RESUME 9: BY LOUISE GARVER, CPRW, CMP, JCTC, CEIP, MCDP, CJSS, CPBS

GREGORY LAWRENCE, C.P.A.

445 Sunset Lane
Vernon, NY 60194

glawrence@yahoo.com

Mobile: (914) 962-7835
Home: (914) 918-3499

CORPORATE ACCOUNTING • PUBLIC ACCOUNTING • TAXATION

Certified Public Accountant with business management experience and a master's degree in accounting and taxation. Critical thinker and creative problem solver with excellent planning, organizational, analytical, and financial management strengths. Technical skills: MS Office (Word, Excel, Access, PowerPoint), JD Edwards, and Peachtree Accounting.

KEY SKILLS

General Accounting … Cost Accounting … Financial/Business Analysis … Asset and Liability Management
Cost/Benefit Analysis … Financial Modeling … Auditing … Risk Assessment … Working Capital

CAPABILITIES—ACCOUNTING/FINANCE

Education and training provided a solid foundation in:

- Setting up balance sheets, income statements, and cash-flow statements in compliance with GAAP.
- Analyzing financial performance of business operations, tracking and analyzing costs, and creating and implementing cost-control systems to achieve corporate objectives.
- Developing and administering budgets; familiar with capital budgeting process. Versed in the different types of corporations, consolidations, and tax advantages.
- Determining valuation of business assets, stock and bond prices, depreciation schedules, and pro forma statements. Creating capital asset pricing models and financial models.
- Calculating P/E ratios, DCF, EPS, discounted cash flow, and beta for equity security analysis.
- Devising portfolio asset allocation strategies and conducting risk assessments; developing business plans.
- Developing financial management and investment strategies for both individuals and companies.

EDUCATION

SIMMONS COLLEGE, NEW YORK, NEW YORK
M.S. in Accounting and Taxation, 2009
B.S. in Business Administration with concentration in **Finance,** 2000

Relevant Courses: Advanced Accounting, Intermediate Accounting, Managerial Accounting, Governmental Accounting, Auditing, Finance, Business Law, Cost Accounting, Tax Accounting

Certified Public Accountant—State of New York, 2009

BUSINESS MANAGEMENT EXPERIENCE

Store Manager (2001–present) / **Assistant Manager** (1998–2001): **Value Stores, Inc., New York, New York**

Promoted to manage financial and day-to-day operations of $3 million business, including P&L, sales, merchandising, customer relations, inventory, security, human resources, and training. Scope of responsibility encompasses auditing financial records, processing payroll, managing cash, balancing drawers, entering inventory on computer system, adjusting inventory retail values, and preparing bank deposits and reconciliations.

Accomplishments:

- Significantly improved store's financial performance, bringing it from 10% under budget to 3% above budget within the first month as manager by
  - Assessing and realigning employee skills with appropriate tasks/functions.
  - Improving inventory levels and product mix on sales floor.
  - Reducing turnover, hiring and training quality candidates, and implementing a succession plan.
- Boosted profits 20% over prior year, sales by 4% annually, and budgeted profit forecasts by 6% per year.
- Winner of 3 Paragon Awards out of 15 managers in the district for achieving excellence in customer service and exceeding profitability/sales targets. Tapped as mentor, developing and training 25 new store managers.

Career Change: *From retail manager to accountant.*

Strategy: *Lead off the resume with a concise summary of background, key skills, and new goal, followed by detailed information about his proven capabilities. In presenting work experience, emphasize financial skills related to his goal.*

RESUME 10: BY IGOR SHPUDJEKO, BSIE, MBA, CPRW, JCTC

Saul M. Lieb

113 Foster Road, Teaneck, NJ 07430
(201) 226-8745 • E-mail: slieb@aol.com

ACCOUNTING / FINANCE / ADMINISTRATION

PERSONAL STATEMENT: After 16 years as a practicing physician, I'm changing career directions to follow my lifelong interest in finance and accounting. To that end, I am currently enrolled at the University of Maryland, where I am completing (12/10) my BS degree in Accounting. Following completion of this program, I plan to sit for my CPA exam and obtain my MBA from Rutgers State University and Master's in Accountancy from the University of Maryland.

My ultimate career goal is a senior-level corporate finance position. However, to achieve that level of position and responsibility, particularly considering my unique background in the health care arena, I realize that I need to start in a more junior position where I can gain practical, hands-on experience in corporate accounting and finance.

Key Qualifications

- 3.8 GPA in accounting coursework.
- Completion of 150-credit course on the Business of Medicine.
- Review and analysis of all financial and accounting statements of private practice.

EDUCATION AND TRAINING

- **Bachelor of Science in Accounting,** University of Maryland, College Park, MD, 12/10—GPA 3.8
- **Business of Medicine Executive Certification Program,** Florida State University, Tallahassee, FL, 11/09
  - Marketing and the Management of Service Quality
  - Managing People/Development Strategies
  - The Business Environment of Health Care
  - Data-Driven Management
- **MBA** to be completed 6/12, Rutgers State University, New Brunswick, NJ
- **Master's of Accountancy** to be completed 11/12, University of Maryland
- **MD,** Northeastern Ohio School of Medicine, Rootstown, OH, 1991
- **Bachelor of Arts in Biology,** University of Rochester, Rochester, NY, 1985
- **Graduate Residency**—Family Practice, St. Thomas Hospital, Akron, OH, 1994

COMPUTER SKILLS

- **Microsoft Excel Certification,** Career Blazers Computer Application Software Training
- **QuickBooks Pro Class,** 6/08

PROFESSIONAL EXPERIENCE

RAMSEY MEDICAL GROUP   Ramsey, NJ   1993–Present
Partner / General Practitioner
Large family practice. One of three partners. Responsible for patient care and practice management. Review and analyze all financial and accounting statements. Monitor monthly statements for accuracy and timeliness.
- Implemented new computer system to allow for online billing.
- Negotiated with HMOs for competitive rates.

VALLEY MEMORIAL HOSPITAL   Ridgewood, NJ   2000–2004
Chairman—Department of Family Medicine

VALLEY MEMORIAL HOSPITAL   Ridgewood, NJ   2000
Member—Executive Committee

VALLEY MEMORIAL HOSPITAL   Ridgewood, NJ   1998
Member—Hospital Credentialing Committee

NEW JERSEY MEDICAL SCHOOL   Newark, NJ   1994–2006
Assistant Professor

Career Change: *From physician to accounting/finance professional.*

Strategy: *Lay out the rationale for the career change in an interesting "personal statement"; highlight the commitment to change by listing extensive relevant education, both completed and planned.*

CARLISLE GOODWIN

10238 San Ramon Drive • Tucson, AZ 85701
520-453-6607 • cagoodwin@gmail.com

ACCOUNTING / AUDITING / TAX SPECIALIST

Critical thinker improving operations through judicious decision-making,
meaningful interactions, and strong understanding of financial and accounting principles.

Well versed in general accounting practices, compilations, cash management, financial planning/analysis/ reporting, tax preparation, and budget projection/management. Expertise in conducting audits on reporting, systems, procedures, and records; analyzing results; and proposing recommendations. Working knowledge of income tax law and tax related accounting; able to utilize various resources to research and answer questions.

CORE COMPETENCIES

- Tax & Accounting Consultation
- Financial Statement Analysis
- Auditing & Process Redesign

- Research & Investigations
- Legal/Regulatory Compliance
- Customer Service & Relations

- Profit & Loss Management
- Managerial Decision Making
- Meticulous Recordkeeping

EDUCATION

MBA, Accounting – University of Arizona, Tucson, AZ (GPA: 3.92), 2009
BS, Finance – San Diego State University, San Diego, CA, 1990

PROFESSIONAL EXPERIENCE

Financial Manager: Managed financial resources for 15+ years with direct accountability for P&L, payroll, hiring, scheduling, budget, and spending decisions. Verified deposits and held accountable for extremely large sums of cash.

- **Achieved corporate financial goals for $800M business.**

Financial Analyst: Comparatively analyzed financial reports and made necessary adjustments to meet budget requirements and corporate goals. Calculated sales projections and made expense account decisions accordingly. Set margins to reach profit line.

- **Planned and controlled budgets for start-up of $100M retail outlets.**

Tax Accountant: Built income tax return service business from the ground up. Steadily grew business through networking, reputation, and referrals. Proficiently utilized Drake tax accounting software. Joined National Association of Tax Professionals.

- **Completed tax forms/returns with absolute accuracy within tight time constraints.**

Auditor: Performed internal audits, searching for and identifying cash and recordkeeping discrepancies or dishonesty. Launched investigations to rectify problems and prevent future occurrences. Assembled and led auditing teams.

- **Routinely conducted audits and uncovered lack of controls that led to financial loss. Oversaw procedural changes to resolve issues.**

Operations Controller: Drove profitability of multi-unit operations with responsibility for up to 4,000 employees. Heightened productivity, efficiency, and quality of operations via staffing, training, customer service, inventory, and cost-saving initiatives.

- **Managed and analyzed P&L to maximize financial performance of 10 retail units.**

Career Change: From retail manager to accountant/auditor/tax specialist.

CARLISLE GOODWIN

PAGE TWO

EMPLOYMENT HISTORY

GOODWIN TAX AND ACCOUNTING   2007 to 2009

Income Tax Consultant – Mira Mesa, CA

Provided a broad range of technical tax guidance and support for a diverse client base regarding pre-filing and filing processes.

TARGET STORES   1993 to 2007

Market Manager – San Diego, CA (2 years)

In charge of 10 stores in metropolitan San Diego, comprising 4,000 employees and generating $800M in revenue per year.

District Manager – San Diego, CA (4 years)

Directly accountable for $450M of retail business, 6 stores, and 2,200 employees. Opened 3 new stores, including multi-level retail center in San Diego.

Store Manager – Escondido / Rancho Bernardo / Poway, CA (7 years)

In charge of $60M to $80M stores with 325 to 495 employees. Opened *Target's* first multi-level store, which served as model for future stores nationwide.

Store Manager – Tucson, AZ (1 year)

Managed $72M retail operations and 320 employees. Maintained profit around 5% and shrinkage under 1%.

COSTCO   1990 to 1993

Merchandising Manager – San Diego, CA

Led comprehensive merchandising efforts for $15M wholesale-format retailer. Supported warehouse manager's activities and oversaw approximately 200 employees.

~ Excellent References Available upon Request ~

Strategy: *Focus the resume on recent education (MBA in Accounting) and use functional headings in the Experience section to identify relevant skills and accomplishments before revealing employment history on page 2.*

RESUME 12: BY DON ORLANDO, MBA, CPRW, JCTC, CCM, CCMC

Stanton Kerry

222 Pine Drive   Coreyville, Alabama 36000   stantonk@bellsouth.net   ☏ 205.555.5555

PROFIT-BUILDING CAPABILITIES I CAN OFFER **TopLine** AS YOUR NEWEST
TRANSPORTATION MANAGER

❑ Building and maintaining teams that want to do well—as a point of honor

❑ Matching the right person to the right job

❑ Investing judiciously in training that produces a return on investment

❑ Limiting liability

❑ Keeping loyalty by showing each employee the tie between his job and his
company's future

RECENT WORK HISTORY WITH EXAMPLES OF PROBLEMS SOLVED

❑ Sales Representative *promoted ahead of 10 more experienced competitors to be*
Service Manager, Saturn of Centerville, Centerville, KY   90 to 09

*Because we were one of Saturn's first service departments, my work was closely
monitored not just by the dealership owner, but by some corporate levels at
Saturn's headquarters. The shop I managed produced $700K in annual sales.*

Served as direct reporting official for 21 service technicians, oil changers, and
detailers; 2 service writers; and a cashier.

"Rescued" a top-performing employee whose work had deteriorated. Earned
his trust by helping guide him through family problems. Gave him key tasks I knew he
could do well. Then boosted his confidence by having him train others. *Payoffs:* His
morale and productivity soared. He remains one of the company's **top-producing**
technicians.

Redesigned our workload so employees saw their stake in doing a key job that had
limited their earnings for years. My fix was ready in a week. *Payoffs:* **Costly repairs
fell. People felt management cared** about them. That's why employees **worked on
their own time** to do the job well.

Listened to my people and our customers well enough to design and execute new work
schedules that helped everyone. Overcame owner's resistance with solid "homework."
Payoffs: Generated **more money with fewer man hours.** Raised morale. Avoided
overtime. My system became **the example for other dealerships.** All done **without
extra funding.**

Helped transform a good policy into an excellent money maker. Worked closely with
sales to match the right responsibilities with the right people. *Payoffs:* Customers
liked our longer hours. Customer **complaints fell to their lowest point in 8 years.**

Changed the way we rewarded our workers by **transforming** customer service goals
from threats to rewards. Overcame initial objections that centered on the cost of
the celebration parties that were a key part of my plan. *Payoffs:* We **did so well,**
corporate headquarters encouraged other dealers to copy our methods.

*More indicators of performance **TopLine** can use ...*

Career Change: *From auto service manager to corporate transportation manager.*

Strategy: *Emphasize management skills and showcase ability to produce results.*

Stanton Kerry   **Transportation Manager**   205.555.5555

❑ Mechanic and **Assistant Transportation Supervisor** *promoted to* Automotive Technology Instructor, Cross County Board of Education, Cross, AL   85 to 90

Took full responsibility, as an instructor, for the performance of 48 students, many of whom were unskilled.

Ran, as an Assistant Transportation Supervisor, a fleet of 88 school buses and support vehicles.

Overcame a chronic funding problem by turning "junk" engines people usually throw away into classroom learning aids for our students. Used the success of that plan to persuade a local manufacturer to donate 6 brand-new engines for my kids to work on. *Payoffs:* When I told students the refurbished engines would be theirs if their work was excellent, **they became top candidates for jobs** in local industry.

Broke up a clique of disruptive students—just like the groups that sometimes hamper industry—by being ready to be "tested" by the ringleader. Saw beyond his bullying to let him grasp the greater rewards of performing well. *Payoffs:* Praised him when he did good work—and made sure others heard my words. **Not only won him over, but got the support of several more** good students at the same time.

❑ Previous employment includes night manager at a motel and 8 years of service with the United States Army.

RELEVANT EDUCATION AND PROFESSIONAL DEVELOPMENT

❑ MS, **Personnel Counseling,** Coreyville State University, Coreyville, AL   Jun 84
Earned this degree while working full time and carrying a full academic load.

❑ AS, Automotive, STRATTON COMMUNITY COLLEGE, STRATTON, AL   MAY 81
Worked full time while attending school full time.

❑ B.G.S., Psychology, ALOHA UNIVERSITY, KIHEI, HI   JUN 77
Completed this degree by attending night school and working full time.

❑ Comprehensive 2- to 5-day training in all phases of **managing skilled, semi-skilled, and unskilled work forces,** Saturn Corporation, Alcoa, TN   90 to 09

COMPUTER SKILLS

❑ Near expert in proprietary work order and customer contact software suite; proficient in Internet search protocols; working knowledge of Word.

Page two

Keith R. Henderson, Jr.

3777 Kintuk Road, Madison, PA 15663   412-555-1212 ▶ krhenderson@hotmail.com

MANAGER ▶ SUPERVISOR ▶ TEAM LEADER

- ▶ Self-motivated individual with exceptional leadership, organizational, and supervisory skills, encompassing key values of integrity, honesty, appreciation, teamwork, growth, and results-orientation with an eye toward continuous improvement.

- ▶ Respected team leader with excellent interpersonal skills. Interact well with individuals from diverse cultures and all professional levels. Teach, train, mentor, motivate, and evaluate personnel to achieve the highest quality standards.

- ▶ Lead special projects and provide strategic insight into operations. Effectively manage and prioritize multiple responsibilities. Ensure adherence to policies and procedures to achieve objectives in safety, quality, production, good manufacturing practices, and cost.

- ▶ Knowledgeable in
  - Personnel Supervision
  - Human Relations
  - Organizational Management
  - Field Management
  - Records and Information Management
  - Problem Resolution
  - Mechanical Maintenance
  - Hazardous Materials Handling
  - Principles of Instruction
  - Office Administration
  - First Aid
  - Military Science

EXPERIENCE

United States Army   *1990–2010*

Master Sergeant *(2001–2010)*   Specialist Fourth Class *(1991–1992)*
Sergeant First Class *(1999–2001)*   Private First Class *(1991)*
Staff Sergeant *(1994–1999)*   Private Second Class *(1990–1991)*
Sergeant *(1992–1994)*   (Honorable Discharge, *2010*)

- ▶ Fast-track promotions in recognition of leadership, valor, discipline, and attainment of highest test scores.

Senior Military Science Instructor, Pebble University (ROTC)
- ▶ Managed ROTC program for 4 years. Trained cadets in military subjects with emphasis on land navigation, first aid, small unit tactics, marksmanship, physical fitness, drill, and ceremony. Coordinated and implemented all field training exercises. Led Pebble ROTC to top 10% ranking nationwide. Led Ranger Challenge Team to finish in the top 1 or 2 position in each of three years.

First Sergeant, Ft. Panera, North Dakota
- ▶ Served as senior enlisted soldier of Basic Combat Training Company consisting of 18 teams training approximately 240 Initial Entry Training Soldiers every 9-week cycle. Provided continuous guidance, counseling, and assistance to permanent-party and training soldiers. Served as Master Trainer; organized and directed Noncommissioned Officer Professional Development Program. Supervised all company personnel, logistics, and administration.

Senior First Sergeant, Drill Sergeant, Ft. Panera, North Dakota
- ▶ For 3 years, trained 55 initial-entry soldiers in each 8-week cycle to become highly motivated, skilled, and physically fit. Directed logistics and administrative support; monitored discipline and morale.

Platoon Sergeant, Ranger Squad Leader, Team Leader, 7 years, Ft. Haderus, Iowa

Instructor / Squad Leader, 4 years, Ft. Swanson, Missouri

Career Change: *From a career in the military to corporate supervisor or manager.*

Strategy: *Use headline to call attention to career goals; include documented personal attributes that will make him an excellent leader and manager in the corporate world.*

Keith R. Henderson, Jr.   412-555-1212   Page 2

PERFORMANCE REMARKS

- Consummate team player
- Consistently sound judgment; works long, hard hours
- Highest degree of loyalty, integrity, and competence
- Instills skill, spirit to achieve, and a winning attitude
- Meticulous attention to detail
- Obtains maximum results in personnel's performance
- Makes safety decisions in best interest of personnel while maximizing training efforts

- Sets standard for personal and professional conduct
- A master at training and developing personnel
- Superior physical stamina and mental toughness
- Possesses diverse skill set: smart, hands-on, tough
- Prolific problem-solver; outstanding planner/organizer
- Accomplishes assigned tasks with superb results

CERTIFICATIONS / AWARDS

Emergency Medical Technician, National Registry of EMTs
HazMat Certification
Recipient of numerous performance awards, including Bronze Star for Valor and Purple Heart

EDUCATION / TRAINING

U.S. Army Training:

School of Cadet Command	Long-Range Surveillance Leader	Ranger / Airborne
Drill Sergeant	Basic Noncommissioned Officer	Infantryman / Pathfinder
Combat Lifesaver Training	Advanced Noncommissioned Officer	Primary Leadership Development
Military Freefall Jumpmaster	Packaging of Hazardous Materials	Outward Bound, Certified Trainer
Instructor / Trainer	for Transportation	(Group Training as well as One-on-One)

Graduate, 1990, Easton High School—Easton, PA

PERSONAL STRENGTHS

Descriptive terms of personal strengths in the workplace based on professional Personality Profiling

Competitive ▶ Pioneering ▶ Challenge-oriented ▶ Accomplishes goals through people ▶ Confident

RESUME 14: BY LOUISE KURSMARK, MRW, CPRW, JCTC, CEIP, CCM

Donna Mazzei
donna_mazzei@hotmail.com

Project Leader

Analysis • Creativity • Leadership • Communication • Presentation

Effective communicator, presenter, and project leader with strong planning, analysis, and implementation skills. Proven ability to lead teams, coordinate complex/detailed programs, and drive initiatives to successful conclusion. Exceptional skills as a presenter, influencer, and consensus builder; able to interact and build rapport with individuals of all ages and diverse cultures.

Relocating to Boston Spring/Summer 2010

Experience & Achievements

Instructor – Multicultural Classroom – U.S. Department of Defense, Illesheim, Germany, 2008–Present

- **Planning & Execution:** Strategically plan classroom activities and special projects to prepare students for next level of learning; design curriculum from the ground up and consistently above standards.

- **Communication:** Design and produce monthly newsletter; initiate regular formal and informal communication with students' families.

- **Project Management:** Selected as co-chair of annual fund-raising event, a community-wide talent show. Coordinated auditions, supervised team of 20–25 volunteers, negotiated hundreds of dollars worth of donated services, generated publicity (TV, radio, print), and managed all facets of high-visibility event.

- **Strategy & Analysis:** Participate on Improvement Committee, analyzing data and crafting reports and strategy recommendations for future direction in the areas of staffing, facilities, community relations, and administration.

- **Leadership:** Gain full support and cooperation of parents, achieving 100% participation in open house and conference evenings.

- **Creativity:** Successfully teach the scientific method to young children and incorporate all steps into diversified classroom projects and activities.

Instructor – U.S. Department of Defense School System, Ft. Bragg, NC, 2004–2008

- **Planning & Execution:** Created and implemented original lesson plans to ensure delivery of defined curriculum.

- **Project Management:** 1) Teamed with another staff member to write, direct, and produce an original play for African-American History Month; managed teams of adult volunteers and directed student actors. 2) Adapted and produced original musical and directed its performance before soldiers being deployed to Iraq; earned favorable publicity.

- **Leadership:** By word of mouth/reputation, increased class size 68% (35% above average). Managed 2 teachers' aides.

- **Teamwork:** Worked with Improvement Committee to develop recommendations and then with staff at all levels on project implementation.

- **Creativity:** Launched innovative year-long program to build students' knowledge base of musical theater.

Career Change: *From elementary school teacher to business project manager.*

Strategy: *Use functional headings to call attention to highly related skills used in her job as a teacher; downplay use of elementary education language.*

RESUME 14, CONTINUED

Donna Mazzei
donna_mazzei@hotmail.com

continued

Drama and English Teacher – Columbia High School, Columbia, SC, 2004
- **Teamwork:** Worked closely with team of teachers to implement the drama program across all grade levels.

Drama Director, Instructor, and Actor – South Carolina Youth Detention Facility; Dixieland Theater Academy; U.S. DoD School, Columbia, SC, 2003–2008
- **Performance:** Recruited for role in Dixieland Theater production of *Bridge to Terabithia*. Performed throughout region.
- **Creativity:** Conceived and executed original teaching methodology to improve language skills of at-risk youth. Success led to quick transition of volunteer role to part-time paid position.

Board Member/Member – Junior League of Columbia, Columbia, SC, 2005–2008
- **Leadership:** Elected by new class of members to head up major community project, a holiday toy drive that served 120 area children. Created project plan, delegated responsibilities, scheduled activities, and coordinated distribution.
- **Project Management:** Spearheaded annual scholarship drive that awarded 3 grants to outstanding local youth. Managed applications, coordinated judges' panel, and secured publicity.
- **Recognition:** Named *Provisional of the Year* for contribution to the organization, 2005–2006.

Board Member/Member – Downtown Club, Columbia, SC, 2005–2008
- **Project Management:** Chaired a key initiative to drive young adults to downtown enterprises. Secured 15 business sponsorships.

Board Member – South Carolina Youth Detention Center, Columbia, SC, 2004–2006
- **Strategy & Analysis:** Analyzed the organization's financial records, budget, and curriculum to develop long-term strategy for best use of facility and resources.

Campaign Volunteer – City Councilor Debra Clegg, Columbia, SC, 2007
- **Teamwork:** Participated in grassroots campaign effort that resulted in 2-to-1 victory for new city councilor.
- **Project Management:** Coordinated volunteers and helped manage fund-raising events.

Education

University of South Carolina, Columbia, SC
- Master's in Early Childhood Education, 2006
- Certification in Theater Education, 2003
- Bachelor of Arts in Theater, 2002 — *Theater Student of the Year, 2002*

ADAM MANNING
amanning@teampolaris.com

(home) 651-555-3865
(cell) 651-555-4290

18 Lake Shore Parkway
White Bear Lake, MN 55110

SPORTS BUSINESS EXECUTIVE
Running organizations at maximum effectiveness to satisfy the public's passion for sports

Versatile management professional with 9-year track record combining strategic, business, and communications skills to build top-performing organizations. Polished communicator with commanding presence and impeccable negotiating abilities honed through extensive client representation. Insightful leader with strong media relations, legal, and financial management background; a huge enthusiasm for sports; and the ability to energize teams.

CORE QUALIFICATIONS

Executive Business and Administrative Leadership
P&L Management, Strategic Planning, Budgeting, Finance, Legal Oversight
- Provided legal review and financial management for several multimillion-dollar business investments that consistently delivered profitable results.
- Pioneered a financing solution for large software purchases by clients unable to obtain traditional credit source.

Communications and Marketing
Strategic Marketing and Communications Plans, Branding, Positioning, Public Relations, Media Relations, Negotiations
- Shaped strategic communications and PR plans for Fortune 500 clients to advance their corporate goals.
- Crafted high-impact marketing materials that produced $1M in funding in 12 months.

Operations Management
Project Management, Team Leadership, Facilities Management, Operations Streamlining
- Laid a blueprint for new business ventures by establishing sound operational frameworks and policies.
- Improved clients' financial outlook by recommending cost-cutting measures and operational streamlining.
- Directed sales staff and communications teams to meet revenue and project goals.

PROFESSIONAL EXPERIENCE

POLARIS MANAGEMENT LLC, Minneapolis, MN   2005–Present
Partner
Launched and grew successful 2-partner private equity investment and management consulting firm. Steer business initiatives as both equity investor and business advisor to produce rapid profit growth and operational improvements.

Project Highlights

- **Positioned 2 fitness centers to achieve positive cash flow within 18 months.** Directed operations of 2 gyms with 3,500 members and combined valuation of $1M, setting strategic direction for marketing, advertising, and workforce planning activities. Drove successful negotiations for advantageous franchise, partnership, and operating agreements.

- **Masterminded innovative financing solution to overcome current credit crisis and close multimillion-dollar software sales.** Guided legal and financial management of company partnered with Sun Microsystems. Achieved $11M in contracts to high-profile clients including Dynatrac Technology Systems, United Medical Solutions, Northstar Health, and FedEx.

- **Transformed operations of restaurant group to generate 11% bottom-line improvement within 12 months.** Advised owners of 4 Twin Cities–area fine-dining restaurants to implement cost-cutting initiatives and productivity improvements, paving the way for opening a fifth restaurant.

Career Change: *From attorney to sports industry executive.*

Strategy: *Begin with a sports-oriented branding statement followed by a strong section of "Core Qualifications" that quickly summarize his strengths in executive business leadership.*

ADAM MANNING • amanning@teampolaris.com • (cell) 651-555-4290   Page 2 of 2

KRUGER FOR CONGRESS, St. Paul, MN   2003–2004
Finance Director • Policy Director
Held dual roles in congressional campaign organization: to create a positive image and elevate public awareness of candidate, and to raise funds to finance campaign operations. Aligned messaging and policy priorities with national party committees and other affiliated groups. Supervised 3 communications/research staff.

- Envisioned and executed successful fund-raising plan, producing $1M within 12 months through multifaceted campaign including multiple direct-mail appeals, telephone calls, and events.
    - Crafted 9 targeted direct-mail pieces with powerful and compelling messages that delivered high response rates.
    - Orchestrated attention-generating fund-raising events that swelled attendance numbers through appearances by former President Bill Clinton.

- Spearheaded policy research and development activities across wide-ranging topics including Homeland Security, Tax and Economic Policies, Defense, Healthcare, Social Security, Education, and Transportation.
    - Propelled candidate's name recognition by authoring press releases and op-ed columns as well as talking points and briefing materials for speeches; debates; and television, print, and radio interviews.

THE VANGUARD GROUP, Washington, DC   2002–2003
Associate
Recruited by president and founder of boutique government relations firm to create all media and communications strategies for Fortune 500 clients. Wrote client policy papers, press releases, and talking points for media interviews. Monitored proposed legislation and devised proactive legislative agendas for clients. Managed 8-member staff.

- Successfully transitioned former employer to contracted government relations services and subsequently attracted numerous BDA member firms as new clients.

- Excelled in bringing together client representatives and key federal leaders for executive meetings to advance legislative agendas.

BIOTECH DEVELOPMENT ASSOCIATION (BDA), Washington, DC   2001–2002
Director of Government Affairs/General Counsel
Represented biotech trade group on Capitol Hill, spearheading all media and communications activities to promote group's goals. Cultivated relationships with 150 business members including 50 Fortune 500 companies.

- Advanced understanding of the biotechnology industry's value to House and Senate commerce committees and to U.S. Department of Commerce leaders through testimony and policy papers.

RHOADES FOR SENATE 2000, Minneapolis, MN   2000
Deputy Communications Director
Directed event planning for state senator's reelection campaign; orchestrated rallies, speeches, and town hall meetings. Drafted speeches, campaign literature, and summaries of field activities. Supervised 8 staff and 1,000+ volunteers.

EDUCATION & AFFILIATIONS

J.D. — WILLIAM MITCHELL COLLEGE OF LAW, Minneapolis, MN
B.A. in Political Science — ST. OLAF COLLEGE, Northfield, MN
Member — Minnesota Bar

COMMUNITY SERVICE

Board Member — Twin Cities Athletic Scholarship Foundation

ANDRE MITCHELL

513-249-0090   9787 Covington Place, Apt. 7, Cincinnati, OH 45005   am@cinci.rr.com

Facilities Manager

Efficient and effective manager with experience in multiple facets of building construction, maintenance, and management and exceptional performance in critical areas of building safety, security, and tenant satisfaction. Maintenance/management experience includes multi-tenant commercial properties, food-service facilities, and entertainment venues as large as 25,000 square feet.

Skilled/licensed carpenter, HVAC technician, sheet metal fabricator, and auto mechanic with additional experience maintaining electrical and plumbing systems. Licensed real estate agent proficient at showing property and managing tenant relations.

General Manager: The Blue Note, Cincinnati, OH   2001–Present

Direct all business operations for 15,000-sq.-ft. nightclub with weekly revenues exceeding $100,000. On board since start-up; put in place the operating procedures, security standards, and revenue safeguards that have been pivotal to long-term success and profitable operation of the club.

Recruit, train, and manage 42 staff. Manage financial operations, including monthly budgets, payroll, assessments, and inventory. Ensure compliance with all building and safety codes; oversee building maintenance, including A/C, plumbing, and electrical.

- ☑ **Site selection & construction:** Assisted owners in locating and selecting site in up-and-coming downtown neighborhood. Oversaw building construction and club layout. Represented owners at community meetings and before licensing boards.

- ☑ **Revenue protection:** Established foolproof ticketing system that eliminates non-paying guests and guarantees revenue accountability. Set demanding standards for door staff and hold them accountable.

- ☑ **Safety & security:** Created effective security system that minimizes use of illegal substances and promotes a safe environment—since launched, zero incidents. In demand as consultant to introduce similar systems in other Tristate-area clubs.

- ☑ **Community relations:** Instituted street-side crowd control to minimize neighborhood disturbances. Personally visible and accessible to all neighbors.

- ☑ **City agency relations:** Personally secured and maintained up-to-date city licenses for fire safety and building security. Built excellent relationships with Cincinnati police and fire departments.

- ☑ **Staff loyalty & reliability:** In high-turnover industry, retained staff long term. Constantly improve staff skills through training. Create a positive, team-oriented culture.

Property Manager: Downtown Spaces Realty, Cincinnati, OH   2003–2007

Managed multi-unit commercial property with close attention to safety, building maintenance, and swift resolution of tenant issues.

- ☑ **Maintenance:** Created maintenance schedules and performed or supervised all aspects of maintenance, repairs, cleaning, and rules enforcement.

- ☑ **Management:** Showed property to prospective tenants; managed leasing and evictions; maintained excellent tenant relations through professional approach to building management.

Career Change: From nightclub general manager to building/facilities manager.

513-249-0090   **ANDRE MITCHELL**   am@cinci.rr.com

Construction / Supervisor: Buckeye Mechanical Systems, Toledo, OH   1995–2000

Performed wide range of activities related to installation and servicing of residential and commercial HVAC systems.

- ☑ **Special skills:** Fabricating and installing sheet metal; rebuilding, servicing, and installing steam turbines and absorption units; all areas of pipe fitting for refrigeration and hot water boilers.

- ☑ **Staff & project management:** Supervised work crews to ensure efficient and timely project completion. Trained workers in all aspects of the job.

Manager: Lakeside Inn, Port Clinton, OH   1998–2000

Turned around unprofitable, inefficient, poorly managed seasonal facility and created a profitable inn/restaurant/nightclub that was so successful, owners invested in Cincinnati club (The Blue Note) and brought me on as GM from day one.

- ☑ **Operational turnaround:** Revamped entire operation for better efficiency; replaced 90% of staff; introduced new computer system for cash registers and office functions; instilled strict operational policies and procedures. Transformed lax operation to consistently profitable "tight ship."

- ☑ **Safety & security:** Implemented and maintained new security practices for bar, nightclub, and hotel.

Manager: Alhambra Nightclub, Toledo, OH   1993–1998

Worked in all areas of nightclub operations, beginning as busboy and advancing to manager of 25,000-sq-.ft. establishment with 1,800-patron capacity.

Managed stock and ordered inventory. Handled all employee payroll accounts. Hired and trained staff at every level. Managed all special events as well as day-to-day functions of the nightclub.

Licenses / Certifications / Technical Skills

- ☑ Cincinnati Fire Department certifications: Fire Drill Conductor, Maintenance, Public Assembly.

- ☑ Cincinnati Health Department License for Food Service.

- ☑ Certified auto mechanic. Sheet-metal worker, fabrication and installation.

- ☑ Former union carpenter (employed full-time with Local 129 from 1989–1991). Scaffolding and rigging experience on high-rises.

- ☑ Licensed refrigeration and air-conditioning technician. Electrical and plumbing experience.

- ☑ Ohio Real Estate License; related education through College of Mount St. Joseph:
  — Changing Dynamics of Real Estate (11/08)
  — Real Estate Law (11/06)
  — The Management of Residential Property (11/06)
  — The Management of Commercial Property (10/06)

Strategy: *Pull out just the relevant experience from the most recent position, which involved broader sales, marketing, and supervisory experience than is detailed in this resume. Include part-time property manager role as key experience.*

RESUME 17: BY CINDY KRAFT, CPBS, COIS, CCMC, CCM, JCTC, CPRW

717-222-8988
fisher@email.com
2283 Atlantic Avenue, York, PA 17404

MICHAEL FISHER, MBA, CPA

SENIOR MANAGEMENT EXECUTIVE
Finance ... Change Management ... Procurement ... Purchasing

Visionary strategist with a demonstrated ability to deliver corporate objectives. Solid 13-year career creating market advantage, reducing and controlling expenses, and fostering a culture of teamwork, shared mission, and dedication to customer satisfaction. Key strengths ...

> *"You quickly jumped in with both feet and made an immediate contribution to our team. Specifically, your analysis and projections of our financials and operational metrics within our group have been right on track."*
>
> John Jones
> General Manager

> Michael *"improved his revenue standing as the manager from the #6 position to the #2 position in about 60 days."*
>
> Loren Hughes
> Director,
> Consumer Ops

Leadership ... Pioneered a service program to improve customer service ratings that exceeded quarterly targets and captured the #1 position among 7 teams. The program was adopted by corporate and rolled out in 21 offices.

Cost Reductions ... Collaborated with intradepartmental managers and senior executives to implement a cost-reduction plan companywide. Negotiated a telecommunications contract that generated $1.8 million in savings annually.

Change Management ... Drove the organization's ranking from #6 out of seven to #2 in sales performance within 60 days by introducing an empowering, team-based management style.

Vendor Sourcing ... Consolidated temporary services sourcing from 50 providers to one national contract, generating $200,000 in annual expense savings.

Team Building ... Championed employee development, recognition, and open communication that positioned the call center as #1 in product retention within a 9-state region in 5 months.

New Product Launch ... Introduced incentives and measurement tools that positioned the territory as #1 in telephone sales within a 5-territory region.

Participative Management ... Partnered with the Communications Workers of America (CWA) union to create a performance-based work environment, establishing best-in-class benchmarks for management practices.

Training & Development ... Key member of a 6-person team tasked with developing sales effectiveness training and implementing a certification process. Drove 15% annual sales increases post-implementation, garnering the VP/GM "Shining Star" Award.

PROFESSIONAL EXPERIENCE

BANK OF AMERICA, York, Pennsylvania

Director of Customer Service Operations — 2007 to Present
Recruited to take over leadership of a department with a history of ineffective leadership, lack of performance, escalating expenses, and excessively high budgets. Manage a 15-person staff and $100 million expense budget; report directly to the Controller.

- Reduced expenses by $2.5 million through detailed reports and analysis of travel, telecom, express mail, copier leases, office supplies, document management, and cell phone policies.
- Partnered with the Human Resources Director to negotiate a 10% contract reduction on a national temporary services contract, yielding an annual expense savings of $200,000.
- Pioneered the department's first-ever incentive performance plans.

Career Change: From call-center manager to finance executive.

Strategy: Create a skills-based resume to pull out financial accomplishments; add quotes from supervisors to provide even more emphasis on his qualifications in his target area.

RESUME 17, CONTINUED

MICHAEL FISHER	Page 2	717-222-8988

VERIZON, Tampa, Florida

Hired as a Financial Analyst, launching a successful 10-year career holding increasingly responsible management positions with this Fortune 100 communications services company. Recruited for a special assignment as Finance Manager with P&L responsibility for a $200 million expense budget.

Manager of Sales/Service/Retention, Consumer Services — 2006 to 2007
Selected to drive sales and ensure customer service and retention. Managed 12 direct reports and 100 union-represented employees.

- Personally selected by senior management from among 1,000 candidates to participate in the Gateway Leadership Program.
- Completely turned around sales performance, taking the team from #6 to #2 in 60 days. Maintained the second position for the balance of 2006.
- Initiated the customer service and satisfaction program that took ratings from #3 to #1 in 60 days.
- Built team unity and empowered employees to achieve corporate goals, establishing the team as #1 in product retention and beating the company's regional retention rate by 8%.

Manager of Sales Excellence, Consumer Services — 2005 to 2006
Personally chosen for leadership, product knowledge, vision, and financial expertise for this newly created position.

- Developed the Sales Effectiveness Training program that standardized training, strengthened the overall regional sales organization, and led to annual revenue increases of 15%.

Finance & Call Center Manager, Consumer Services — 2002 to 2005
Promoted to Finance Manager and within 12 months assumed additional responsibilities directing a 13-person team in the special-needs call center.

- Resolved a $20 million shortfall in sales goals to finish #1 in booked revenues by benchmarking internal performance, reallocating revenue goals between sales and service departments, and employing performance metrics for sales representatives.

Financial Analyst, Consumer Services Finance — 1997 to 2002
Conducted post-promotion marketing reviews for profitability; recommended marketing and operations funding prioritizations; reviewed income statement categories to evaluate financial trade-offs; and analyzed activity-based costing system results.

PRIOR RELEVANT EXPERIENCE

Financial & Compliance Auditor, FLORIDA AUDIT DEPT., Tallahassee, Florida — 1995 to 1997
Staff Accountant, Audit Staff, ERNST AND YOUNG, Nashville, Tennessee — 1994 to 1995

EDUCATION

Master of Business Administration, University of Florida, Gainesville, Florida — 2006
Bachelor of Science in Accounting, Purdue University, West Lafayette, Indiana — 1994

CERTIFICATIONS

Certified Public Accountant (CPA) • Certified Internal Auditor (CIA)
Certified Information Systems Auditor (CISA)

DEREK STEPHENS

215 Churchill Street, Pittsburgh, PA 15212
412.322.1258
dstephens@msn.com

* MANAGEMENT CONSULTING *
Certified Six Sigma Black Belt

Consummate Research Scientist with a **synergistic proficiency between technical disciplines and Six Sigma strategies** to successfully integrate analytical insight and business knowledge. **Highly motivated** with a responsible work ethic and a **solutions-oriented** focus within a demanding environment to impact long-term process improvements. A **professional communicator** with the ability to build relationships based on mutual respect, trust, and benefit.

Business Analysis and Team Development

- Apply cross-functional communications to interface with high-profile business clients, consultants, teams, agencies, professors, and students.
- Integrate strong quantitative and analytical skills to re-engineer business processes using the **Six Sigma methodology** leading to optimum business efficiency.
- Present scientific data and information to non-scientific communities while leading and participating on project teams.
- Play instrumental role in bringing new products to market. Improve processes to make products more robust.

Technical Expertise

- Design experiments for product analysis and formulate strategies to reduce process variation.
- Recognized internally as **technical expert** in optical thin films. **Submitted three intellectual property applications.**
- Apply highly developed technical discipline to create process improvements through data-driven decision making.
- Astute understanding of air-sensitive and solid-state chemical manipulations.
- Extensive hands-on experience utilizing chemical vapor deposition, solvo/hydro-thermal, high-pressure synthetic, glass-blowing, glove-box, and vacuum-line techniques.
- Computer Skills—Statistical analysis software: JMP
      Silicon graphics crystallographic software: SHELXTL and Cerius2

WORK EXPERIENCE

SR. RESEARCH SCIENTIST, **RRT Industries,** Pittsburgh, PA	2007–PRESENT
RESEARCH ASSISTANT, **University of Michigan,** Ann Arbor, MI	2005–2007
RESEARCH ASSISTANT, **Arizona State University,** Tempe, AZ	2003–2005
TEACHING ASSISTANT, **Arizona State University,** Tempe, AZ	2003–2005
SYNTHETIC POLYMER CHEMIST, **RRT Industries,** Oak Creek, WI	2002–2003
RESEARCH ASSISTANT, **Carroll College,** Waukesha, WI	2001–2002

EDUCATION

PH.D., University of Michigan, Ann Arbor, MI   *Emphasis:* Materials Chemistry
   Project: Synthesis, design, characterization, and study of highly porous metal-organic materials for use in heterogeneous catalysis, gas and liquid separation, and storage applications.

M.S., Arizona State University, Tempe, AZ   *Emphasis:* Inorganic Chemistry
   Project: Synthesis and design of single-source molecular precursors for chemical vapor deposition of group III nitrides for use in light-emitting diodes.

B.S., Carroll College, Waukesha, WI   *Major:* Chemistry   *Minor:* Business Administration

Career Change: *From research scientist to management consultant.*

Strategy: *Create a layered resume with the option to use either two or three pages depending on the specific opportunity. Page 1 contains qualifications gleaned from past experiences; page 2*

DEREK STEPHENS

215 Churchill Street, Pittsburgh, PA 15212
412.322.1258
dstephens@msn.com

Page 2

KEY PROJECT MANAGEMENT & LEADERSHIP

Challenge: **New Product Development**—To generate ideas and applications for new products that define value-added opportunities.

Actions: (1) Designed and developed novel materials for next-generation products.
(2) Assessed novel materials for unique product opportunities.
(3) Led technical activities within team environments.

Results: Inventor of **Solarshade** self-cleaning glass product.
Launch Date: February 2009.
Built intellectual property position—Application #US 5,215,348.

Challenge: **Market Development**—To analyze problems and creatively generate solutions to overcome production issues.

Actions: (1) Developed process strategies and possible capabilities for producing materials.
(2) Performed online design of experiments at production facility.
(3) Established trends using **Six Sigma methodology.**
(4) Designed pathways to eliminate problematic issues.
(5) Provided technical input to assist and influence customer.

Results: Employed novel approach to overcome process issues.
Inventor of **Visiongate** statistical software to track and eliminate problematic technical issues.
Launch Date: December 2010.
Built intellectual property position—Application #US 6,451,730.

Challenge: **Academia Collaborations**—To leverage expertise within academia to bring new technology to RRT Industries.

Actions: (1) Collaborated with Materials Science and Environmental Engineering departments to initiate ideas to leverage expertise.
(2) Provided appropriate materials and assisted with analysis to finalize project goals.
(3) Assessed results using **Sigma Logic methodology** to define products and opportunities.
(4) Translated university work to RRT process technology.
(5) Recommended ways to improve RRT process.

Results: Defined products and opportunities.
Built intellectual property position—Application #US 9,296,197.

RECOGNITION AWARDS

Two awards for **technical project update presentations** to the CEO and Executive Committee of RRT—awarded by R&D Director of RRT.

Idea Generation Committee Award for **contribution and leadership** in uncovering new ideas for product opportunities—awarded by R&D Associate Director of RRT.

Successful online design of experiments that revealed process limitations to overcome product qualification hurdles—awarded by Manager of Glass Coatings Process Control Group of RRT.

Rackham Dissertation Fellowship (University of Michigan)—departmental fellowship awarded to most promising dissertation.

shows in-depth project leadership using the CAR approach; and page 3 documents publications and scientific instrumentation knowledge.

DEREK STEPHENS

215 Churchill Street, Pittsburgh, PA 15212
412.322.1258
dstephens@msn.com

Page 3

PRESENTATIONS / PUBLICATIONS

Presentations: "Precursors for Strongly Bonded Three-Dimensional Frameworks," D. Stephens, _Abstr Pap Am Chem Soc_. 220: 354-Inorg. Chem. Part 1, August 20, 2006.

"Synthesis of Cl_2InN_3, Br_2InN_3, and Related Adducts," D. Stephens, Departmental Seminar, Arizona State University, April 3, 2005.

"Combustion of Liquid Organic Compounds in a Bomb Calorimeter," D. Stephens, _Abstr Pap Am Chem Soc_. 213: 511-Chem. Ed. Part 1, April 13, 2003.

Publications: "Synthesis, Characterization, and Sorbtion Comparisons of $Tb_2(B_{10})_3$, $Tb_2(AnDC)_3$, and $Tb_2(DHDC)_3$." _Submitted._

"Mixed Metal-Organic Frameworks Constructed from Benzene Tricarboxylic Acid." _Submitted._

"Highly Porous Three-Dimensional Metal Formates." _Submitted._

"Design of Secondary Building Units Using Functionalized Terephthalates." _Submitted._

"Synthesis of New Azidoalanes with Heterocyclic Molecular Structures," J. Williamson, J. Miller, D. Stephens, Main Group Met. Chem., 24 (2): 77–84 Apr. 16, 2007.

"Synthesis and Structures of Heterocycle Azidogallanes $[(CH_3)ClGaN_3]_4$ and $[(CH_3)BrGaN_3]_3$ en route to $[(CH_3)HGaN_3]_4$: An inorganic precursor to GaN," J. Williamson, J. Miller, D. Stephens, T. Reiter, J. Huber, Inorg. Chem., 39 (17): 3805–3809 Aug. 21, 2006.

"Synthesis of Cl_2InN_3, Br_2InN_3, and Related Adducts," D. Stephens, J. Miller, J. Williamson, Inorg. Chem., 39 (7): 1615 Apr. 3, 2006.

"H_2GaN_3: A Facile Approach to GaN," J. Miller, K. Burnside, D. Stephens, J. Williamson, Inorg. Chem., 37 (26): 6638–6644 Dec. 28, 2004.

Complete publication and abstract bibliography available on request.

INSTRUMENTATION

Extensive experience
- FTIR spectroscopy
- High/low temperature X-ray powder diffraction
- Thermogravimetric analysis
- Mass spectroscopy
  Electron impact ionization
  Fast atom bombardment
- Gas chromatography
- Ultraviolet spectroscopy

Fluent background
- Single crystal X-ray diffraction
- Scanning electron microscopy
  BSE/SEI/EDS
- Solid state and solution NMR
  $^{13}C/^{31}P/^{15}N/^1H$
- Rutherford backscattering spectrometry
- Ultra high-vacuum chemical vapor deposition film growth processes

CHAPTER 5

Resumes for Career Changers Seeking Technology Positions

Despite outsource, offshore, and downsizing initiatives, the demand for qualified technologists continues to grow. It is important to have the right qualifications to be considered for these opportunities. Note how many of the resumes in this chapter emphasize recent training and list specific technologies and skill sets. These resumes represent the following specific career and industry changes:

- Carpenter to network administrator
- Graphic designer and musician to video game audio engineer
- Librarian to information technology professional
- Certified surgical technologist to network administrator
- Business owner to Web designer
- Manufacturing engineer to Web applications developer
- Account analyst to computer graphics designer
- Telecommunications account executive to video game producer
- Sales manager to Chief Information Officer

WILL GATEM

wgatem@construct.net

105 Outlook Drive   Nashville, Tennessee 37239   615.792.1412

NETWORK ADMINISTRATOR

➢ Versatile, hardworking individual; driven to meet or exceed expectations.

➢ Passion and exceptional aptitude for working with computers. Skilled in troubleshooting and identifying procedures needed to maintain a reliable and efficient network to keep the organization running smoothly and profitably.

➢ Knowledgeable in designing gates in hardware and software to allow free exchange of data, custom applications, and the computer power to process this information for authorized users; also skilled in setting up firewalls to protect proprietary information from outsiders.

➢ Effective interpersonal skills; work well as a team member with people at all levels of an organization and of various cultures. Equally capable working independently.

➢ Computer proficiency includes Microsoft Office (Word, Excel, Access, Outlook, PowerPoint), QuickBooks Pro, backup protocol, and scanning documents/graphics.

EDUCATION / TRAINING

Coursework in **Computer Technology,** 2009 4.0 GPA
Vanderbilt University—Nashville, TN

Coursework in **Microcomputer Familiarization,** 1990
Coursework in **Mechanical Engineering,** 1988
The Ohio State University—Columbus, OH

CERTIFICATION

Microsoft Certified Systems Engineer, 2010
Microsoft Certified Professional, 2009
- Networking Essentials
- Proxy Server
- Windows 2008 Server
- NT Server in the Enterprise
- Internetworking with Microsoft TCP/IP on Windows 2000 Server

EMPLOYMENT

Brant Construction Co., Inc.—Nashville, TN   1989–Present
  CARPENTER FOREMAN—1996–present
  CARPENTER—1992–1996
  LABORER—1989–1992

Earned respect of co-workers and supervisors in family-owned business through diligent observation and application of skills learned. Demonstrate remarkable work ethic.

- Supervise 3–10 carpenters and laborers in construction/renovation/maintenance of residential/ commercial buildings. Schedule subcontractors. Ensure accuracy of work.

- Calculate space estimates regarding material costs, labor costs, and time from start of project to completion. Organize job site and ensure tasks are completed in a timely and cost-effective manner.

Career Change: *From carpenter to network administrator.*

Strategy: *Emphasize recent education and use the introduction to detail transferable skills gained from multiple experiences.*

sam elliot

148 W 219th St., Torrance CA 90502
(310) 555-1212. samuel@samuelelliot.com

Keyboardist/Programmer/Engineer for The Memory Chain

— transitioning to video game audio engineering —

profile

Built extensive original F/X library. Wrote, performed, engineered, and produced four albums. Advanced skills in session dialing for basic tracking, overdubs and voice-overs, Foley, mixing and mastering, and live mixing for clubs and national tour venues. Strengths include

**Sound Effect Creation ... Sampling/Looping ... Music Composition ...
Audio Engineering/Production ... Orchestral Scoring ... MIDI ...
Digital Audio Studio ... Musician: Guitar, Keyboards, Drums ... Audio Editing**

Skilled in a variety of studio applications including: **Pro Tools, Cubase SX, Sound Forge, DirectMusic Producer, Acid, Reason, Logic, SoundDiver, ReBirth, and Studio Vision Pro.**

selected reviews

"The Memory Chain takes sampling to a new level…. Sam Elliot has done it again."
LA Times, May 2008

*"The Memory Chain's latest album is the one where Sam Elliot finally takes center stage
… and if this album is any indication, he should have been there long ago."*
Q magazine, October 2007

"Sublime keyboards … Sam Elliot is a musician's musician."
Musician magazine, June 2006

musical career

Keyboardist/Programmer/Engineer, The Memory Chain, 2002–2008
Released four CDs as sound designer and performer with this critically acclaimed band. Toured U.S., Asia, and Europe extensively. Played keyboards on four CDs and 600+ live performances.

Clear Sounds Audio, 2nd Engineer, Paid Internship, 2004
Recorded, edited, mixed, and produced multi-track audio productions for major label artists and advertising agencies. Assisted outside engineers.

other experience

Freelance Designer, Graphics and Web Design, 2007–Present

education

BA in Music. Emphasis in Electronic Music and Recording

— Member ASCAP —

Career Change: *From graphic designer and musician to video game audio engineer.*

Strategy: *Use name recognition of well-known band to capture interest; combine this with emphasis on technical abilities and deemphasize design experience even though it is recent.*

MELANIE MARTINSON

34 Straight Path Avenue
Brentwood, New York 11717
(631) 887-0990
MMIT@techway.net

Transitioning from Library Science to Information Technology, bringing the following transferable strengths:

- Advanced Research Strategies
- End-User Support
- Staff Training & Supervision
- Information Systems Management
- Systems Infrastructure
- Customer Service Excellence
- Vendor Sourcing & Relations
- Purchasing/Inventory Control
- Expenses/Budget Control

CREDENTIALS

Info-Tech Training Center, Huntington, New York
A+ Certified Technician, 2010

Adelphi University, Garden City, New York
Master of Science, Library Science, 1996

C.W. Post at Long Island University, Brentwood, New York
Bachelor of Arts, Sociology, 1992

PROFESSIONAL EXPERIENCE

Career track in information science and business management, bringing the following transferable experience:

Information Systems/Database Management
- Developed reference tools for collecting, organizing, interpreting, and classifying information.
- Successfully trained users on Internet navigation techniques for use in complex reference searches.
- Accessed proprietary vendor databases with demonstrated expertise of complex infrastructure navigation.
- Applied advanced media, including the Internet, virtual libraries, and remote resources.
- Developed a strategic database-driven system that proved effective for generating Internet results.

Business Management/Customer Support
- Established brick-and-mortar and Internet-based bookstores with total responsibility for business operations.
- Cost-effectively purchased and resold books from publishers and wholesalers for global distribution.
- Maintained a strong vendor base to ensure a broad selection and availability of used and hard-to-find books.
- Recruited, trained, and supervised personnel in areas of product knowledge, research, and customer service.
- Delivered quality customer service tailored to individual customer needs, ensured open lines of communication between all concerned, and handled all aspects of financial management and reporting.

WORK HISTORY

Reference Librarian, Kennedy University, Coram, New York	2007–Present
Reference Librarian, Sheridan Community Library, Islip, New York	2003–2007
Reference Librarian, Lincoln Public Library, Brentwood, New York	1996–2002
Managing Owner, Skies The Limit Books, Deer Park, New York	1991–1996

Career Change: *From librarian to information technology professional.*

Strategy: *Emphasize profile and keywords using a functional format that really highlights transferable experience.*

RENÉE ROVAN

4405 Georgia Avenue NW, #412, Silver Spring, MD 20901 ▪ (301) 291-8512 ▪ rrovan@email.com

NETWORK ADMINISTRATION PROFESSIONAL

Pursuing **Cisco Certified Network Associate (CCNA)** and **Network+** credentials.

Proficient in Microsoft Office applications in a Windows 7/XP environment.

EDUCATION

Information Systems (IS),
IS Management Specialization (Honors Graduate), Avery College, Arlington, VA 2010

Northern Virginia College, Alexandria, VA 2006–2007

Medical Specialist/Surgical Technology, U.S. Armed Forces Health & Sciences College, Irving, TX 2004

APPLIED RESEARCH PROJECTS

Completed **Applied Research Projects (ARPs),** in conjunction with IS degree requirements, covering all aspects of design and management of organizational technical resources, as follows:

➢ **Organizational Culture and Leadership** (2010): Evaluated the organizational culture of Briarwood Surgery Center's endoscopy unit and operating room (OR) in order to ensure that the mission and vision statements were being appropriately applied at the staff level.

➢ **Human Resources (HR) Management** (2010): Established a comprehensive orientation package for the Briarwood Surgery Center's clinical staff.

➢ **Strategic Management and Planning** (2009): Conducted internal/external environmental assessments in order to identify an approach for Briarwood Surgery Center to expand its OR facilities.

➢ **Financial Accounting** (2009): Created a quarterly operating budget for the Briarwood Surgery Center and implemented an expenditure tracking system.

➢ **Database Management Systems** (2009): Created an inventory-control system that optimizes inventory maintenance in a cost-effective manner.

➢ **Networking and Telecommunications** (2009): Identified solutions to integrate Briarwood Surgery Center's two local area networks (LANs) into a single LAN.

➢ **Systems Analysis and Design** (2009): Created a project plan to automate and streamline Briarwood Surgery Center's cataloging of surgical supplies.

➢ **Management Support Systems** (2009): Identified solutions to resolve inventory-control vulnerabilities at minimal cost for Briarwood Surgery Center.

➢ **Statistics and Research Analysis** (2008): Generated graphics to illustrate the Merrifield Hospital Center's assisted-reproduction success rate statistics.

PROFESSIONAL EXPERIENCE

CERTIFIED SURGICAL TECHNOLOGIST

Briarwood Surgery Center, Silver Spring, MD 2009–Present
Merrifield Hospital Center, Vienna, VA 2007–2009
U.S. Army Reserves, Allen Reece Medical Center, Washington, DC 2005–2007
Kelway Ambulatory Surgery Center, Irving, TX 2004–2005

MILITARY EXPERIENCE

U.S. Army Reserves 2004–Present

Career Change: *From certified surgical technologist to network administrator.*

Strategy: *To paint the picture of an accomplished professional, focus on the numerous applied research projects she completed in conjunction with her IT/IS degree requirements.*

RESUME 23: BY LORETTA PETERS, ACRW, MRW

KATHERINE ESPERIAN

191 South Main Street ❱ Manchester, CT 06042 ❱ (860) 685-9148 ❱ Kathy@SBCGlobal.net

WEB DESIGNER

Strategic Design ❱ Interactive Media ❱ Consultation
View my portfolio at www.StrategicWebDesign.com

PROFILE..

A highly creative, energetic Website and Content Professional with solid computer graphics experience dedicated to taking a leadership role in helping to expand company growth and profits. Ability to assess all aspects of a website project and deliver results that meet client expectations in a reasonable time. Proactive in recognizing brand identity gaps in print promotional materials and online. Strengthen market presence through visual concepts and targeted message by working with client to meet marketing goals.

QUALIFICATIONS...

- SEO/SEM Management
- Corporate Branding/Identity
- e-Commerce Store Development
- Project Management
- Email Marketing/Newsletters
- Strategy and Positioning
- Site Map and Navigation
- Testing and Delivery
- Planning and Scheduling

TECHNICAL SKILLS...

Adobe InDesign • Dreamweaver • HTML • Cascading Style Sheets (CSS) • Fireworks • Microsoft Office • Adobe Illustrator • Flash • CSS Tableless Layout • Adobe Contribute • Microsoft FrontPage

PROFESSIONAL EXPERIENCE ....

Esperian Designs, LLC, Manchester, CT   2002–Present
Web Designer
Assess needs, develop cost-effective web solutions, and deliver presentations to secure new business. Serviced more than 100 clients in B2C and B2B markets.

- Captured the vision of new business owners by designing and delivering valuable websites, producing and editing content, and creating print promotional materials.
- Created websites from start to finish through strategy, conceptual design, launch, and debugging.
- Coordinated implementation with browser compatibility, accessibility, SEO, and keyword search.
- Designed high-impact logos for new and existing businesses.
- Maintained and grew relationships by delivering great customer service and staying in contact.

Graphic Designer—Freelance   1998–2002
- Recruited business through self-marketing tactics and referral system.
- Drafted proposals for Internet development, consultation, logo, and graphic design projects.
- Prepared file formats, optimized image files and artwork, and delivered HTML to clients.

EDUCATION ....

- **Bachelor of Fine Arts and Art History—Summa Cum Laude**
  University of Hartford, Art School, West Hartford, CT   1997

CERTIFICATIONS ....

- Certified Internet Webmaster Associate
- Photography

Career Change: *From business owner to Web designer.*

Strategy: *Because Katherine owned a Web design business, her resume focuses on her functional activities in designing Web sites and downplays her business ownership responsibilities.*

John Joseph Derry
176 Woodhaven Drive, Eatontown, NJ 07724
(732) 927-5555 ▪ JJDer@bol.com

Web Applications Management
e-Commerce ▪ B2B ▪ Project Management

KEY QUALIFICATIONS

✓ **Technical Strengths:** Up-to-date, diverse training in e-Business Management coupled with years of experience in analytical, technical process engineering profession.

✓ **Project Coordination and Teamwork:** Highly productive in team environments as both team member and team leader. Efficient in handling multiple project priorities.

✓ **Communication:** Able to communicate technical information in an easily understandable way. Recognized for relationship building with team members and clients. An effective listener.

✓ **Personal Attributes:** Innovative problem solver. Committed to goal achievement. Dependable.

EDUCATION

✓ Cybersoft Internet Professional—CIP 1, Cybersoft, Inc., Woodbridge, NJ
December 2009, **Certified e-Business Architect, e-Business for Managers**
December 2008, **Certified Cybersoft Communications 1000** including Fundamentals of Networking, Database, Web Development, Web Design, Multimedia, and Internet Business

✓ Bachelor of Science, Industrial Engineering, Connecticut Institute of Technology

TECHNICAL SKILLS

e-Commerce: e-Business and B2B Infrastructures and Consumer Payment Protocols
Applications: ERP, e-Procurement, Selling Chain Management, Customer Relationship Management
Software Tools: MS Word, MS Excel, MS Access, HTML, Dreamweaver, JavaScript
Operating Systems: Windows 7/XP/Vista/2000

PROFESSIONAL EXPERIENCE

1994–2009 ENGINEERING SYSTEMS, INC., Astro Space Division, Eatontown, NJ
Manufacturing Engineer, Production Engineering Department

Provided assembly documentation and engineering floor support throughout all phases of production flow, including fabrication, assembly, and test operations, for manufacture of diverse satellite products contracted by major government clients (USSA and U.S. Air Force).

ACCOMPLISHMENTS

▪ Promoted to Team Leader for new equipment installation and upgrades. Performed research and analysis, and tested in production mode. Full authority to sign off on fully tested equipment.

▪ Reduced cycle time by 30% through development of assembly and test tolling. Improved recycle characteristics and cut hazardous emissions into atmosphere by 40%.

▪ Collaborated with 60-person design engineering team to ensure that designs were producible in manufacturing environment. Provided cost-effective manufacturing recommendations.

▪ Trained 8 entry-level engineers in 4-month period to prepare efficient, labor-effective work plans for multi-line production floor in 80,000-square-foot facility.

Career Change: *From manufacturing engineer to Web applications developer.*

Strategy: *Showcase recent education and technical skills while also highlighting abilities in team collaboration, project coordination, communications, and problem-solving gained from prior experience.*

Christine Steile

2 Denver Court
Brentwood, NY 11717
(631) 766-1003
webdesigner@grafx.net

Seeking a position in Computer Graphics with an emphasis in Web Design

Education

Adelphi University, Garden City, NY
Certificate of Completion, Web Design, 2010

Preston School of Art and Design, New York, NY
Bachelor of Fine Arts, 2006
Concentration, Computer Graphics

Accomplishment
As one of Preston's web project leaders, guided a team of student webmasters recruited to design the school's 125-page website. Successfully optimized the site, achieving top-10 placement in all major search engines.

Computer Proficiencies

Platforms
Macintosh; Windows 7, Vista, XP, 2000

Web/Graphic Design
Adobe InDesign, Illustrator, Premiere; QuarkXPress; Macromedia Flash, Dreamweaver, Director; Microsoft FrontPage; JavaScript; HTML

General Software
Microsoft Word, Excel, PowerPoint, FoxPro, Outlook; EasyMail SMTP Express

Experience Overview

➢ Managing customer service and office support functions within banking and retail sales environments.

➢ Efficiently processing orders, invoices, and job orders.

➢ Streamlining workflow efficiencies and training others.

➢ Interfacing between customers and vendors, exercising strong follow-through and problem-solving skills.

➢ Maintaining account information on data-tracking systems.

➢ Contacting merchants and financial institutions to investigate and resolve transaction disputes.

➢ Monitoring and reconciling account discrepancies.

➢ Received numerous employee recognition awards.

Graphics / Web Design

➢ **Internship Experience**
Produced designs that captured the essence of marketing identities. Demonstrated an eye for color, shape, size, texture, and layout in the creation of promotional materials.

- MAGAZINE LAYOUTS
- COMMERCIAL WEBSITES
- CORPORATE LOGOS
- E-PORTFOLIOS
- BUSINESS CARDS
- E-GREETING CARDS
- BOOK/CD COVERS
- BANNER ADVERTISING
- BROCHURES
- ONLINE NEWSLETTERS

➢ **Academic Experience**
Completed extensive mock projects that incorporated the use of HTML, dynamic databases, templates, images, audio clips, and animation to create online and print materials.

Work History

Account Analyst, Montgomery Bank, Hauppauge, NY, 10/05–Present
Intern Graphic Designer, Dream Designs, Commack, NY, 4/05–10/05
Customer Service Representative, Fashion Frenzy, Huntington, NY, 9/02–4/05
Customer Care Associate, Precision Watches, Hauppauge, NY, 6/99–9/02

Career Change: *From account analyst to computer graphics designer.*

Strategy: *Express creativity while clearly categorizing relevant education, internship experience, and software proficiencies.*

GREG DAVIES
189 Delaware Street
Columbus, OH 43206
(614) 204-9912
gregdavies@net.net

ASSOCIATE PRODUCER
– Video Game Industry –

Combine a passion for video games with exceptional project
management skills and an absolute determination to succeed in the game industry.

Results-oriented individual committed to building a successful career in the video game industry. Offer a strong background in technical project management, problem-solving expertise, and a proven ability to coordinate the work of teams. Dynamic and entrepreneurial with a track record of meeting deadlines in extremely stressful, fast-paced environments. Strengths include

- ✓ Highly organized with a hands-on approach to project management
- ✓ Extremely knowledgeable about games and the game industry
- ✓ Experienced managing contract and in-house staff
- ✓ Exceptional creative problem-solving skills
- ✓ Frequently recognized for outstanding work performance
- ✓ Strong background in staff development and training

SUMMARY OF QUALIFICATIONS

Consistently excel when faced with new challenges, especially
when working under pressure or to tight deadlines.

✓ **Organization:** Organized previously chaotic technical consultancy into highly efficient operation. Changes reduced turnaround time from 3 weeks to 7 days and generated a 14% return on sales.

✓ **Self-Development:** Obtained 4 technical certifications, without company sponsorship, by studying after work and on weekends while paying all associated costs.

✓ **Performance Excellence:** Received several awards for performance excellence and consistently ranked among the top 10% of regional account executives.

✓ **Staff Development:** Developed training for new hires in 2 different companies in order to increase productivity and reduce errors.

✓ **Problem Solving:** Frequently selected to solve challenging technical-support issues despite the presence of more-experienced technicians on staff. Used reverse engineering to resolve many longstanding customer issues that no one else had been able to solve.

✓ **Relationship Building:** Turned around problematic relationships with major computer hardware manufacturers such as HP and IBM, with the result that SemTech received valuable assistance and technical support at no cost.

Industry Change: From telecommunications account executive to video game producer.

GREG DAVIES · gregdavies@net.net · **PAGE 2**

PROFESSIONAL HISTORY

Commitment and exceptional work ethic have brought success in diverse positions and industries.

PACIFIC COMMUNICATIONS, INC., COLUMBUS, OH · **2006–PRESENT**
Commercial Account Executive

Generate new sales and manage existing accounts in the small to mid-market corporate IT/telecommunications environment.

- Generated $1.3 million in top-line revenue, an increase of 22% over region's prior performance, while consistently ranking among the top 10% of regional account executives over a 2-year period.
- Designed training on proprietary CRM software to ensure that new sales reps could produce quickly. This training program was subsequently adopted by Human Resources for use with all new hires.

LEVEL10 COMMUNICATIONS, COLUMBUS, OH · **2004–2006**
Network Operations Technician

Recognized and resolved problems within legacy network, IP infrastructure, and worldwide frame-relay architecture, which represented 45% of Fortune 500 WAN connectivity.

- Consistently selected to solve challenging technical-support issues. Used reverse engineering to resolve complex customer issues that had been open for more than 3 days.
- Coordinated and developed new-hire training agenda to teach required technical skills to new associates. Program reduced orientation time from 6 weeks to 14 days.

SEMTECH, COLUMBUS, OH · **2003–2004**
Consulting Engineer/ Practice Manager

Managed PC hardware troubleshooting and repair for 7 major corporations. Maintained database of service calls, product returns, and parts inventory. Diagnosed and fixed technical issues.

- Reduced turnaround time from 3 weeks to 7 days and generated a 14% return on sales by implementing new systems that transformed this previously chaotic technical consultancy.
- Received Compaq 5-star ratings for "outstanding service and customer support" for 2 consecutive quarters. Awarded SemTech Consultant of the Month twice in 10 months.

EDUCATION

Demonstrated a continued commitment to personal development since earning degree.

CompTIA A+ Software Certification (2006)
CompTIA A+ Hardware Certification (2005)
CompTIA Network Plus Certification (2005)
Cisco Certified Network Associate (2004)

BS Management Information Systems and Finance, The Ohio State University, Columbus, OH (2003)

PROFESSIONAL ASSOCIATIONS

Member, International Game Developers Association (IGDA), 2006–Present

Strategy: *Present accomplishments in areas that will be relevant to senior managers in this industry that is notoriously difficult to enter; include personal qualities to help him stand out as an individual.*

RESUME 27: BY DIANE BURNS, CPRW, CCMC, CCM, CEIP, JCTC, CLTMC, CFJST

Jane M. Goodson

2398 Melancholy Lane • Columbia, MD 21045 • 410-555-3490 • jmgood@hotmail.com

CAREER FOCUS

Chief Information Officer ~ IT Director

PERSONAL & PROFESSIONAL VALUE OFFERED

Optimize your business investments with realistic IT solutions, build high levels of customer satisfaction, and bridge the gap between management and techies with a skilled business manager and IT professional proficient in the following:

· Policy Development	· Strategic Planning	· Leadership & Team Management
· Organizational Skills	· System Administration	· Computer Espionage & Security
· Financial Management	· Operational Procedures	· IT Implementation & Operations
· EDI Management	· Training/Staff Development	· Problem Solving & Analysis
· Web Design & Hosting	· High-Level Briefings	· Quality Customer Service
· Interpersonal Skills	· Federal & Corporate Contracts	· Oral & Written Communications

Career Highlights

- More than 15 years of experience as a proven leader in technology management with working knowledge of computer platforms, applications, measurement systems, and performance standards. Able to teach/train others in such technology. Consistently worked in high-technology industries.

- **Certified CIO through the Office of Personnel Management and the University of Virginia.** Only three universities offer this new CIO Certification program, which is supported and backed by the U.S. federal government to bridge the digital divide within government agencies. Familiar with researching, analyzing, identifying, and developing strategic plans and objectives for the implementation and use of IT.

- Accomplished professional lauded for refined interpersonal and public communications abilities. Poised and polished public speaker. Articulate writer.

PROFESSIONAL EXPERIENCE

Motorola, U.S. Federal Government Market Division (USFGMD), MD   2000–Present
* Motorola is a major manufacturer and seller of two-way communication equipment.

Sales Account Manager, 2006–Present
- Manage 300 Department of Labor, Army Corps of Engineers, U.S. Navy, and Naval Ship accounts. Consistently generate new accounts. Started 2001 with a $3M quota and exceeded the quota by 30% by summer 2001, growing accounts by more than 26%.

- Determine strategies for the development of two-way communication systems, including wireless LANS, VoIP, and VPNs. Assess technologies and the IT direction of each client. Formulate plans, determine upgrades or migrations for systems, and implement solutions to facilitate and strengthen the cost-effectiveness and efficiency of IT and wireless solutions.

- Provide clients with superior customer service. Develop quotes, manage customer service problems/issues, and follow up on delivery. Conduct user training, on site or via telephone.

- Suggest appropriate systems, operations, and integration of new systems. Guide customers in understanding where new technology can add value while supporting or transforming program operations. Provide immediate technical support for information systems or telecommunications systems.

EDI Manager (Concurrent Assignment), 2005–Present
- Independently researched, built, and maintain Electronic Data Interface transactions with federal government agencies with more than 500 accounts and web-based technology for two Motorola divisions.

Career Change: From sales manager to Chief Information Officer.

Strategy: Focus on IT and management skills, with technology expertise and recent certification as added value.

RESUME 27, CONTINUED

Collection Manager & Web Master, 2000–2005

- Spearheaded the division's EDI objectives and maintained the department's web page. Worked with a web development team to determine content, placement, and accomplishment timelines. The company desired to be presented as superior in a web display to the world.

- Created the idea for a web page and brought the division in line with current-day technology with a web-based presence. Led a team to create, develop, upload, and maintain the department's web page.

- Provided a superior level of customer satisfaction related to the maintenance and collection of accounts receivable generated by the sale of Motorola Parts and Equipment to the federal government. Supervised, trained, and evaluated a staff of four. Interfaced with division and field finance personnel.

- Instrumental in the creation and implementation of strategies and action plans. Co-wrote the collection and credit policy, and revised and updated outdated regulations. Managed international business and updated/implemented international collections policy, a subset of departmental policy. Handled European transactions and led a team responsible for Asia, South America, and Africa.

- Wrote a user-friendly collections guidance manual for junior employees, reducing the confusion in the department. Streamlined procedures to one plan and eliminated employees asking repeated questions.

- Member of the Critical Differences Total Customer Satisfaction (TCS) Team and Legacy. Discussed and recommended working solutions to complex customer problems and difficult customer issues.

Desktop Publishing Specialist, 1999–2001

- Assigned to Motorola, Inc., as a Macintosh subject-matter expert and Temporary Credit Analyst. Troubleshot programs and ensured computers were up and running. Designed a policy manual.

United States Marines, Active Duty, The Pentagon	**1995–1999**
Reserves	**1999–present**

Intelligence Specialist (TS/SBI Clearance), Active Duty **Soldier of the Year,** 1998 *(Distinguished Professional)*

- Supervised and trained a team of 6 personnel that produced and distributed a daily, 18-page classified newsletter for the White House and Joint Chiefs of Staff.

- Presented high-level briefings and prepared briefing products and reports. Enforced cyber-security measures. Implemented communications security protocols.

- Instrumental in the integration of a new state-of-the-art desktop publishing system.

- Developed and published a comprehensive series of Standard Operating Procedures that served as a valuable tool for the conduct of the office during manpower turnovers and shortages.

- Participated in setting up the initial operating procedures for the secure video teleconferencing link that supported the daily morning brief to the Director of Marine Intelligence and his staff.

- Quickly mastered the procedures maintaining the office ADP system. Trained all incoming personnel.

EDUCATION

- **MS in Information Technology,** University of Virginia, Richmond, VA, May 2009
- **Certified CIO,** Office of Personnel Management and the University of Virginia (21 continuing-education credits), July 2008
- **BS** in Business Administration, University of Virginia, Richmond, VA, May 2000

CHAPTER 6

Resumes for Career Changers Seeking Sales, Marketing, Advertising, Public Relations, Writing, and Events Management Positions

To facilitate a successful transition to a sales or marketing career, resumes in this chapter highlight relevant knowledge and—wherever possible—proven abilities in the important functions of communication, persuasion, and presentation.

- Network engineer to sales representative
- Hospital services specialist to medical sales professional
- Police officer to sales representative
- Flight attendant to pharmaceutical sales representative
- Chiropractor to medical/pharmaceutical sales representative
- Teacher to sales representative
- Training manager to sales professional
- Counselor to pharmaceutical sales representative
- Financial industry analyst to sales or business development manager
- TSA screener to travel industry marketing/event manager
- Retail manager to sales representative or sales manager
- Auto technician to marketing professional
- Pharmacist to marketing professional
- Fashion designer and medical office projects manager to marketing/PR
- Teacher to public relations/marketing communications professional
- Retail manager to marketing professional
- Massage therapist to writer/editor
- Academic advisor to writer
- Underwriter to event manager
- Entrepreneur to marketing and events management professional

Part II: Sample Resumes for Career Changers

RESUME 28: BY MICHAEL LEVY, CPRW, CEIP, MCDP, PHR, GCDFI

JOHN E. COOPER

822 Clayton Street
N. Las Vegas, Nevada 89032

Residence: (702) 938-5802
Cell: (702) 573-8137

Email: JohnEcooper@cox.net

TECHNICAL SALES REPRESENTATIVE
TECHNOLOGY / COMMUNICATIONS / MANUFACTURING
First-class customer service—increased company revenue $3 million

AS400, Cisco, WAN, Routers, Hubs, Switches, Network Servers, Lotus Notes, Visio, ATM

- Account Development
- Customer Needs Assessment
- Global Marketing Strategies
- Client Relationship Management
- Team Building and Leadership
- Vendor Negotiations
- Consulting
- Revenue Growth
- Technical Knowledge

Organized and self-directed manager with 15+ years of experience in the technology industry. Excellent communicator and sound decision maker with proven people skills. Consistently delivered multimillion-dollar projects on time and within budget. Trained new technicians and developed processes.

PROFESSIONAL EXPERIENCE

Network Design Engineer   2005–Present
Sprint, Las Vegas, NV

Developed and maintain up to 225 business-to-business sales accounts both nationally and internationally. Supervise a team of 14. Coordinate with departments to prepare cost-effective solutions, provide buyer satisfaction, and create profits for the company.

- Achieved 25% reduction in customer turnaround and product delivery time—set a benchmark standard.
- Teamed with department heads to create an automated PC tool that enhanced tracking, coordination, and process flow.
- Brought customer service back online within 72 hours after major region-wide power outage.

Network Design Engineer   1994–2005
Qwest Corporation, Denver, CO

Managed multi-network accounts throughout the United States, Europe, and South America. Prepared design and managed delivery to customers; assisted the sales teams in product review for cost-effective solutions for customers; monitored customer networks to ensure 100% usage of circuits.

- Enhanced the profit picture by ensuring 100% accountability for 200+ client accounts.
- Created a test system to identify potential configuration problems—saved time and expense.
- Reduced wasted duplication, met deadlines, and improved efficiency of information by maintaining close communication with other department managers.

Network Technician   1992–1994
Level 3 Communications, Denver, CO

Lead technician overseeing technical training, keeping informed of latest technology, managing customer accounts, and solving high-level problems.

- Developed a technician hands-on training process that reduced learning curve of new technicians.
- Initiated a high-speed upgrade project to support 800+ branch offices—the project was self-funded, was completed 6 weeks ahead of schedule, and returned $3 million to the company.

OTHER EXPERIENCE

Line Chief, Jet Maintenance, United States Air Force

EDUCATION AND CERTIFICATIONS

Louisiana State University, Baton Rouge, LA
Studies in Business (2 years completed)

Pace University, New York, NY
Certified in Network Skills (12-week course)

Career Change: From network engineer to sales representative.

Strategy: Emphasize relevant technical knowledge, along with proven ability to work with people as demonstrated by delivering training and developing vendor and business relationships.

Bill M. Turner

Marshall, Washington (greater Spokane) ▪ Turner@Spokane.rr.com ▪ 509.245.7309

HEALTHCARE INDUSTRY PROFESSIONAL

HOSPITAL ACCOUNT MANAGEMENT ▪ MEDICAL EQUIPMENT TRAINING

Clinical experience includes work as EMT and extensive use of medical equipment, including dialysis machines (Fresenius E, H, K), Minntech Reuse equipment, Zyzatech Portable ROs, defibrillators, and centrifuges. Numerous long-term relationships with hospital accounts in greater Spokane. Extensive experience training medical staff and physicians. Great work ethic; worked full and part time while achieving college degree. Longer-term career goal of sales management. Career reputation of quickly transitioning into a "trusted resource" for customers.

Endorsements:
- "Bill has the traits of the elite medical sales reps; he's a catch for your sales team." – **Dr. William Norris, Neurologist, Kaiser Hospital**
- "He has tremendous interpersonal skills … enhanced the relationship between LCC and St. Thomas Hospital … very conscientious and has an excellent work ethic … I recommend Bill to you without reservation." – **Janis Hunter, RN, McLeeland General Hospital**

PROFESSIONAL PROFILE

LCC Donor Network, Bellevue, WA   2005 – Present
Hospital Services Specialist
Develop relationships with hospital administrators, nursing staff, and physicians to promote organ donation programs.
- *Overcome challenges* inherent to program integration and ensure compliance of programs with HCAHO and UNOS requirements.
- Manage several larger accounts, including Spokane-based Providence Scared Heart Medical Center & Children's Hospital, Deaconess Medical Center, and Providence Holy Family Hospital; also manage Bass Medical Center in Coeur d'Alene, ID, and St. Joseph's Regional Hospital in Boise, ID.
- Call on neurosurgeons, neurologists, transplant physicians, hospitalists, hospital ethicists, medical directors, CCU staff, pharmacists, transplant administrators, and nursing administrators.
- Provided support key to St. Thomas Hospital, winning awards for donation performers; enabled conversion rate rise from initial 60% to a record 80%.

Northwest Medical Care Group, Spokane, WA   1998 – 2005
Medical Equipment Trainer / Patient Care Technician
Showcased ability to quickly learn new technology and establish key relationships. Promoted 3 times during this period and awarded Certificate of Appreciation by peers.
- Received several letters of recommendation from healthcare industry customers served during this tenure; letters attested to professionalism, work ethic, and interpersonal skills with all members of medical staff.
- *Overcame the challenges* of working 18-hour shifts while resolving difficult medical challenges.
- Gained invaluable insight to medical-related programs, processes, challenges, and opportunities.
- Established excellent skills in public speaking and effective communication with doctors and nursing staff.

Spokane Fire District, Spokane, WA   1995 – 2004
Emergency Medical Technician (EMT) / Firefighter
Established essential insight to emergency medicine protocols, including elements of ER and OR
- Awarded "Firefighter of the Year" in 1997.
- Worked full and part time to finance college education during this period.
- Served as a Wildland Firefighter for Lewis National Wildlife Refuge (1997) and Idaho Department of Lands (1998).

EDUCATION, CERTIFICATIONS & TRAINING

B.A., Organizational Management — Washington University, Spokane, WA
Graduated Cum Laude with GPA of 3.82

Certifications Include: Basic Life Support Certified Instructor (CPR/AED), Nationally Certified Clinical Hemodialysis Technician (CCHT), Semi-Automatic Defibrillator Certified Operator (DCO), and Washington Emergency Medical Technician (EMT0-B).

Career Change: *From hospital services specialist to medical sales professional.*

Strategy: *Emphasize health care background and include powerful endorsements from medical professionals.*

TERENCE KEENAN

344-02 Parsons Blvd., Flushing, NY 11355 • 718-660-9033 • TKeenan@netway.net

SALES / ROUTE DISTRIBUTION

Five years of experience in route distribution preceding a 20-year career in law enforcement. Offer an impeccable New York State driving record and a proficiency in 18-wheeler operations. Work well with diverse populations and expertly handle potentially threatening situations throughout urban communities. Maintain a high energy level and strong stamina required for lifting heavy loads and working long hours in inclement conditions.

Select Areas of Qualification:

– Beverage Route Distribution – Promotional Display Merchandising – Purchasing/Inventory Control
– Product Sales & Marketing – Customer Needs Assessment – Receivables/Collections
– Customer Service Excellence – Security Enforcement/Theft Control – Vehicle Maintenance/Repair

Relevant Experience — *Route Distribution*

ROUTE DRIVER / SALES REPRESENTATIVE
Long Island Beverage Distributors, Bay Shore, NY, 1985–1990

- Recipient of 15 quarterly recognition awards for *Top Sales Production* and *Performance Excellence.*
- Managed a route distribution of Barley's Brew throughout competitive Suffolk County sales territories.
- Serviced an account base of 25–40 daily stops that included bars, restaurants, supermarkets, and delicatessens.
- Monitored and replenished daily/weekly inventory levels, and consistently met delivery schedules on time.
- Expertly managed tailgate deliveries and forklift operations for volume product loading and unloading.
- Effectively negotiated sales agreements and terms with potential and existing clients.
- Maintained ongoing expenses for inventory and vehicle maintenance; collected accounts receivable.
- Supported customers' merchandising needs with window displays and relevant promotional materials.
- Responded to customer requests, resolving problems directly and through appropriate channels.

Career History — *Law Enforcement*

POLICE OFFICER
109th Precinct, Flushing, NY, 1990–Present

- Currently work with the New York State Police Department/New York State Parole Department as part of a Joint Task Force to track and apprehend parole violators throughout all areas of the 5 boroughs.
- As part of the Department's specialized training, recently completed extensive criminal investigative studies in Forensic Science, Automotive Crime, and Organized Crime through the New York City Police Academy.
- Throughout career, worked collaboratively with all Bronx County precincts (9) and numerous Brooklyn North precincts on diverse cases and assignments in high-crime vicinities throughout all 5 boroughs.
- Trained Academy recruits in all aspects of foot, car, and scooter patrol of high-crime areas.
- Extensively experienced in undercover surveillance work in connection with robberies and drug trafficking.

Education

John Jay College of Criminal Justice, New York, NY
Associate in Applied Science, Criminal Justice, 1990

Career Change: *From police officer to sales representative.*

Strategy: *Bring to the forefront similar experience, even though it occurred more than 20 years ago.*

DIANE M. SEYFERTH

122 N. Telegraph ▪ Southfield, MI 48024
(248) 555-3456 ▪ seyferth@aol.com

Highly motivated and results-driven professional seeking **Pharmaceutical Sales Representative** position to accelerate sales growth through effective product education and extensive relationship building.

SUMMARY OF QUALIFICATIONS

- ✓ Persistent in pursuit to build sales and provide solutions according to identified customer needs.
- ✓ Strong customer-service orientation as demonstrated by commendations earned while working for high-profile corporations, including Southwest Airlines—recognized for unparalleled service.
- ✓ Familiar with medical terminology and able to convey complex concepts in simpler terms.
- ✓ Frequently chosen for prime assignments based on performance and job dedication.
- ✓ Professional, confident demeanor; excellent public-speaking skills; willing to work extended hours.

Strengths: Goal Attainment ▪ Persuasion Skills ▪ Needs Assessment ▪ Time Management

RELATED EXPERIENCE

SALES

- One of selected few chosen to participate in sales campaign designed to promote new services within new-growth market. Utilized consultative-sales approach to educate customers on service packages and incentive programs, emphasizing advantages and features. Employed suggestive-selling strategy to maximize individual sales while selling travel packages to customers.

CUSTOMER SERVICE

- Recruited to serve needs of international dignitaries of presidential stature based on outstanding customer-service skills. Supported diverse needs of up to 137 customers daily through attentive, responsive service. Responded effectively to inquiries of up to 150 phone customers daily. Remained current on service packages and options to ensure accuracy of rapidly changing service information.

MEDICAL

- Assisted with medical situations of passengers suffering from cardiac arrest, strokes, hypoxia, diabetic comas, and Alzheimer's. Interfaced with doctors and medical professionals during medical situations. Volunteered for Airline Crisis Team to assist in emergency-recovery efforts. Participated in annual training seminars to remain current on medical procedures.

COMMUNICATIONS / PRESENTATIONS

- Educated groups of 100+ individuals on policies and practices. Communicated clearly and effectively with dignitaries, executives, colleagues, and customers. Wrote copy to generate interest in current events and stories presented by anchors of news station (during internship).

WORK HISTORY

Flight Attendant, Southwest Airlines, Detroit, MI, 2004–Present
Customer Service Representative / Flight Attendant, America West Airlines, Detroit, MI, 2000–2004
Corporate Flight Attendant, Execujet / Aramco Associated Company, Detroit, MI, 1998–2000

EDUCATION / TRAINING

Bachelor of Arts in Communications, University of Michigan, Ann Arbor, MI

Career Change: *From flight attendant to pharmaceutical sales representative.*

Strategy: *Bring relevant experience to the top and enhance its value by emphasizing other related areas that contribute to her capabilities. The bold subheadings call attention to the necessary skills.*

RESUME 32: BY CAROL ALTOMARE, MRW, ACRW, CPRW, CCMC, CJSS

ROBERT EVANS, D.C.

18 Lee Boulevard ◆ Woodbridge, VA 22192 ◆ 703-884-2060 ◆ evansdc@gmail.com

SALES REPRESENTATIVE
MEDICAL/PHARMACEUTICAL SALES
Sales & Marketing / New Business Development / Product Promotion
Client Relationship Management

Well-regarded chiropractic doctor with strong network of medical contacts and proven expertise in promoting products and services in medical settings. Skilled relationship manager; a knowledgeable medical resource who is effective in building trust and retaining client accounts long term. Solution-oriented service provider with skill in identifying need and articulating value to clients in terms they can understand and embrace. Driven team player with a passion for achievement and a commitment to delivering results.

Core Competencies:
➤ Leveraging knowledge of medical operations to open doors and cultivate receptive audiences.
➤ Promoting products and services through persuasive presentation of features and benefits.
➤ Managing client accounts, providing exceptional service to build loyalty and retain business long term.
➤ Building and maintaining productive business relationships to expand sales and achieve revenue goals.

PROFESSIONAL EXPERIENCE

WOODBRIDGE CHIROPRACTIC, Woodbridge, VA   1995 to present
Managing Owner/Chiropractic Doctor
Oversee all business operations while providing services to 35 to 40 patients per day in thriving solo practice.

- Successfully launched and grew practice, implementing multi-pronged marketing strategy that included direct-mail and print advertising campaigns to build awareness of services and generate business.

- Built robust network of referring doctors and other medical professionals, cultivating relationships through onsite visits to establish productive pipeline for ongoing expansion.

- Promoted and won approval to present wellness seminars at corporate locations, gaining audiences with prospective clients at companies such as Alexandria Insurance and Apple Credit Union. Currently negotiating deal to provide seminars for industry giant American Express.

- Built strong record in managing client relations, effectively developing, explaining, and promoting on-target, well-conceived care plans to win client business while providing top-notch service and support to maintain client accounts long term.

ARLINGTON CHIROPRACTIC CENTER, Arlington, VA   1988 to 1995
Associate Chiropractic Doctor
Provided chiropractic services, including spinal exams and screenings, X-ray interpretations, care plans, and treatments. Delivered weekly seminars. Authored reports for attorneys and insurance companies.

EDUCATION

Doctor of Chiropractic, Palmer Chiropractic College, Port Orange, FL, 1988
Bachelor of Arts, Biology (Pre-med with physiology specialization), University of Delaware, Newark, DE, 1985

Career Change: From chiropractor to medical/pharmaceutical sales representative.

Strategy: Emphasize marketing, sales, relationship-building, and client account management aspects of his work as a self-employed chiropractor.

Edward King

5 Falling Ledge Lane • The Woodlands, Texas 77381 • (936) 273-6785

QUALIFICATIONS PROFILE
Sales & Business Development

Well-educated professional offering a unique combination of professional skills. Successful educator and sales manager with core competencies in sales development, sales presentations, competitive market positioning, customer relationship management, teaching, training, and coaching. Excellent communication, organizational, and planning skills.

SALES EXPERIENCE

DIAMOND INTERNATIONAL, INC., Ontario, Canada   2009–Present
Area Manager & Distributor, Plink-o
Recruited by this Canadian-based vending machine manufacturer as an exclusive distributor to sell/lease a new product, "Plink-o Money Machine," to restaurants, convenience stores, and other retail establishments in the Houston area. Assumed full responsibility for cold-calling and canvassing, sales presentations, contract negotiations, product delivery, and follow up. **Exceeded sales goal by 15%.**

TEACHING EXPERIENCE

Fifteen years of experience as a **Special Education Teacher** employed on educational grants within Texas, Massachusetts, New York, and New Hampshire. Taught all academic subjects and social and life skills to learning-handicapped, cognitively disabled, and emotionally disturbed youths in grades 5–12.

Houston School District, Houston, Texas	(2008–2009)
Nashua Children's Home, Nashua, New Hampshire	(2007–2008)
Worcester Public Schools, Worcester, Massachusetts	(2005–2007)
Seacoast Learning Collaborative, Kingston, New Hampshire	(2002–2005)
Crockett Intermediate School, Conroe, Texas	(2000–2002)
FM Black Middle School, Houston, Texas	(1999–2000)
Erasmus Hall High School, Brooklyn, New York	(1998–1999)

ACCOLADES FROM SENIOR MANAGERS

"Ed was extremely conscientious and worked hard to develop support programs for students…a dedicated professional."
Krista Osborn, Principal, Houston School District

"Ed shows a general desire to serve the children in his care…always presents himself in a professional manner."
Joanne Burdett Dion, Educational Director, Nashua Children's Home

"Ed's lesson plans were some of the best from my school, and he implemented them with success…his teaching style is firm yet flexible, caring and professional."
Jo Ann Beken, Principal, Worcester Public Schools

"You were our anchor in the BAC program…you did a great job in a tough situation."
Bourke Meagher, Principal, FM Black Middle School

EDUCATION

St. John's University, New York, New York, **MS, Special Education**
St. John's University, New York, New York, **BS, Management**
State of Texas General Special Education Certification • Certified Special Olympics Coach

Career Change: *From teacher to sales representative.*

Strategy: *Concentrate on recent part-time sales experience and downplay teaching career. Use quotes as strong endorsements.*

RESUME 34: BY MICHAEL DAVIS, ACRW, CPRW, GCDF

GARY DAY

M: 317-555-5911
H: 317-555-2057

gday@in.rr.net

852 East Prospect
Indianapolis, IN 46201

SALES & MARKETING LEADER

Building Strong Organizations, High-Performance Employees, and Profitable Operations
Through Strategic Leadership, Vision, and Action

Powerful professional career with domestic and international experience building top-performing sales & marketing and training & development organizations. Innovator in conceiving strategies and launching programs to boost sales performance, capture new revenue, and expand channel penetration. Thrive in challenging, fast-paced organizations. Achieve business objectives through expertise in the following:

Core Qualifications

- Channel Marketing Management
- National Distributor Relations
- Team Recruitment / Development
- Negotiation of Customer Agreements

- Client Needs Analysis / Solutions Delivery
- Multi-Location Direction / Leadership
- Performance Improvement / Metrics / ROI
- Global Training Program Implementation

Executive Performance

DALCO, INC., Indianapolis, IN   2007–Present
Designs, develops, and delivers a full range of sales training and go-to-market development programs that enhance employee performance in the electronic hardware industry.

Account Manager
Member of team traveling nationwide teaching and training account managers to negotiate, recognize opportunities, perform SWOT analysis, and deliver final recommendations to customers.

- Increased sales performance by more than 11% over 12 months by streamlining selling approach, clearly defining products, and establishing pricing and promotions.

LORRILLARD TOBACCO COMPANY, Jersey City, NY   1980–2007
Nation's oldest tobacco company, founded in 1760.

Senior National Training Manager
Coordinated first national company meeting after sale to Carolina Group, then assumed position as Senior National Training Manager to develop and deliver sales training programs for global organization.

Sales & Marketing Leadership
- Achieved 25% increase in sales, 12% increase in calls per day, and 33% increase in placements of temporary displays through revitalization of underperforming business unit.
- Increased section's operating performance from 21st position to 4th in 3 years through better goal definition, training, and personnel positioning.
- Achieved more than 9.7% increase in calls per day by eliminating inefficient activities.
- Realized 15% growth in signage placements and POP advertising through better communications.

Training & Development
- Managed trade training programs for parent organization across 136 end markets worldwide.
- Liaised and managed external vendors who assisted in developing selected training programs.
- Achieved 47% reduction in training time through implementation of design and execution strategy for online, interactive website.

EDUCATION

M.S., *Marketing,* INDIANA UNIVERSITY, Bloomington, IN

B.S., *Business Administration,* RUTGERS UNIVERSITY, Camden, NJ

Career Change: *From training manager to sales professional.*

Strategy: *Focus on career achievements and emphasize how they relate to sales.*

RESUME 35: BY DEBBIE ELLIS, MRW, CPRW

John J. Cochran

16533 Sky Ranch Road
San Diego, CA 92138

Office: 619-555-6257 jjcochran@aol.com Mobile: 619-555-5740

TERRITORY SALES—CUSTOMER SERVICE—BUSINESS DEVELOPMENT
PHARMACEUTICAL, MEDICAL EQUIPMENT, HEALTHCARE MANAGEMENT ORGANZATIONS

PROFILE

Results-driven professional with a career distinguished by consistent performance within both small and large organizations—focus on service organizations—operating in diverse business cultures, industries, and markets. Offer high-caliber cross-functional management qualifications and proven leadership talents. Strong orientations in business development, relationship management, and performance improvement. Highly motivated, innovative, and creative, with a big-picture perspective. Analytical, logical, and resourceful in approach to prospecting, relationship building, problem solving, and decision-making. Honest, ethical, and effective.

— Licensed Professional Counselor —

CORE QUALIFICATIONS

Strategic Business Planning
Organization & Follow-through
New Business & Account Development
Customer Relations & Negotiations
Account Revitalization

Team Building & Leadership
Purposeful Listening & Needs Assessment
Solutions & Relationship Sales
Persuasive Communication Skills
Large Group / Small Group Presentations

PROFESSIONAL EXPERIENCE

JOHN J. COCHRAN, MA, LPC COUNSELING, INC.—San Diego, CA   1998–Present

Owner, Licensed Professional Counselor serving largely physician and executive client base using cognitive-behavioral psychotherapeutic approaches and methodologies.

- Increased client base 300% in first two years of practice using aggressive, six-step solution-selling technique: approach, interview, demonstrate, validate, negotiate, close.

HUMANA HOSPITAL ACADEMY OF MENTAL HEALTH—San Leandro, CA   1986–1998

Executive Director, reporting to the Board of Directors, responsible for its 260-outpatient base, providing individual and group counseling on addictive behaviors.

EDUCATION & PROFESSIONAL ACTIVITIES / AFFILIATIONS

MA, Counseling—CALIFORNIA SCHOOL OF PROFESSIONAL PSYCHOLOGY, Los Angeles, CA
BS, Industrial Engineering—UNIVERSITY OF ILLINOIS, Chicago, IL

Keynote speaker—January 2006, New York Life Insurance Co.—*"Tying Self-Motivation to Performance"*
Ethics Committee Chair, California Counseling Association (CCA)

PROFESSIONAL REFERRALS

"Through his private practice, John has worked together closely with physicians and medical offices. He is well apprised of the intricacies of the medical services environment as well as familiar with the pharmacological therapies used for disorders of the nervous system. He is an excellent candidate for a medical-type services sales representative position ... I am sure that he will meet and exceed all expectations."
—*Clarissa Schick Howisson, Ph.D., DABR, Chief, Division of Radiotherapy Medical Physics, University of California Medical Sciences Medical Center*

"I have been in the practice of medicine for 34 years and have dealt with pharmaceutical representatives for all of them. I have known John for 12 years and have always been impressed with his communication skills and his ability to build and sustain an outstanding rapport with a wide range of professionals. I believe he will be much superior to the 'typical' sales representative that I see on a daily basis. I can guarantee that he will be an asset to any company."
—*Richard G. Sullivan, MD*

Career Change: *From counselor to pharmaceutical sales representative.*

Strategy: *Relate professional experience in the health care field to the challenge of a sales career. Enhance the resume with strong professional referrals from individuals in the medical field.*

MARK JONES

5301 S. Yosemite
Greenwood Village, CO 80112

(303) 600-8603
jones@mail.com

SALES MANAGEMENT / BUSINESS DEVELOPMENT

Guaranteed to spur outstanding sales results by leveraging more than 10 years of experience in increasing profitability via innovative prospecting, mesmerizing client consultations, and long-term relationship building.

B2B, Division & Territory Sales | Internet & Online Sales | Multimillion-Dollar Accounts

Integrity-driven and forward-thinking leader with a naturally charming ability to engage clients, keenly gauging and targeting their needs. Intuitive at pairing clients with the right service/product. Extensive B2B (business to business) sales. Stellar communicator, presenter, and negotiator, persuading and influencing clients over competitors and earning hard-to-attain accounts. Managed **400+** client accounts worth up to **$60M.**

Expert in full sales cycle: Researching demographics, prospecting, cold calling, networking, overcoming objections, closing tough sales, and building sincere relationships through solution-based selling, plus the following:

* *Sales Planning & Execution*
* *Staff Training & Development*
* *Client Account Optimization*

* *Territory Development & Growth*
* *Creative Profit Growth Strategies*
* *Web 2.0 Marketing / SEO*

* *High-Impact Sales Presentations*
* *Competitive Market Analysis*
* *Technology Knowledge*

CAREER SUMMARY & ACHIEVEMENTS

Prospecting, presenting, abolishing apprehensions, and closing as an <u>Investment Analyst</u> ♦ **2006 to 2010**

FINANCIAL SECURITIES, Greenwood Village, CO

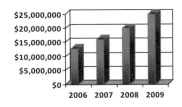

Coordinated all aspects of managing client accounts worth up to **$25M** for up to **300** clients. Served as primary contact, strengthening communications and customer service. Informed and engaged clients, developing sales plans with clear and defined strategies. Implemented creative and vigorous account-gathering strategies.

> *"The challenge of being a successful salesman is relating to the client and keenly identifying their needs. I embrace this challenge and teach others how to capture attention, hold, connect, and sell."*

* Increased account value by **20%** each year by executing successful **B2B** practices previously overlooked by others, such as routinely prospecting in person and customizing sales approach to align with client goals.
* Prospected face-to-face, earned appointments, and became consultant to **$4M** in local business.
* Captured a **30%** client referral increase by demonstrating genuine care for client satisfaction through meticulous following up on all leads and consistent delivery of promises (*"a broken promise is a lost deal!"*).

Marketing, customer service, and profit growth planning as a <u>Director/Sales Manager</u> ♦ **2006 to 2008**

MEDIA INC, Centennial, CO

Conceptualized and launched a business, concurrently promoting and managing multiple websites providing "hot" content to surfers and targeting corporations as advertisers. Set sales projections. Monitored and optimized website traffic and conversion sales. Presented persuasively, influencing and netting advertisers.

* Captured the attention of the *U.S. Army, Paramount Pictures,* and *Amazon.com,* closed them as advertisers, and increased CPM revenue **200%** by doubling targeted traffic.

Career Change: *From financial industry analyst to sales or business development manager.*

Strategy: *Use an eye-catching graph to show sales results even though he wasn't technically a salesperson. Make the most of a short-term entrepreneurial venture that involved sales.*

MARK JONES

(303) 600-8603   Page 2   jones@mail.com

Market penetration and client-focused presentations as <u>Senior Financial Advisor/Consultant</u> ◆ **1999 to 2006**

LIFE & CASUALTY, Colorado Springs, CO
SCOTT, LLC, Englewood, CO

Recognized by peers and clients as strategist who consistently succeeded in driving profitability within challenging markets. Led a unique team that conducted monthly client seminars, earning clients' trust and producing continued success. Continuously revamped consultant training and development to keep up with market demands and maintain solid team performances. Independently mounted an aggressive and tactical sales campaign. Personally consulted prospects, skillfully balancing a numbers-driven goal with integrity-driven sales closings.

- Outperformed others by differentiating selling technique: Offered unique strategies to meet individual needs. Exceeded annual goals, increasing gross **25%** each year to more than **$300K** per year.
- Trained and built driven, high-performance teams that captured more than **$1M** in new assets each seminar and a **$10M** case through impactful presentations.

EDUCATION

UNIVERSITY OF DENVER
(BA) Bachelor of Arts

RESUME 37: BY ANN BOYER, M.ED., CCMC, ACRW

THOMAS M. WILLIAMS

4424 Deer Valley Road • Rossville, MD 21237
901-916-5432 • tmwilliams25@att.net

TRAVEL INDUSTRY PROFESSIONAL
Marketing • Promotions • Event Management

More than 20 years of experience delivering unsurpassed customer service in the cruise line, airline, and fine-dining industries. Seeking an opportunity to utilize strong conceptual and promotional abilities in combination with diverse hospitality experience and industry operational knowledge. Expertise in:

- Cruise Line Operations & Procedures
- Tour Arrangement & Planning
- Tourism Promotion Strategies

- Direct/Indirect Sales
- Event Planning
- Banquet Operations

- Food & Beverage
- Photography/Layout/Design
- Staff Supervision

EDUCATION / CERTIFICATIONS / LICENSES

Bachelor of Science, Travel and Tourism Management, South Florida University

Special Projects:

- **Old Town Historical Tour**—Conceptualized and implemented a historically accurate tour. Conducted all research, photography, layout, proofing, and editing activities for printed materials and exhibits. Assisted with public relations that launched a successful advertising and marketing campaign.

- **Heritage Center**—Designed a permanent exhibit showcasing a collection of historic artifacts. Cataloged, photographed, and displayed artifacts in a historically correct and artistic backdrop.

- **Broward County Fair**—Coordinated large-group travel arrangements for annual event that required oversight of travel dates and times, party size, and cost calculation.

Certifications and Licenses:

- Merchant Mariners Document (MMD)
- Occupational Safety & Health Administration (OSHA) Certification
- United States Public Health (USPH) Certification

EMPLOYMENT

Transportation Security Officer   2008–Present
Department of Homeland Security, Transportation Security Administration, Baltimore, MD

Conduct security screening of passengers and carry-on baggage at Baltimore Washington International Airport (BWI). Monitor walk-through metal detector and X-ray equipment while adhering to strict government surveillance guidelines. Instruct passengers on security procedures.

- Sustain vigilant surveillance while maintaining professional and courteous demeanor, in spite of time pressure, surges in traveler volume, and unpredictable security issues.

- Implement decisive measures during peak traffic and/or security alert conditions to allow timely processing of passengers and bags. Received "**Incident Management Award**" for cooperation and teamwork during a maintenance emergency.

Staffing Coordinator/Service Captain   2007
Wine Country Catering Company, Fredericksburg, VA

Hired as a server and promoted to oversee event management for an award-winning catering company serving Wine Country and Northern Virginia. Coordinated the staffing and scheduling of 60+ employees for large weddings and formal events serving up to 300 guests. Assumed service captain duties during event: Assigned stations to staff, oversaw service, tended bar, and served guests.

- Contributed to successful event catering through strategic staffing and timeline planning.

Career Change: *From TSA screener to travel industry marketing/event manager.*

Strategy: *Highlight relevant education and earlier experience in the travel industry, although in a lower-level customer service position rather than current goal of marketing/event management.*

THOMAS M. WILLIAMS • tmwilliams25@att.net   Page Two

Bartender   2004–2007
Coral Cruise Lines (CCL), St. Petersburg, FL

Assigned to *Sea Spirit,* a 12-deck, U.S.-flagged cruise ship with capacity for 2,000 passengers and 900 crew. Hired as bar server; promoted to bartender within 9 months. Rotated bartending services among 12 bars.

- **Supervised** up to 10 wait staff; ensured workstation assignment was properly executed.
- Increased weekly sales revenue 10%–15% through the promotion and upselling of drink specials and soda programs. Minimized bar inventory costs through accurate inventory planning.
- Received **"Excel Award"** for special assignment achievements: Captured cruise line experience through portrait and outdoor photography; mounted, displayed, and sold pictures.
  —Increased photography department revenue 20% through photo package upgrade sales.
- Completed CCL training with demonstrated competency in crowd management, fire fighting, environmental protection, wine selection, and stewardship.

Customer Service Agent   2000–2003
US Airlines, Baltimore Washington International Airport (BWI), Baltimore, MD

Initially employed as an airline reservation agent at the Baltimore Call Center. Provided travel information regarding schedules, fares, and seat availability. Made reservations and processed payments. Transferred to BWI ticket counter; assumed passenger check-in and boarding responsibilities.

- Received **"Top Performance Award"** in recognition of ticket sales that exceed $350,000.
- Successfully managed influx of passengers when airlines experienced irregular operations. Worked promptly and efficiently to identify satisfying rebooking and rerouting solutions.

Tour Coordinator   1995–1999
City View Tours, Inc., Washington, DC

Coordinated tour scheduling and transportation logistics for corporate clients during local and regional excursions for a destination management company.

- Subcontracted administrative services with Intercontinental Corporation, a conference support company. Recognized by management for demonstrated ability to address customers' diverse traveling and administrative requests.

VOLUNTEER EXPERIENCE

Community Service Volunteer   2000–2003
American Service Corps, Rossville, MD

Contributed to the marketing campaign of Mobile Classroom, a preschool reading program sponsored by one of the nation's largest antipoverty service programs.

- Expanded program's promotional materials: Designed logo, business cards, and letterhead stationery; wrote public service announcements; and produced an 8-minute promotional video.

RESUME 38: BY GAYLE HOWARD, CERW, CCM, CPRW, CRW

MICHAEL BLACK

33 Fairbairn Drive
Rocklin, CA 94677

Email: mickblack@verizon.net

Mobile: 415-205-3940
Residence: 415-939-2004

SALES & MARKETING MANAGEMENT

A **resolute desire to sell and achieve,** a passion for influencing consumer buying habits, and proven strengths in building sustainable market share have been the foundation of career successes over an impressive, achievement-filled career. Rare talent for simplifying and executing strategic ideas has generated widespread support, delivered strong revenue growth, and complied with budget constraints. Confidence, integrity, discipline, and vision have been key drivers in expertly nurturing relationships with team members, clients, senior management, and vendors.

Professional Strengths

- Market & Segment Expansion
- Strategic Marketing Plans
- Staff Recruitment
- Key Account Management
- Financial Management
- Market Intelligence
- Customer Retention

- Change Management
- Branding Concepts/Rollouts
- Team Development
- Multichannel Distribution
- Sales Force Motivation
- Customer Needs Assessment
- High-Impact Presentations

- Profit & Loss Accountability
- Campaign Management
- Contract Negotiations
- Supplier Relations
- Competitive Product Positioning
- Margin Improvement

EDUCATION

Bachelor of Science, Business Administration (Marketing)
University of California at Los Angeles

EMPLOYMENT NARRATIVE

PAINTGLOW PAINTS, Rocklin, CA
State Retail Manager

2007–Present

Appointed to steer statewide operations during a period when lack of strategic planning, pricing restrictions, and an absence of cohesive teamwork were limiting market expansion. Skeleton staffs of traveling sales representatives restricted campaigns to trade accounts, and multi-branded independent distributors were failing to make desired headway against aggressive competition in a static market. A total revitalization strategy was critical.

Immediately established a tactical rollout plan, spearheaded intense market research into competitor placements, and managed performance expectations by devising a series of key performance indicators to act as benchmarks for staff achievement.

Results were impressive:

- State revenues **up 20% over preceding year.**
- Market share increased from **6.8% to 7.5% statewide.**
- **Capital expenditure and setup costs** delivered **25% under budget.**
- Rental **expenses 30% below budget.**

Key Contributions—In-depth

- **Reinforced team focus** towards core fundamentals of customer service, product quality, and competitive pricing. Despite a stationary market, clients remained receptive to opportunities for aggressive, value-added service with competitive advantages.
- Coordinated advertising and promotional campaigns to maximize impact and results.
- **Grew customer base by 20% per month** over 12 months by introducing cutting-edge sales prompts into the POS system and injecting new "customer-care" performance initiatives into shop-floor roles.

> **SNAPSHOT**
>
> **Report to:**
> CEO and National Sales and Marketing Manager
>
> **Direct reports:**
> 4 Decorator Center Managers and 5 Trade Sales Representatives
>
> **Operating Budget:**
> $2M per year
>
> **State Revenues:**
> $21.1M

Career Change: *From retail manager to sales representative or sales manager.*

Strategy: *Use a chronological format but minimize references to the specifics of his retail experience and focus on client accounts, marketing and promotional campaigns, and management skills.*

MICHAEL BLACK	Mobile: 415-205-3940 mickblack@verizon.net	Page 2

EMPLOYMENT NARRATIVE
C O N T I N U E D

PAINTGLOW PAINTS
State Retail Manager (continued)

- Launched greater market presence, establishing company-owned outlets with one "exclusive" brand.

- Spearheaded lucrative **relationship-marketing initiative** with RACV, Delfin Property Group, several health insurers, and Master Painters' Association.

- Recruited 20 new staff and rolled out a series of rewards and recognition programs that raised the bar for **sales performance excellence.** Incentive programs in conjunction with active succession career planning has set benchmarks for sales retention—**currently steady at 95%**.

- Reversed ad hoc approach to inventory control that had prompted overstocking, understocking, and widespread inefficiencies. Devised formula to optimize stock turns, and attained a **previously unprecedented rate of 86% OTIF** (on-time-in-full).

- Negotiated six leases, overseeing council planning permits for usage, parking, and signage.

Store Manager 2005–2007

Presided over a period of significant revenue growth that reflected a series of incremental yet substantial changes to key business processes, expense controls, and goal attainment.

Revamped marketing programs; instilled "Market Best" service standards; produced new branding strategies; devised an integrated approach to advertising, marketing, and promotions in retail and trade markets; and spearheaded a staff revitalization program that rewarded superior efforts for attaining newly conceived goals.

Results & Key Contributions

- Sustained operating expenses to 82% of budget, **steering savings in logistics** through improved warehousing and inventory controls.

- Propelled **sales revenues 34.6%** over previous year to $25.4 million.

- Boosted **staff retention** by more than one-third to achieve a **95% rating.** Alleviated the "brain drain" of high-performance staff through training, incentives, and recognition for goal achievement.

- Orchestrated renewed focus on company-owned decorator centers that flourished under lower commissions and rebates. Decision proved significant, **increasing profitability by 38+%** to $3.2 million.

- **Increased market share** from 11% to 12.7% of the California market.

- Conducted group training sessions for up to 40 staff. Presentations **fostered a dynamic environment** where participants brainstormed new ideas—many of which were revenue-positive.

- Analyzed market and architected a doubling of the product range offered to customers, providing alternatives and value-added packages.

> **SNAPSHOT**
>
> **Reported to:**
> California State Manager,
> National Decorator
> Center Manager
>
> **Direct reports:**
> 12 California Decorator
> Center Managers across
> 12 locations and 7 Trade
> Sales Representatives
>
> **Operating Budget:**
> $3M per year
>
> **State Revenues:** $25.4M
>
> **Key Clients:**
> AV Jennings, Q-Build,
> Rocklin City Council,
> Main Roads Rocklin

Trade & Retail Sales Representative 2002–2005

Distinguished from colleagues for securing the lucrative Q-Build Industries account, contributing $1 million annually. The account spurred credibility in the California marketplace, being utilized for virtually all government maintenance projects.

Identified flaws in opposition strategy, focusing successfully on product performance and services in negotiations with major builders across Rocklin. Secured key accounts from major government contractors, project builders, and prominent hardware and paint groups.

Recognized for achieving maximum budget incentives 3 years consecutively, and doubling territory sales in 2 years.

Excellent References & Client Testimonials Available

James T. Manville

jimmyman@network.com

4609 Miller Street • Mt. Clemens, MI 48043 • 586.555.8730

Profile
♦ Committed to pursuing a career in marketing or public relations.
♦ Strong interpersonal skills and ability to build rapport with others.
♦ Creative and artistic.
♦ Computer skills include Word, PowerPoint, Excel, and other spreadsheets.

Education

Oakland University • Rochester, Michigan
Bachelor of Business Administration—Marketing   2008

Eastern Michigan University • Ypsilanti, Michigan
Course work in **Business** and **Afro-American Studies**   2005–2007

Specs Howard School of Broadcasting • Southfield, Michigan
Radio/TV program   2005

Relevant Experience

Pontiac School District—Owen Elementary • Pontiac, Michigan
Bridges to Success Instructor   2008–Present
• Teach African-American Studies to 4th- and 5th-graders two days
per week under auspices of grant-funded after-school program.
• Adapt curriculum to students' levels; research and develop handouts to
supplement lessons.

National Basketball Association • Atlanta, Georgia
Marketing Assistant (Volunteer)   Winter 2008
• Assisted staff at NBA All-Star Weekend Jam Session.
• Interacted with children and families; encouraged participation with
the "Got Milk?" program.

Employment History

Ford Motor Co. Vehicle Operations Division • Allen Park, Michigan
Technician *and* **Team Recorder**   2002–Present
• Conduct tests and inspect parts per QS-9000 guidelines.
• Elected by peers to record minutes during meetings on quality, throughput,
safety, and communications. Generate weekly report based on meetings.

S&R Clothing • Detroit, Michigan
Assistant Manager   2000–2002
• Assisted with daily operations of trendy retail store.
• Performed merchandising; monitored inventory.

Community Affiliations

♦ P.A.L. (Police Athletic League)
♦ Zeta Phi Beta Fraternity (community service)

— *References available on request* —

Career Change: *From auto technician to marketing professional.*

Strategy: *Emphasize relevant education as a primary qualification and include a Relevant Experience section even though this is not his primary work experience.*

JOHN MARTIN

2400 Greenville Place
Atlanta, Georgia 30040   jlm@earthlink.net   770.555.5555 (Home)
770.555.6666 (Office)

WHAT I CAN OFFER **TopLine** AS YOUR NEWEST **MARKETING PROFESSIONAL**

❑ Translate marketing analysis into sales ❑ Introduce the right product to the right market—faster than the competition ❑ Leverage market savvy into every aspect of corporate success ❑ Keep close enough to customers to anticipate their needs

RECENT WORK HISTORY WITH EXAMPLES OF PROBLEMS SOLVED

❑ **Pharmacy Manager,** ShopMart, Conyers, Georgia   05–Present

My pharmacy operates 54 hours a week sharing a tough market with 8 competitors. We fill more than 54K prescriptions each year.

Supervise directly two full-time and one part-time pharmacy technicians.

Improved market data to realign expensive **inventory with customer demand.** *Outcomes:* Cut inventory costs by 29%—the lowest level in years—yet kept customer satisfaction very high.

Used informal demographic analysis to identify the benefit that captured most consumers in this very tough market: minimum waiting time. Redesigned our workflow and then retrained our workforce. *Outcomes:* We **gained market share**—and it **didn't cost us an extra dime.**

❑ Staff Pharmacist *promoted over 10 competitors in just 6 months to be* **Pharmacy Department Manager,** LuckyAide, Lilburn, Georgia   02–05

Brought this new store online. Entered a market already dominated by 20 competitors. We wrote more than 62K prescriptions annually.

Kept valuable customer relationships completely intact even as I changed corporate identity and location. *Outcomes:* **Exceeded corporate production standards by 240%** from the first quarter on.

❑ **Owner and Manager,** Winter Drug Company, Montgomery, Alabama   92–02

Operated two locations that employed a pharmacist and store manager, a bookkeeper, two pharmacy technicians, and six cashiers. Competed successfully against 20 competitors—some partially underwritten by nationwide corporations.

Compared national market trends with local demand to offer a new service. *Outcomes:* Market analysis was good enough to return my investment in just 9 months. New service became **our highest marked-up** product line.

More indicators of performance TopLine can use …

Career Change: *From pharmacist to marketing professional.*

Strategy: *Focus on recent MBA and show how the business he ran benefited from his marketing skills.*

John Martin   **Marketing Professional**   770.555.5555

Stayed close enough to our customers to offer a new service faster than our competition could react. *Outcomes:* **Dominated** one new **segment for 2 years.** In another case, became a new organization's **sole provider for 5 years.**

❑ Staff Pharmacist *promoted over 3 very much more senior team members to be* **Director of Pharmacy,** General Hospital, Kronigsburg, Alabama   85–92
My operation supported a 157-bed acute-care hospital.

Supervised a secretary, 5 pharmacy technicians, and an IV technician.

Applied market savvy to internal customers. Addressed the needs of holdouts and overcame all their objections. My plan for a closed formulary won corporate approval. *Outcomes:* Much **more cost effective—without compromising quality and service.**

EDUCATION

❑ MBA, Georgia State University, Atlanta, Georgia   Expected Spring 10
Paying my own way to earn this advanced degree while working up to 45 hours a week. **GPA 4.0.**

❑ BS, Pharmacy, Samford University, Birmingham, Alabama   85
Carried a full academic load and worked 25 hours a week.

COMPUTER SKILLS

❑ Expert in **proprietary pharmaceutical software,** PROScript and Rx200 (industry-standard, **comprehensive, LAN-based business software** suite optimized to pharmacies), Microsoft Word and Outlook.

❑ Proficient in Adobe Acrobat; Internet search engines; Microsoft Excel, PowerPoint, and Access.

PROFESSIONAL AFFILIATIONS

❑ Co-founder, Georgia Independent Drugstore Association   00–02

Found, marketed to, and captured an overlooked niche from scratch. *Outcomes:* **Grew** membership **rapidly from 3 members to 250 in just 2 years**—all with very little money and time to spend.

❑ Former Board Member, State of Georgia Medicaid Drug Utilization Review Board   97–01

❑ Former Committee Member, State Employees Insurance Board's Drug Program   97–01

CERTIFICATIONS AND LICENSURE

❑ Registered Pharmacist, State of Georgia Board of Pharmacy

Page two

Chantal Luz

24612 Railroad Lane
Fillmore, California 91333
chantal@hotmail.com

Home: 805-263-8611   Mobile: 661-263-1651

**MARKETING / BUSINESS DEVELOPMENT / ACCOUNT MANAGEMENT
ADVERTISING / MARKETING COMMUNICATIONS
PUBLIC RELATIONS / SPECIAL EVENTS**

Creative, dynamic, results-driven professional with expert qualifications in identifying and capturing market opportunities to accelerate expansion, increase revenues, and improve profit contributions across broad industries, markets, and accounts. Energetic, organized, self-motivated individual who is able to comprehend and manage multiple details while focusing on the overall picture. Natural communicator with strong motivational skills and the ability to build, produce, and succeed. Extensive travel.

- Proven ability to spot and analyze trends across product/services spectrum.
- Evolution of concepts into achievable business strategies.
- Product research, analysis, and justification for production.
- Negotiation and relationship-building skills; project planning and execution.
- Drive, visual creativity, and ability to reach objectives under demanding circumstances.
- Strong analytical and problem-solving skills with a focus on workable solutions.
- Creative and strategic planning abilities with solid implementation skills.
- Computer literate.

Career Highlights

SPECIAL PROJECTS COORDINATOR / PARTNER   2004–2010
Surgery Center—Granada Hills, CA

Authored the firm's strategic communications plan and orchestrated successful effort to establish corporate vision, mission, and values statement. Transitioned marketing focus to core customer types and segments. Architected new corporate advertising and client testimonial trade campaigns. Developed human resources materials such as employee handbook (researched laws with assistance of attorney) and confidentiality agreements; participated in hiring process for office manager.

- Built physician's name as **brand value.**
- Conceptualized ideas and worked with ad companies to develop ads and brochures.
- Developed marketing and advertising materials to attract new patients, educate the community, and build referral base among physicians.
- **Special events:** Set up educational seminars for the community and prospective patients, held both in office and at area hotels.
- Performed grassroots marketing to Chamber of Commerce, spas, gyms, salons, and other local businesses.

DESIGNER / OWNER   2007–2009
Claire de Lune by Chantal Luz—Montrose, CA   (concurrently)

- Started business from ground up. Designed a 30-piece line of fun, hip, contemporary sleepwear. Handled all creative, PR, and administrative functions. Retained and trained required staff to produce line.
- **Developed brand label** and showroom representation for market events.

Career Change: From fashion designer and medical office projects manager to marketing/PR.

Strategy: Demonstrate her talent for delivering practical business solutions through her interpersonal skills and ability to manage complex projects, meet deadlines, and meet high quality standards.

Chantal Luz

Successful background developing, establishing, managing, and maximizing profitability based on loyal client, vendor, management, and staff relationships.

BUYER   2003–2004
Marie Springs—Houston, TX

Oversaw advertising and organized store events. Bought better contemporary dresses for this women's designer specialty store.

DESIGNER   2001–2003
Cecilia—Los Angeles, CA

Designed line of social-occasion dresses for better contemporary sportswear and dress manufacturer. Selected all fabrics and trims, developed styles from first sketch through production, managed sample room and extensive fittings.

FASHION COORDINATOR / MERCHANDISER   1999–2001
Nicole Delbain—New York, NY

Developed color stories, fashion concepts, and presentation boards for each season. Shopped print market and developed original designs. Worked closely with managers and buyers to create a collection look for their stores.

- Visited European and New York stores to provide constant flow of ideas and fashion trend information. Designed specific groups for direct vendors in Asia.
- Directed domestic manufacturers to develop merchandise appropriate for Nicole Delbain.

Prior to 1999

DESIGNER, Macy's Corporate Buying, New York, NY
ASSISTANT DESIGNER, Nicole Miller, New York, NY

Education

Bachelor of Science, Design
College of Design, Architecture, Art & Planning
University of Cincinnati, Cincinnati, OH

Courses in Microsoft Windows, Word, and Excel
Valley College, Valley Glen, CA

NOLAN MATTHEWS

993 Rocky Hill Rd., Waterbury, CT 06701
203-785-4567 (Mobile)
nolanmatthews@hotmail.com

CAREER FOCUS: PUBLIC RELATIONS / MARKETING COMMUNICATIONS

Qualifications: Master's Degree and 6+ years of leadership experience in diverse professional environments including education, business, and service/not-for-profit. Areas of expertise include

- Event Coordination / Fund Raising
- Needs Analysis / Lead Generation
- Project Management
- Business Development
- Relationship Management
- Strategic Partnerships

Strengths: Articulate and persuasive. Creative and team-oriented, with proven ability to think strategically, overcome obstacles, and initiate action to meet deadlines. Recognized as a visionary leader who inspires others to achieve extraordinary results. Adaptable, resourceful, and goal-oriented.

EXPERIENCE SUMMARY

Communications / Media / VIP Customer Service
- Served as communication liaison between media personnel and politicians as Project Director for a global relief organization.
- Managed strategic communications with field personnel and collaborated with international and local non-governmental organizations (NGOs), hospitals, health networks, and government ministries in overseeing on-the-ground support.

Marketing & Public Relations / Account Management / Business & Nonprofit Development
- Developed client relationships with wholesale distributors in the outdoor equipment, industrial supply, and pharmaceutical industries as an Account Executive.
- Co-founded educational foundation dedicated to raising money for underfunded music programs. Established mission statement, branding, Web presence, and public relations/communications strategy.

Project Management / International Relations
- Coordinated on-the-ground logistics administration for on-site disaster management programs as an Account Executive/Project Director for an international relief foundation.
- Traveled extensively throughout the U.S. and Eastern Europe and served as point of contact to ensure timely response and on-time delivery of relief supplies through customs.

Leadership & Organizational Development
- Conducted one-on-one, small-group, and large-group instruction/presentations, tailoring content to different audiences to successfully engage and motivate participants.
- Provided leadership as Instructional Team Lead, Student Council Administrator, and Head Coach/Manager for track and field program.
- Provided one-on-one training/coaching on USGA golf techniques/strategy to youth at all skill levels.

EMPLOYMENT HISTORY

Instructor (Social Studies), Central High School, Waterbury, CT, Aug 2008–June 2010
Co-Founder/Director of Communications, Kids 4 Kids, Inc., Waterbury, CT, June 2006–July 2008
Trainer/Coach, Westside Golf Camp, East Hartford Public Schools, Summers 2008–2009
Instructor (Middle Grades), East Hills Middle School, East Hartford, CT, Aug 2005–June 2008
Retail Sales Associate, High Country Outfitters, Meriden, CT, 2002–2005 (part-time while in school)
Account Executive/Project Director, Care International, Storrs, CT, Summers 2000–2002

EDUCATION

Master's Degree in Education (MEd), University of Hartford, East Hartford, CT, 2008
Bachelor of Arts Degree in Psychology (BA), University of Connecticut, Storrs, CT, 2005

Career Change: *From teacher to public relations/marketing communications professional.*

Strategy: *Use a functional format to highlight relevant areas of expertise and related accomplishments.*

Mark Adams

61 Havenhurst
Pasadena, CA 91101

markadams@aol.com

Home: 818-138-0108
Cell: 818-572-9428

MARKETING MANAGEMENT / BUSINESS DEVELOPMENT

Creative, energetic, multifaceted professional with an MS degree in marketing and a career of successful accomplishments. Proven record of achieving significant sales and business-development goals. Ability to increase productivity and efficiency by building and effectively supervising strong teams. Knowledgeable leader and trainer with excellent communication and interpersonal skills. Experienced in all aspects of customer service. Work within budget requirements to meet or surpass company goals. Capable of substantially improving sales and operations by developing and implementing creative solutions.

AREAS OF EXPERTISE

Retail Sales	Product Promotions	Merchandising
Business Development	Operations Management	Strategic Planning
Policies & Procedures	Leadership / Team Development	Creative Display Building
Forecasts / Budgets	Training / Supervision / Motivation	Communication
Staff Scheduling / Coordination	Productivity / Quality Improvement	Customer Service
Inventory Control / Warehouse	Purchasing / Cost Containment	Problem Resolution
Contract / Union Negotiations	Process & Efficiency Improvement	Shipping / Receiving

PROFESSIONAL EXPERIENCE

ALPHA BETA, Pasadena, CA

1990–Present

GM/Drug Manager (2006–present)
GM Manager (1992–2006), Clerk (1991–1992), Courtesy Clerk (1990–1991)

Management/Operations:
- Hold leadership and strategic planning responsibility for total store operations.
- Implement company guidelines, policies, and procedures and set an example for others.
- Resolve problems and issues related to the store, employees, and customers.
- Monitor and evaluate staff productivity to ensure achievement of sales goals.
- Inspire coworkers with the organization's vision and culture.
- Initiate new ideas and solutions to meet the objectives of my position and the store.
- Prioritize daily activities and projects to maximize productivity.
- Anticipate problems and opportunities and make timely and appropriate decisions.

Customer Service:
- Ensure that all store personnel provide excellent-quality service to customers.
- Address problems quickly and furnish efficient solutions.
- Continuously promote our store by cultivating and developing customer relations.

Staff Training:
- Supervise, motivate, schedule, and train 12 staff members to increase their efficiency and productivity.
- Utilize team-building strategies, including coaching and constructive feedback, with an emphasis on training and development.
- Encourage a cooperative and cohesive work group by inspiring staff members to set and reach goals.
- Delegate authority and responsibility to others in an appropriate and effective manner.
- Exhibit a constructive team-spirit approach to attain individual and group goals.

Sales:
- Total profit-and-loss responsibility for Pasadena store with $3 million in annual sales.
- Continuously build the Pasadena Alpha Beta into a more profitable, higher-volume store.

Merchandising:
- Build and oversee the construction of displays for promotional and seasonal items.
- Plan, direct, and coordinate all special events and promotions in the store.
- Ensure visual standards of in-store merchandise and displays.

Career Change: *From retail manager to marketing professional.*

Strategy: *Emphasize recent marketing degree and incorporate relevant skills into a strong profile. Use category headings in the experience section to help the reader focus on key points.*

Mark Adams   818-572-9428   Resume—Page 2

2009 YEAR-END PERFORMANCE REVIEW SUMMARY_____

- Rated outstanding in meeting and exceeding sales projections 2 out of 4 quarters; sales were up more than 8% in all 4 quarters.

- Exceeded earnings and gross in all 4 quarters.

- Outperformed expectations in customer-service shop score 3 out of 4 quarters, with total score above company guidelines.

- Rated **Outstanding** in Customer Service, Change Management, Action and Speed Management, Continuous Improvement, Education, People Development, Leading by Example, Decision Making, Communications, Planning, Goal Reaching, and Overall Performance.

- Rated **Above Expectations** in Positive Leadership, Diversity, Recognition & Reward, and Partnerships.

EDUCATION_____

Master of Science: Marketing (2009)
California State University, Fullerton, CA

Supervisory Skills and **Management Training** (2009)
Sponsored by Alpha Beta

Bachelor of Science: Marketing (2008)
California State University, Fullerton, CA

INSTRUCTOR / TRAINER / MENTOR_____

Train and coach future Alpha Beta store managers (2009)

Conducted Management Training in Operations, Inventory, Ordering, Scheduling, Reporting (2007–2009)

RESUME 44: BY MICHELLE MASTRUSERIO REITZ, CPRW

KATHERINE D. SCHOLLINGER

51027 Deerview Drive • Cleves, OH 45002
Phone: (513) 792-6127 • Mobile: (513) 505-6180 • kdswriter@aol.com

OBJECTIVE

Full-time, part-time, or freelance work involving

➢ Writing and editing articles, business biographies, marketing materials, newsletters, brochures, articles, and short stories
➢ Research and interviewing services for writers, publishers, and journalists
➢ Reading and evaluating manuscripts

QUALIFICATIONS

Demonstrated ability to develop prose that is clear, concise, and inviting to read. Exceptional interpersonal skills; proven ability to put people at ease and interview effectively. Experienced in conducting research through printed materials, online resources, and interviews. Well organized; efficient in coordinating multiple simultaneous projects and meeting tight deadlines. Accurate, prompt, dependable, and attentive to detail. Proficient with Microsoft Word.

RELATED EXPERIENCE

OHIO MANUFACTURING, Cheviot, OH   1994–2003
Newsletter Editor/Administrative Assistant—Performed research, conducted interviews, and wrote articles for company newsletter that was instrumental in keeping employees informed and motivated. Reviewed and edited articles submitted for publication. Composed letters, memos, and other correspondence. Prepared reports in formats that were well organized and eye-appealing. Organized and maintained files. Position required the ability to prioritize multiple simultaneous projects, meet deadlines, and work well independently.

SOUTHWEST REGIONAL SCHOOL DISTRICT, Cleves, OH   1991–1994
Teacher's Aide—Assisted teachers with all facets of classroom management, including researching, preparing lessons, grading papers, recording grades, and preparing written materials. Tutored individual students and small groups in all subject areas. Gained the ability to simplify subject matter, adapt lessons to fit different learning styles and levels of ability, and make lessons interesting.

DAILY JOURNAL NEWS, Hamilton, OH   1985
Proofreader, Advertising Department—Proofread copy, delivered proofs, and worked with advertisers to ensure copy was accurate. Consistently met all deadlines.

SUBJECT INTERESTS & RESEARCH EXPERIENCE

• Sociology, family, women's issues
• Health: psychology, holistic approaches to wellness, addictions, massage therapy, nutrition
• Nonfiction (biographies, American history, current events, self-help), literature, mysteries, historical novels

Continued...

Career Change: From massage therapist to writer/editor.

Strategy: Use a combination format that brings older, relevant experience to the fore.

KATHERINE D. SCHOLLINGER

Page 2

ADDITIONAL EXPERIENCE

TRI-STATE HEALTH NETWORKS, Cincinnati, OH—Massage Therapist	10/07–Present
DAYLIGHT SALON & DAY SPA, Lawrenceburg, IN—Massage Therapist	11/05–9/07
OHIO REGIONAL CLINIC, Blanchester, OH—Addictions Technician	12/04–6/05
UNIVERSITY GENERAL HOSPITAL, Cincinnati, OH—Addictions Technician	5/04–12/04
PERFECT DAY SALON, Cincinnati, OH—Massage Therapist	11/02–5/04

Massage Therapist—Provided massage therapy for clients in support of major national and regional health plans in Ohio and Indiana. Administered therapeutic Swedish and deep-tissue massage. Coordinated appointments with other professionals. Identified opportunities and cross-sold other salon services with a professional, customer-focused, and low-key approach.

Addictions Technician—Provided administrative support for drug and alcohol counselors. Observed and charted patient behaviors, including notation of physical and emotional issues, new medications, and other pertinent facts. Position required the ability to handle confidential information with absolute discretion.

EDUCATION

UNIVERSITY OF CINCINNATI, Cincinnati, OH   Present
Bachelor of Arts in progress. Major: English Literature. Minor: American History.
Attending school part-time to allow full-time employment. Degree expected December 2010.

- **GPA: 3.7**
- **Dean's List**
- **Relevant Courses:** Writing from Research • English Composition I & II • Interpersonal Communication

Additional Training

Additional studies: *Mastering Research Using the Internet,* computer training (Windows, Word, and Excel), and several psychology seminars.

Center for Holistic Therapy Studies, Independence, IN   2002
Healing Massage Techniques: Completed 168-hour program.

Charlotte School of Massage Therapeutics, Charlotte, IN   2001
Completed comprehensive 427-hour program, approved by the American Massage Therapy Association and accredited by the State of Indiana. Curriculum provided classroom training and practical experience.

RESUME 45: BY GAIL TAYLOR, CPRW, CEIP

Rita Cantor

1250 Vista Diego Road   Santa Clarita, CA 91310   (661) 449-5255   ritawriter@ezmail.com

Business & Creative Writing

Foreword	*"To whom much is given, much is required."* —French proverb

For 14 years, I have enjoyed the privilege of helping others develop their writing abilities. In this time, I have conceived and developed learning tools, conducted classes and writing workshops, and helped students realize potential and achieve goals. Now, I look forward to pursuing full-time my first passion: Writing.

The Writer	*"Ease in writing comes from art, not chance."* —A. Pope

Well-versed in: Business Communications ▪ Speeches ▪ Marketing ▪ Poetry ▪ Nonfiction
Publications: *The Tribute* (Nonfiction, 2009) ▪ *Women of the Decade* (Nonfiction, 2006)
Featured in: *Poetic Path* ▪ *Ascension* ▪ *Living Arts* ▪ *Reader's Choice* ▪ *MasterWorks*

The Teacher	*"Teaching is an instinctual art, mindful of potential."* —A.B. Giamatti

Writing Courses: Advanced Essay ▪ Creative Writing ▪ Business Writing ▪ Writing About Literature
    Writing Proficiency Exam Workshops ▪ Science Fiction & Film
English Courses: Basic Grammar ▪ English & ESL ▪ English Rhetoric ▪ Linguistics

The Change Agent	*"Things do not change; we change."* —H.D. Thoreau

✓ Developed Writing Proficiency Workshop to help students prepare for exam.
✓ Served on Education Planning & Advisory Committee (EPAC).
✓ Created lunchtime classes that helped employees meet degree requirements.
✓ Started well-received annual clothing drives for underprivileged high school students.

Education	*"Education is for improving the lives of others…"* —M.W. Edelman

M.A. and B.A. in English & Creative Writing, Ojai University, CA   1994—Dean's Honor List

Experiences	*"Creativity seems to merge from multiple experiences."* —C. Edwards

Pepperdine University, Malibu, CA
Academic Advisor   2005–2006   /   **Site Manager**   2006–Present
Write all commencement speeches, marketing materials, outgoing correspondence, and recommendation letters for faculty and students. Counsel students and resolve grievances. Manage MBA & MA programs.

Haverhill University, Ojai, CA
English Instructor   1999–2004
Taught English Rhetoric, Writing About Literature, Creative Writing, Advanced Essay Writing, Linguistics, English/ESL, Drama, and Speech. Conducted Writing Proficiency Exam Workshops.

Palm Grove College, Huntington Pointe, CA
English Teacher / ESL Instructor   1996–1999
Initiated and administered an English Language Proficiency program for Japanese & Korean businessmen. Also taught English; tested & assessed language proficiency for military personnel at nearby air force base.

###

Career Change: *From academic advisor to writer.*

Strategy: *Play up literary mindset using an unconventional format, literary style conventions, and quotes. The result is an interesting and attention-getting resume that speaks the language of her target audience.*

MARILYN NOLAN

22 Meadow Lane ▪ Chicago, IL 78966 ▪ (975) 433-5889 ▪ MNolan@media.net

■ PROFILE

Conferences ▪ Fund Raising ▪ Trade Shows ▪ Meeting Planning ▪ Cultural Programs

Creative professional with expertise in all aspects of successful event/program planning, development, and management. Excel in managing multiple projects concurrently using detail, problem-solving, and follow-through strengths. Demonstrated ability to recruit, motivate, and build cohesive teams. Sourced vendors, negotiated vendor contracts, and managed project budgets. Possess superb written communications, interpersonal, and presentation skills.

■ SELECTED ACCOMPLISHMENTS

Special Events Management:

Planned and coordinated conferences, meetings, and events for companies, professional associations, and arts/cultural and other organizations. Developed program content and administered budgets. Arranged all on-site logistics, including transportation, accommodations, meals, guest speakers and entertainers, and audiovisual support. Coordinated participation and represented companies at industry trade shows. Recognized for creating and planning some of the most successful events ever held statewide.

- **Created cultural events for an arts organization that boosted membership enrollment.**
- **Organized 5 conferences for 2 national professional associations, surpassing all prior attendance records.**
- **Designed successful community educational campaigns promoting safety awareness.**

Fund Raising & Public Relations:

Created, planned, and managed all aspects of several major fund-raising campaigns, resulting in a significant increase in contributions raised for each function over prior years. Recruited volunteers and developed corporate sponsorships. Generated extensive media coverage through effective promotional and public-relations strategies. Created newsletters distributed to employees, customers, and others.

- **Co-chaired capital-fund campaign that raised $3.5 million for new facility.**
- **Coordinated 3 auctions that generated more than $140,000 for an educational institution.**
- **Initiated successful publication, generating $25,000 to finance community programs.**

Sales & Marketing:

Selected by management to spearhead opening of regional office, including all logistics, staff relocation, and business development efforts. Designed and implemented creative sales and marketing strategies to capitalize on consumer trends and penetrate new market. Coordinated and conducted sales training.

- **Developed and managed 17 key accounts, generating $10 million annually.**
- **Recognized for managing top revenue-generating program companywide.**
- **Consistently exceeded sales forecast and led region to rank #1 out of 6 in profitability nationwide.**

■ EXPERIENCE

Financial Underwriter—Marcon Financial Services Company, Chicago, IL (1997–2010).

Event/Program Coordinator—Arts Council, Botanical Gardens and Cultural Exchange, Chicago, IL (2005–2009).

■ EDUCATION

B.A. in Business Administration, Springfield College, Springfield, MA

Career Change: From underwriter to event manager.

Strategy: Design a one-page functional resume that showcases experience related to event planning—even though this experience was unpaid. Background in underwriting is downplayed.

RESUME 47: BY MICHAEL LEVY, CPRW, CEIP, MCDP, PHR, GCDFI

KAREN M. MITCHELL

25 Adams Drive
Braintree, MA 02184   kmitchell@yahoo.com   H: (617) 345-1457
                                                          C: (617) 505-4917

Business Marketing and Events Coordinator
Business Services / Hospitality / Business to Consumer / Special Events

PROJECT MANAGEMENT—FINANCIAL CONTROL—TRAINING & COACHING

Creative business manager and entrepreneurial professional with 15+ years of experience in a marketing management capacity. Team coordinator, leader in business development, and director of business operations. Consistently increased profitability and market expansion.

- Entrepreneurial Spirit
- Employee Management
- Staff Training
- Financial Control

- Critical Thinking
- Strategic Planning
- Business Startup
- Time Management

- Problem Identification
- Profit Improvement
- Idea Generation
- Relationship Building

PROFESSIONAL EXPERIENCE

T&T PARTNERSHIP, Boston, MA

Operations Manager, Partner
1992–2010

Directed all operations and marketing activities associated with multi-business partnership. Developed and initiated organization and operating plans; recruited staff; conducted demographic research; and initiated creative marketing strategies that grew second-year business **300%** over year one. Maintained client retention at **90%.** Focused on quality customer service, standards, and price strategies to keep a competitive edge. Controlled financial operations and budgets up to **$500K** for multi-business partnership. Implemented marketing strategies that created and retained new business.

MASSACHUSETTS SPECIAL OLYMPICS, Boston, MA

Co-Director and Coach of Figure Skating
1997–2006

Coached and organized figure-skating events at the Massachusetts Summer Games. Supervised participants and sporting events. Achieved maximum student participation. Organized and recorded all qualifying and winning scores of each athlete in all events.

EDUCATION AND PROFESSIONAL TRAINING

Boston University, BA Candidate (2 years completed)
American Academy of Dramatic Arts, Theatre

Career Change: From entrepreneur to marketing and events management professional.

Strategy: Show strengths and skills related to her goal, highlighting relevant details from business ownership. Use page 2 to detail relevant accomplishments.

KAREN M. MITCHELL   PAGE TWO

SELECTED ACHIEVEMENTS

MARKETING AND SALES

PRESERVED A COMPETITIVE ADVANTAGE WITH A CREATIVE MARKETING APPROACH. Developed an innovative marketing promotion focusing on each client. Increased new-client base by 45% and earned more positive feedback from clients than any other promotion.

ORGANIZED AND DEVELOPED PLAN TO INCREASE SALES IN THE OFF-SEASON BY 20%. Trained staff in areas of in-depth presentation, product specials, and expanded product line. Successfully achieved company goals and improved product awareness.

PLANNED AND COORDINATED REUNION EVENT FOR 600+ ATTENDEES. Researched history of organization 1950–1981. Maintained tight budget requirements. Prepared publicity for local newspapers and television news shows.

MANAGEMENT

SERVED AS COACH AND CO-DIRECTOR OF FIGURE SKATING for the Massachusetts Special Olympics for 9 years. Developed into one of the best-organized events each year at the summer games.

RELIEVED A STRESSFUL SITUATION AND POTENTIAL LOSS OF BUSINESS. Screened, recruited, and trained 3 new employees, quickly responding to unexpected employee turnover. Avoided loss of business and customer dissatisfaction.

APPLIED NEW STATE REGULATIONS. Trained staff to focus on customer needs and how they could help. Enhanced customer and employee awareness.

RECEIVED NUMEROUS REFERRALS AND MAINTAINED 90% CLIENT RETENTION RATE. Recognized by clients and colleagues as a consummate professional with the utmost creativity and personal integrity. Perceptive, patient, and persistent; nurture trust and confidence.

BUSINESS ANALYSIS AND FINANCIAL OPERATIONS

CONTINUOUSLY ACHIEVED 12-MONTH FINANCIAL BUDGET GOALS. High standards of service and products were instrumental in consistent increase of capital for reinvestment in business.

NEGOTIATED A WIN-WIN SITUATION WITH MANUFACTURER. Analyzed prices of manufacturer and its competitors. Resulted in $20,000 annual cost savings.

INITIATED AND EXECUTED PLAN TO PURCHASE SECOND BUSINESS. Designed a market strategy to analyze business finances and local demographics. Commitment to detail resulted in a lower purchase price of business.

EXPANDED STORE SPACE TO ACCOMMODATE RAPID BUSINESS GROWTH. Business exceeded first-year projections by 50%.

CHAPTER 7

Resumes for Career Changers Seeking Health Care, Social Services, and Personal Services Positions

Retraining is often necessary to earn the qualifications and credentials for a switch into the health care industry. Many of the resumes in this chapter make this current education the centerpiece, with prior experience playing a supporting role. These resumes represent the following career changes:

- Priest to human services administrator

- Health educator to surgical technologist

- Customer service representative to a position in social services

- IT recruiter to social worker

- Business owner to speech/language pathologist

- Manufacturing worker to funeral assistant

- Nurse to legal consultant

- Flight attendant to personal assistant

- Magician to nursing assistant

- Police officer to nurse

RESUME 48: BY ELLEN MULQUEEN, CRW

ANTHONY FONTINI

28 Abbotsford Avenue
Springfield, Massachusetts 01118
413.205.5432
fontini2358@mindspring.com

HUMAN SERVICES ADMINISTRATOR

- Highly skilled not-for-profit management professional with outstanding multitasking ability.
- Visionary leadership style that encourages "out-of-the-box" solutions to unique problems and challenges.
- Articulate, accomplished communicator and motivator.
- Strong team-builder, comfortable working with diverse populations in terms of both cultures and ideas.
- Seasoned traveler, fluent in Italian, Spanish, and Polish.

MANAGEMENT

- Chosen to provide strong, decisive organizational leadership through period of change, transition, and revitalization.
- Established and maintained team atmosphere and high morale level.
- Developed successful grassroots fund-raising campaign for major building project; **pledges / donations surpassed goal by 60%.**
- Designed and coordinated reconstruction of three facilities to better suit needs of residents. First stage of construction underway.
- Composed and presented motivational articles and speeches.

TRAINING

- Developed high-performance leadership training for organization volunteers.
- Trained and supervised staff of seven plus 50 volunteers.
- Led public-speaking seminars.
- Introduced in-house language training to meet needs of diverse community.

COUNSELING/ADVISING

- Regularly sought by members for family and marriage counseling.
- Assisted members needing guidance for ethical and moral dilemmas.
- Motivated members to set and accomplish goals.

(continued next page)

Career Change: *From priest to human services administrator.*

Strategy: *Design the resume so that it is not apparent that he is a priest, using a functional format and "secularized" language (for example, "motivational speeches" rather than "homilies" or "sermons").*

ANTHONY FONTINI – PAGE 2

EXPERIENCE

Pastor   2005–Present
St. Cecelia Church, Springfield, MA

Parish Administrator   2004
Corpus Christi Church, Holyoke, MA

Associate Pastor   1998–2004
St. Anthony's Church, Chicopee, MA

EDUCATION

San Carlos Seminary, Rome, Italy
Master of Divinity / Pastoral Theology

University of Connecticut, Storrs, CT
Master of Arts, Counseling. GPA 3.85

Holy Cross College, Worcester, MA
Bachelor of Arts, Double Major: Philosophy and Theology
Graduated Magna Cum Laude

RESUME 49: BY VIVIAN VANLIER, CPRW, JCTC, CEIP, CCMC

BRIANA MARTIN

5555 Las Flores Canyon Rd.   (323) 555-5555
Los Angeles, CA 91406   brianamartin@email.com

Surgical Technology Student
—Qualified for Position Managing Pre- and Post-Operative Care—

- Well-qualified and dedicated professional with 10+ years of related experience in nonprofit healthcare field.
- Work well in a fast-paced environment… proven ability to respond to problems and emergencies in a calm, organized, and effective manner.
- Managed and supervised paid and volunteer teams.
- Performed educational in-services, community outreach, patient care, client relations, grant writing, and training.
- Coordinated wellness fairs, health classes, and prevention workshops, increasing community awareness of health issues and services available.
- Natural communicator with excellent interpersonal and customer-relations skills.
- Quick learner who enjoys challenges and works well both independently and collaboratively in a team setting.

—Working Knowledge of Health-Related Rehabilitation and Medical Management Process—

EDUCATION

Surgical Technologist; GPA 4.0
LOS ANGELES CAREER COLLEGE, Los Angeles, CA; Completion, May 2010

B.A. in Social Services / Minor in Communications
UNIVERSITY OF CALIFORNIA, Los Angeles, CA (UCLA)

Certifications

CPR Certified—American Red Cross
Certified HIV Educator—American Red Cross

PROFESSIONAL EXPERIENCE

Health Resource Educator   2005 to Present
LOS ANGELES COMMUNITY SERVICES, Los Angeles, CA

Child Welfare Specialist
CALIFORNIA DEPARTMENT OF CHILDREN AND FAMILY SERVICES   2002 to 2005

Health Educator
LOS ANGELES COUNTY HOSPITAL, Los Angeles, CA   1998 to 2002

COMMUNITY / VOLUNTEER ACTIVITIES

Red Cross Blood Drive—Blood Drive Volunteer   2006 to Present
Sunlight Foundation—Healthcare Volunteer   2005 to Present
Big Sisters of Los Angeles—Big Sister to Middle School–Aged Girl 2004 to Present

Career Change: *From health educator to surgical technologist.*

Strategy: *Emphasize recent retraining and relevant health care experience.*

JOAN KAMINSKY

4 Baywood Boulevard
Brick, NJ 08723

jkaminsky@aol.com

Home: 732-477-5172
Cell: 908-810-4139

Target: Youth & Family Services Positions
Juvenile Counselor / Home Studies / Foster Child Placements / Victim-Witness Counselor

Energetic, people-oriented professional with excellent listening and communication skills. Respond well to difficult situations and skilled at juggling multiple responsibilities. Earned bachelor's degree in criminal justice with dual minors in psychology and sociology, plus a concentration in juvenile delinquency. Experienced in:

- Government Agency Communications
- Problem Resolution / Informal Counseling
- Positive Relationship Development
- Home Studies / Positive Child Environments
- Community Outreach Program Participation
- Performance Reviews / Written Assessments

EDUCATION

B.S. in Criminal Justice, Dual Minors in Psychology and Sociology, Juvenile Delinquency Concentration
Georgian Court College, Lakewood, NJ, 1997

Selected Courses:

Deviance: Reviewed common juvenile delinquency problems, how to deal with them, and policy enforcement.
Intervention Methods: Discussed juvenile problems, available intervention programs, and counselor roles.
Juvenile Delinquency: Defined which crimes are termed delinquency and when a delinquent is considered an adult, reviewed treatment steps, and explored types of facilities.
Juvenile Justice Independent Study: Conducted in-depth research on impact of juvenile detention vs. jail, damage of trying youths as adults, and crime rates when intervention programs are or aren't available.

SOCIAL SERVICES BACKGROUND

International Adoption (Personal Experience) • Brick, NJ, and Beijing, China • Apr. 2009–Present

Cooperated in 2 home studies and 2 office visits with in-depth interviews to assess family members, lifestyles, and environment for potential adoptive child. Fingerprinted by the INS, the State of New Jersey, and the federal government. Completed multiple in-depth forms. Successfully passed criminal background and medical checks. Performed 2 extended visits to overseas orphanage. Appeared in American courts and embassies. Cooperated in post-placement visits to ensure positive welfare of child.

Volunteer Juvenile Counselor • Ocean County Juvenile Detention Center, Brick, NJ • Jan. 1997–Jan. 1998

Assisted in the supervision of 25 incarcerated juveniles. Enforced rules about attitudes, behavior, and safety. Planned and participated in sports activities to promote teamwork and physical fitness. Attended, observed, and contributed to small, informal group counseling sessions for juveniles. During counseling sessions, listened to problems, helped them to realize why they were incarcerated, talked one-on-one, and offered opinions or advice on changing behaviors or overcoming difficulties.

RECENT EMPLOYMENT HISTORY

Sovereign Bank, Toms River, NJ • Sept. 2000–Sept. 2007

Customer Service Representative • 01/04–09/07
CSR Supervisor • 08/01–01/04 // **Customer Service Representative (CSR)** • 09/00–08/01

Supervised 4 customer service representatives. Assisted with applicant interviews. Served as intermediary to resolve problems between employees and between employees and customers. Assessed employees' performance and completed written reviews. Participated in community outreach programs including United Way, Habitat for Humanity, and Toys for Tots. Received excellent performance reviews from supervisor.

Career Change: *From customer service representative to a position in social services.*

Strategy: *Highlight relevant education and personal experiences that qualify her for the role she is seeking. Eliminate irrelevant information from her employment history.*

RESUME 51: BY DEBRA O'REILLY, CPRW, CEIP, JCTC, FRWC

Marie Samuels, MSW

203-555-5885   160 Terryville Road, Fairfield, CT 06430   samuelsm@email.com

EDUCATION

MSW, Sacred Heart University, Fairfield, CT   May 2005
    Concentration: *Clinical Practice*; Specialization: *Children and Families*   GPA: 3.9
BSW, University of New Haven, West Haven, CT   May 2002
    Graduated *magna cum laude*   GPA: 3.8

SOCIAL WORK EXPERIENCE

Social Work Intern, Claire M. Brousseau Elementary School, West Haven, CT (2003–2004)
    Provided individual and group therapy for children and adolescents with emotional and behavioral disorders, using cognitive-behavioral techniques. Conducted biopsychosocial evaluations; implemented and reviewed clinical services; developed individual programs (IEPs) to maximize therapeutic potential. Coordinated assistance with other social service providers. Communicated with parents to improve family dynamics.

Social Work Intern, Learning for Life School, North Haven, CT (2001–2002)
    Provided behavioral, social, and emotional support for students; implemented behavior-modification curriculum. Participated on interdisciplinary team providing counseling and crisis intervention.

Social Work Intern / Resident Counselor, Desjardins Healthcare, West Haven, CT (2000–2001)
    Conducted psychosocial evaluations / assessments; developed goals and treatment plans. Established rapport with patients, colleagues, and families to support achievement of goals.

Volunteer Facilitator for recreational activities for youth in foster care, New Haven Youth Trust.

ADDITIONAL PROFESSIONAL EXPERIENCE

COMPUTER PERSONNEL, INC., New Haven, CT   2005–2008
Technical Recruiter
    Supported market reps in the recruitment, sourcing, and placement of IT professionals for contract and permanent positions. Conducted candidate evaluations to assess skills, interests, and availability. Maintained communication from initial contact through post-placement follow-up.

MEDICAL SERVICES, San Rafael, CA   *Leader in transtelephonic pacemaker monitoring*   1996–2004
Pacemaker Medical Technologist III
    Advanced through increasing responsibilities. Conducted high-tech EKG monitoring via telephone for patients with pacemakers and ICD devices. Assessed and instructed patients throughout testing process. Analyzed cardiac data; prepared physician reports. Responded to emergencies, notifying medical personnel as necessary. Assisted in technical staff training and quality assurance.

DANCE ABROAD, INC., Los Angeles, CA   1993–1995
Dance Captain / Lead Dancer
    In addition to domestic performances, performed / lived in Far East for two six-month contract terms. Liaison for business relations and show manager.

Computer skills: MS Office, including Word, Excel, Outlook, and Access.

Career Change: *From IT recruiter to social worker.*

Strategy: *Spotlight relevant experience as an intern and only briefly summarize her additional employment experience. Lead off with strong education credentials.*

KATHERINE RICHARDS

8595 Apple Tree Lane   (619) 444-2131
San Diego, CA 92109   krichards@hotmail.com

SPEECH-LANGUAGE PATHOLOGIST

Dedicated professional offering a Master of Arts in Speech and Language Pathology. Hands-on experience providing evaluation and treatment services for adults and children with communication disorders. Easily develop rapport with a variety of clients. Dependable, organized, and creative.

Proficient in PC and Macintosh environments, Excent IEP, Microsoft Word and Excel, and QuickBooks.

Member, National Student Speech Language Hearing Association

EDUCATION / TRAINING

M.A. in Speech and Language Pathology, University of California, San Diego, CA   2010
B.A. in Communication Disorders and Psychology, University of California, San Diego, CA   1990

Professional Development   **Current Certifications**
Excent Computerized IEP Training, 2010   Interactive Learning (INREAL), University of California
Feeding and Swallowing In-Service, 2010   Cardiopulmonary Resuscitation, American Red Cross
Lee Silverman Voice Training (LSVT), 2009   Personal Trainer, American Council on Exercise

RELEVANT EXPERIENCE

Substitute Teacher, San Diego School District, San Diego, CA   2008 to Present
Work in elementary schools covering long-term assignments and daily substitute teaching.

- Substituted full-time for literacy teacher. Taught decoding and reading strategies to K–3 students (long-term assignment, 2009).

Student Clinician, San Diego School District, San Diego, CA   2010
Assumed duties of school speech pathologist. Provided evaluations and developed treatment plans for students ages 5 to 18 with learning disabilities, apraxia, stuttering, articulation disorders, autism, and hearing loss. Prepared progress reports and communicated results at staff meetings.

- Implemented therapy plans for 60 students.
- Established creative treatments that met IEP goals of each student.

Student Clinician, University of California, San Diego, CA   2009 to 2010
Evaluated and diagnosed clients for the Speech, Language, and Hearing Center. Planned weekly therapy for clients with aphasia, dysarthria, apraxia, stuttering, learning disabilities, and organic voice disorders.

- Served on child diagnostic, adult motor disorder, learning disability, and child screening teams.

OTHER EXPERIENCE

Partner/Owner, Richards & Smith Promotions, San Diego, CA   2003 to Present
Assistant Manager/Sales Associate, Hatfield & Company, San Diego, CA   2005 to 2009
Buyer/Sales Associate, Robin's Boutique, San Diego, CA   2001 to 2005

Career Change: From business owner to speech/language pathologist.

Strategy: De-emphasize sales experience by listing it under Other Experience at the end of the resume. Focus instead on education, training, and relevant activities.

RESUME 53: BY JANET BECKSTROM, ACRW, CPRW

James P. Collings

38 Falcon Lane
Cincinnati, OH 45218

jpcoll@isp.net

Home: 513-555-8541
Cell: 513-555-3259

Profile

Eager to meet challenges in a new career that will benefit from effective communication skills and compassion for others. Accustomed to multitasking; flexible and adaptable. Keen eye for identifying inconsistencies and potential problems; reputation for being able to troubleshoot and resolve issues when they occur. Accrued record of near-perfect attendance (1 day absent in 17 years on the job).

Currently pursuing Associate of Applied Science degree in Mortuary Science.

Relevant Experience

CARE, INC. dba Richardson, Gallego, and Cox Funeral Homes • Cincinnati, OH

Funeral Assistant   2009–Present
- Provide assistance to families and guests: Welcome visitors in person, answer questions, respond to telephone requests for information, place flowers in visitation rooms, and troubleshoot problems.
- Drive funeral coach and limousine as part of procession.
- Respond to facilities and residences to retrieve deceased clients.
- Act as courier with legal documents.

Additional Experience

FORD MOTOR COMPANY • Batavia, OH   **Production Worker** – Batavia Assembly Plant   2007–Present
- Perform final assembly of under-vehicle components.
- Coordinated logistics for vehicles identified with defects. Organized 10–300 vehicles in parking lot; adhered to repair schedule by delivering vehicles to respective departments.

UPS • Cincinnati, OH   **Package Handler** (part-time)   2006–2007

OFFICE MAX • Loveland, OH   **Shipping & Receiving/Dock Clerk** (part-time)   2000–2006

VISTEON CORP. • Dayton, OH   **Computer Paint Technician**   1988–2006
- Set up, started up, monitored, and scheduled robotic paint line processing 30,000–40,000 pieces/day.
- Directed the work of 8 hourly production workers.
- Trained employees with focus on safety; line received the Safety Award of the Year (2004).
- Acted as liaison between customer and plant. Traveled to customer locations to evaluate quality issues, determine causes, and identify solutions.
- Trained employees on new equipment following system changes.
- Collaborated with engineers, tool makers, and plant management to design racks and fixtures to accommodate new products.

Education & Training

❑ **Associate of Applied Science** (expected September 2010) – Cincinnati School of Mortuary Science
❑ **Business Management** course work – Middletown Community College
❑ **Leadership Training** – Dale Carnegie

Career Change: *From manufacturing worker to funeral assistant.*

Strategy: *Lead with relevant though short-term experience that he had gained in a volunteer capacity with a local funeral home.*

DONNA DUGAN, RN
E-mail: donnadugan@hotmail.com
663 Shadow Court, Las Vegas, Nevada 89015
Phone: (702) 654-8015 / Cell: (702) 873-4804 / Fax: (702) 564-4605

LEGAL NURSE CONSULTANT
MEDICAL / PARALEGAL / INSURANCES

Knowledge:

Risk Management — Quality Assurance — Regulatory Compliance
Workers' Compensation Torts — Personal Injury — Medical Malpractice

Qualifications:
- Eighteen years in the medical profession.
- Knowledgeable in state and federal regulations.
- Trained in trial law—depositions, discovery, legal research, motions, and client interviews.
- Thorough understanding of medical terms, client/patient assessments, and life planning needs.

Skills:

• Staff Management	• Medical Terminology	• Compliance Manager
• Communication	• Medical Administration	• Case Management
• Clinical Experience	• Disease Etiology	• Community Outreach

PROFESSIONAL EXPERIENCE

Staff Nurse, Sierra Health Services, Las Vegas, NV   2004–Present
Oversee a 14-bed psychiatric unit for acute mentally-ill patients. Directly supervise 4 employees. Perform monthly, bi-yearly, and peer review of unit-based audits ensuring 100% compliance with standards of care requirements. Recognized a decrease in standards of care and implemented a staff training program that is showing increases toward 100%.

Veterans Health Administration, Knoxville, IA   1991–2004

Primary Nurse, MHC	*2002–2004*
Nurse Manager, Psychiatric Unit	*1998–2002*
Acting Nurse Manager, Extended Care Unit	*1997–1998*
Lead RN, Alzheimer's and Related Dementia Unit	*1995–1997*

EDUCATION
Diplomas and Professional Training

Legal Nurse Consultant, Kaplan College of Professional Studies, Boca Raton, FL
Registered Nurse, Iowa State University, Ames, IA

Advanced Health Assessment Course, Parkland Community College, Champaign, IL
Health Assessment Course, Vennard College, University Park, IA

PROFESSIONAL PRESENTATIONS

Keynote Speaker on "Care of a Patient and Caregiver Support for Alzheimer's"
Crescent City, Community Center
Vermilion County Nursing Home
Iowa City Alzheimer's Support Group

AFFILIATIONS

(Active) Secretary, South Valley Ranch Homeowners Association

Career Change: *From nurse to legal consultant.*

Strategy: *Emphasize related experience and industry expertise to position her as an expert in the emerging field of health care legal consulting.*

CLAUDIA WHITE

1001 Homestead Circuit
Victoria, 3803

Email: cwhite@earthlink.com

Mobile: (61) 5566 7898
Residence: (61) 6600 0323

"FIRST IMPRESSIONS"
S P E C I A L I S T

PERSONAL ASSISTANT • BUTLER • CABIN SERVICES MANAGER

First-class customer service, impeccable personal presentation, superior problem- and conflict-resolution talents, and meticulous attention to detail have been the hallmarks of an eight-year career spanning front-line client service and challenging nursing-care assignments. People-focused and logical; intuitive, empathetic, and proactive in responding to emergencies. A spirited leader and team participant; enjoy devising solutions and enhancing business reputation through the quality of personal communications and professional demeanor. Exposure to citizens of all nationalities via extensive global travel has further refined capacity for demonstrating patience, tolerance, and quick thinking.

Professional Strengths:

✓ "Red Carpet" Customer Service	✓ Safety & Security Processes	✓ Crisis Management
✓ Team Leadership & Direction	✓ Staff Training & Development	✓ Issues Resolution
✓ Conflict Resolution	✓ Medical/Nursing Intervention	✓ Catering/Food Delivery
✓ German/English Translations	✓ Cardiopulmonary Resuscitation	✓ Hygiene Protocols
✓ Quality Assurance	✓ Public Speaking	✓ Sales/Product Promotions
✓ Post-Operative Nursing	✓ Risk Evaluations	✓ Counseling/Listening

Technology skill set includes Microsoft Office, Windows, Internet, email.

EDUCATION | TRAINING

Certificate III in Airline Operations
Equivalent: Hospitality Certificate III
Australia Airlines

Advanced German Language
Institute of Languages

Nursing Diploma of Health Science
University of Sydney

Training also includes Security Awareness for Corrective Services.

EXPERIENCE SUMMARY

✓ "Top-scored" in all airline performance evaluations as a Long-Haul Flight Attendant since 2001—outpacing similarly experienced colleagues.

✓ Devised several initiatives for improving levels of safety, functionality, and efficiency across catering, medical, and occupational health and safety areas.

✓ Awarded several "Notices of Appreciation" from airline management recognizing the challenges faced during chartered distress flights that transferred "Bali Bombing" survivors from Bali to Australia.

✓ Conducted group training on safety, service procedures, and cardiopulmonary resuscitation.

✓ Recipient of numerous complimentary letters from passengers praising courtesy, empathy, and understanding displayed during all interactions.

✓ Volunteered to serve as part of the Risk Intervention Team dealing with prison inmates demonstrating suicidal tendencies.

✓ Managed medical ward and coordinated nursing team caring for up to 30 prisoners simultaneously at Short Bay Jail's Correctional Health Services unit.

Career Change: *From flight attendant to personal assistant.*

EMPLOYMENT CHRONICLE

AUSTRALIA AIRLINES   2001–Present
Long-Haul Flight Attendant

Service excellence, safety consciousness, superior grooming, and willingness to "rise to the occasion no matter what the challenge" are attributes cited on each performance evaluation since 2001 and further reinforced through positive feedback from the traveling public.

Regularly supervising up to 12 cabin crewmembers on international flights, provide leadership in areas such as in-flight conflicts, medical emergencies, staff education, and passenger communiqués—overseeing timely observation of departure schedules and the safety and security of all on board.

Contributions, Highlights, Accomplishments:

✓ Demonstrated superior knowledge of emergency aviation procedures during intensive airline operations training, including evacuations, "ditching," fire-fighting, administering oxygen, survival techniques, and hostage resolution.

✓ Selected to perform emergency medical treatments on doctor's verbal authority via air/land Medlink hook-up. Maintained communication stream by constantly briefing doctors on passengers' vital signs and visual observations.

✓ Devised several initiatives for improving levels of safety, functionality, and efficiency across catering, medical, and occupational health and safety areas.

✓ Volunteered services for Australia Airlines distress flights, evacuating "Bali Bombing" survivors back to Australia from Bali. Dispensed counseling and empathy to passengers traveling to seek missing friends and relatives or identify remains post-attack. Managed wounds previously concealed by survivors, administered first aid and comfort, and calmed distressed passengers. Awarded several "Notices of Appreciation" from management and passengers recognizing the challenges faced.

✓ Defused the violence level of an abusive passenger affected by alcohol and intimidating passengers and crew. Built rapport and eventually won agreement for the passenger to abstain from alcohol during the flight's final 2 hours. The calmed and cheerful passenger disembarked without further incident with thanks for a "lovely flight."

✓ Instigated emergency CPR upon a passenger's collapse during descent. Selected a crewmember to assist and, drawing upon qualifications as a registered nurse, continued to administer CPR procedures until landing and ambulance takeover.

✓ Recipient of numerous complimentary letters from passengers citing courtesy, empathy, and understanding displayed during all interactions.

CORRECTIONAL HEALTH SERVICES   1999–2001
Short Bay Correctional Center's health services division
Registered Nurse/Acting Nurse Unit Manager

Senior staff member and Acting Nurse Unit Manager of the challenging "B Ward"—a medical unit of Short Bay correctional facility caring for inmates with a variety of conditions from fractures and post-procedure care through degenerative and chronic conditions, drug dependencies, and mental illnesses. Personal safety and security of the nursing team and officers was a top priority requiring active awareness of surroundings and scrupulous attention to preventative measures such as storage of sharp objects and medications. Dealt professionally with up to 30 prisoners in the ward and a personal caseload of up to 4 patients daily.

✓ Won the respect of many prisoners by providing group training that prepared inmates for eventual release with a range of daily living skills.

✓ Co-produced reports to stringent guidelines when documenting assaults, suicides, or inmate injuries.

✓ Presented security awareness training to nursing staff, including such topics as hostage survival techniques in a correctional facility.

Claudia White   Page 2   Confidential

Strategy: *Avoid typical language for a flight attendant resume and focus instead on a series of examples that showcase her abilities to manage crises, solve problems, and deal effectively with diverse people.*

Maya Havela, CNA

4331 Laurel Canyon Blvd.
Studio City, CA 91604

mayah@aol.com
818-555-1518

Nursing Assistant

Integrating Health Care & Magic to Restore Dignity & Comfort to the Infirm

Perceptive, service-oriented health professional with unique ability to empower and entertain patients while providing highest quality care. Consummate team worker and developer of cooperative relationships with coworkers and stakeholders. Recognized for ability to remain calm in crises. Licensed in California. Member of National Association of Health Care Assistants. Hablo español.

Value to Your Organization

Up-to-date patient-care skills in accordance with established methods, techniques, and recognized standards. Expertise in performing ADLs and maintaining supplies and equipment on nursing unit.

Engaging personality as proven in the care of a relative with advanced Alzheimer's. Used sleight of hand to regain control of car keys, preventing him from driving. Defused a difficult situation with humor and magic while maintaining his sense of independence and dignity.

Ability to see what needs to be done—and the drive and energy to do it.

> *We consider Maya a valuable asset. She is willing and able in whatever we ask of her.*
> *Maya is punctual, considerate, and fun to have around. Richard Withersby, Instructor*

Professional Skills Profile

- Patient Safety & Rights
- Infection Control
- Physical Therapy
- Medical Records

- Medications
- Cognitive & Physical Disabilities
- Patient Ambulating & Transport
- Nutrition & Food Handling

- Emergency Procedures
- Skin & Body Care
- End-of-Life Care
- Death & Bereavement

Proficient with Macintosh and Windows OS and MS Office. Expertise in programming VCR/DVR devices.

Professional Training & Licensures

- **California Certified Nursing Assistant License,** 2009
- **Fundamentals of Caregiving,** Northridge Medical Center, Northridge, CA, 2009
- **Safety Training for Individual Providers,** Northridge Medical Center, Northridge, CA, 2009
- **HIV/AIDS Education,** Health Information Network, Van Nuys, CA, 2007
- **Standard First Aid/CPR Adult,** American Red Cross, Van Nuys, CA, 2007
- **General Education Diploma (GED),** Department of Education, Phoenix, AZ, 1992

Career Change: *From magician to nursing assistant.*

Page 2
Maya Havela, CNA

mayah@aol.com
818-555-1518

Professional Experience

MAYA'S MAGIC
OWNER, Marbella, Spain

Professional magician, comedian, and creative consultant for 20+ years. Highly respected entertainer with formidable magic skills developed through decades of practice and appearances before audiences worldwide. Performer of pro bono shows for local charities and organizations including Ciudad de los Niños, Cruz Roja (Spanish Red Cross), and American Red Cross.

Community Service

KIWANIS INTERNATIONAL
VOLUNTEER, Studio City, CA, 2006–Present

Collaborate with seniors on projects that stimulate their emotional well-being. Assist with making handicrafts and writing books, biographies, and letters to families.

ASSOCIATION FOR CANCER CARE (ACC)
ORGANIZER, Malaga, Spain, 2003

Raised US$8K+ for ACC by organizing first-of-its-kind fashion show for Spanish cancer charity.

> *I am very proud of the success you achieved for ACC on the occasion of our Fashion Show in Malaga. We should make it an annual event!*

Michelle Wilcox, ACC Founder

Strategy: *Position her as a well-trained, caring health-care professional who is particularly responsive to patients' emotional needs. Use her prior "magical" career as a distinguishing characteristic of her new career focus.*

KATHRYN LAWRENCE

8827 Buchanan Drive • Lewisville, Texas 75027 • KathrynLawrence@gmail.com • (214) 555-9628

GRADUATE NURSE / RN, EMERGENCY DEPARTMENT

Quick-thinking, conscientious, and detail-oriented professional with 13+ years of experience helping others as a police officer, including 6 years of experience as an initial responder to serious, multiple-trauma traffic accidents, providing first aid and assisting with triage. Driven self-starter with superior communication and decision-making skills, a passion for helping others, and a career history that demonstrates unwavering integrity and teamwork. Eager and willing to work hard every day, continue learning, and do what is required to become a world-class nurse. Speak some Spanish.

- *Relevant Experience and Keen Observational Skills.* Practical knowledge serving a multicultural population from diverse socioeconomic groups, teaching people about personal safety and drug awareness, providing detailed documentation and report writing, and ensuring regulatory compliance and appropriate resource allocation. Extensive knowledge and experience working with substance abusers and the mentally ill.

- *Unique Qualifications to Succeed in High-Stress Situations.* Highly regarded for ability to deal with life-and-death situations, provide quick and accurate assessments, make prompt and responsible decisions, and provide calm and attentive customer service.

- *Dedication and Reliability.* Known as a caring, compassionate, dependable public servant and community volunteer. Understand being "mission essential," i.e., rising 2 hours early to drive to work when the roads are icy.

- *Professional Honors and Awards.* Meritorious Service Commendation, 2006; Mothers Against Drunk Drivers Officer of the Year, 2000; Victim's Rights Coalition's Officer of the Year, 1999.

EDUCATION, HONORS & ACTIVITIES

RN PROGRAM: ASSOCIATE DEGREE, NURSING   Will Graduate and Test for RN License 3/2010
University of North Texas, Denton
Cumulative GPA: 3.47 out of 4.0
- **Named to Dean's List** 2 out of 3 semesters.
- **Served as Chair** for Bone Marrow Donation Drive between Cook Children's Hospital and North Central Texas College.
- **Participated in National Student Nurses' Association** as an Executive Board Member and Class Representative.

BASIC LIFESAVING (BLS) FOR HEALTHCARE PROVIDERS CERTIFICATION, Denton Fire Department   2008
ADVANCED CARDIAC LIFE SUPPORT CERTIFICATION, Denton Regional Medical Center   2009

BACHELOR OF SCIENCE, BIOLOGY, and BACHELOR OF ARTS, PSYCHOLOGY
Grove City College, Grove City, Pennsylvania

PROFESSIONAL EXPERIENCE

STUDENT NURSE
North Texas Medical Center, Lewisville, Texas   1st Semester
Lewisville Medical Center, Lewisville, Texas   2nd Semester
Baylor Grapevine, Grapevine, Texas   3rd Semester
Baylor Grapevine Emergency Department, Grapevine, Texas   Accepted for 4th Semester
- **Recognized as 1 of only 3 students to win coveted position** in Baylor Grapevine's Emergency Department.

POLICE OFFICER, City of Plano, Plano, Texas   1997–Present
Capably serve the public, working 12-hour shifts and interacting comfortably with a multicultural population. Developed a reputation for responding admirably in high-stress situations, performing quick assessments, utilizing resources, making swift decisions in accordance with departmental procedures, and providing detailed and accurate documentation.
- **Won numerous awards** for outstanding dedication and service.

COMMUNICATIONS OFFICER, U.S. Army, Seven Posts, including Fort Hood, Texas   6 Years
Managed hundreds of staff members and ensured the safety of millions of dollars of high-tech property.

SOCIAL WORKER, Collin County Community Mental Health, Plano, Texas   2 Years
Worked with 70 mentally impaired clients and a team of health professionals, facilitating interdisciplinary coordination.

• • • • •

Career Change: From police officer to nurse.

Strategy: Start with a strong summary showcasing both hard and soft skills and follow with sections detailing recent education and briefly listing employment experience.

CHAPTER 8

Resumes for Career Changers Seeking Training, Human Resources, Teaching, and Educational Administration Positions

Many jobs contain elements of teaching, training, and human resources functions even when this is not the primary role of the position. People seeking to transition to this role full time need to bring relevant experience to the forefront on their resumes. Quite often they can successfully position themselves as an experienced professional with relevant skills and achievements, rather than a career-transition candidate who needs to show transferable skills. It's all in how you present the material! This chapter contains examples for the following transitions:

- Teacher to corporate trainer
- Talent manager to communications trainer
- Sales manager to human resources generalist
- Securities broker to corporate trainer
- Prevention counselor to training and development professional
- Adoption specialist to employee relations and recruitment professional
- Office administrator to recruiter
- Marketing professional to teacher
- Boiler operator to teacher
- Farmer/rancher to teacher
- Technical writer to teacher
- Retail salesperson and manager to teacher
- Police officer to teacher
- IT consultant to college instructor
- Military officer to university administrator

Lorraine T. Wilson

919-223-8888
wilson@email.com

2813 Twilight Avenue
Raleigh, NC 27613

Training & Development

Expert in delivering training programs that drive productivity and performance improvements.

Dynamic training professional with an outstanding reputation for integrity and results. Effective interpersonal skills with an ability to meet and train people at their level. Skilled in facilitating groups through complex problem solving to action and improvement. Enthusiastic with a positive and motivating management style. Core competencies include …

- Strategic & Tactical Planning
- Performance Management
- Cross-Cultural Communications
- Train-the-Trainer Development
- Needs Assessment & Analysis
- Mentoring Programs

Lorraine "is a highly skilled professional with a wealth of experience in working effectively with individuals and groups across the district to effect change."

Coordinator
North Carolina Diagnostic &
Learning Resources System

"She is an extremely well-planned and structured individual. She models perseverance and encourages others to do the same…. Lorraine has an articulate ability to convey even complicated information in a very clear and concise manner."

Susan Smith
Guidance Counselor

Notable Highlights

- Repeatedly selected by the county to serve as a consultant to *develop training materials for alternative assessments and lead training workshops.*

- Following the requirement of federal- and state-mandated training procedures, *selected by the school district to develop the training modules and train 5,000 teachers to retain critical governmental funding.* Created the highly regarded and very effective PowerPoint presentation, "Solving the Puzzle," incorporating all learning modalities for ease of learning.

- *Created highly successful community-based training program to prepare disabled students for the workforce.* Established long-term, mutually beneficial relationships with major employers, including Sheraton, Marriott, St. Joseph's Hospital, Walmart, Kash n' Karry, and Target. Served as the administration liaison monitoring student progress. *Enjoyed an unprecedented success rate in getting students hired into long-term employment.*

- *Chosen to author the curriculum and teach English to foreign-born nationals.*

- *Recruited to "train the trainer,"* authoring the program to successfully coach experienced teachers in the art of mentoring new teachers to reduce turnover.

- *Recruited by University of North Carolina to develop the "Classroom Manager," standardized web-based lesson plans.*

- *Invited by North Carolina State University* to participate as a key member of the Special Education Consortium conducting alternative assessment field testing for its Life Career Center *as a precursor to becoming a state-certified trainer.*

Career Change: *From teacher to corporate trainer.*

Strategy: *Focus on career accomplishments beyond the classroom and incorporate third-party comments as powerful endorsements of her training abilities.*

LORRAINE T. WILSON   Page 2   919-223-8888

Evaluation Form Excerpts:

"Excellent presenter. Lively presentation of DRY topic!"

"Lorraine has an awesome personality."

"Wonderful job, Lorraine. Very informative, yet fun!"

"Fantastic job."

"Very informative and helpful."

"Good workshop. Brought everything together. Fun activities."

"Excellent! Excellent! Excellent!"

"Great instruction and activities."

"Good information. Well presented."

Professional Experience

GREEN COUNTY SCHOOL DISTRICT, Raleigh, NC

Teacher — 2005 to 2010
EMH Teacher, Central High School — 2004 to 2005
VE/ESE Class Instructor, Springville Adult School — 1998 to 2004
ESOL Instructor, Springville Adult School — 1994 to 1998
ESE Department Head, Washington High School — 1988 to 1994

Broad-based experience in training teachers and students within the 13th largest school district in the nation. As Department Head, supervised and mentored paraprofessionals; served as liaison with outside agencies; and developed effective training materials.

- Developed the coaching programs that resulted in new teacher orientation and professional day training policies.
- Chosen numerous times to serve on committees aimed at improving teacher training.
- Proven record of success in teaching and graduating the most dysfunctional students.
- Repeatedly selected by the district as a model classroom for visiting foreign educators.

Certification

North Carolina Certified Associate of Behavior Analysis (CABA)

Education

Master of Administration — Ohio University, Athens, OH
Bachelor of Arts — Pennsylvania State University, York, PA

PATRICK J. KELLY

86 Redstone Road ▪ Danbury, CT 06810
H: 203.325.9951 ▪ C: 203.911.9073 ▪ pkelly@kelly.com

Executive Training ▪ Workshops ▪ Presentations ▪ Fortune 500 ▪ Speakers Bureau Training

COMMUNICATIONS & TRAINING SPECIALIST
Raising the Bar for Performance, Productivity & Profits

Driving effectiveness of individuals and organizations by delivering communication skills training to broad audiences, including executives and sales staff. More than 12-year track record of **setting new standards and getting people to perform, consistently achieving "the impossible"** with regard to skills improvement, booking high-profile speakers, and sales goals. Recognized by employers for succeeding where others fail.

Training expertise in persuasive speaking, negotiations, sales, and public speaking in one-on-one and group settings. Master's degree in Speech and Theater. Available for travel.

Key Areas of Strength

Executive Presentation Skills	Process Streamlining	Talent Management/Production
Professional Development	PR/Media Management	Sales Presentation/Negotiation
Persuasive Speaking	Speech Coaching	Consultative Selling Skills

CORE EXPERTISE & ACHIEVEMENTS

Executive Training

- Trained Fortune 500 executives in boardroom presentations, employee and stakeholder communications, and media relations.

Negotiations, Sales & Persuasive Speaking/Training

- Conducted sales seminars in one-on-one and group environments of up to 50; sales improved 35% within the next few months.

Public Speaking/Workshops/Seminars

- Presented lectures on topics including health, business, and government affairs for broad range of audiences: corporate, academic, and nonprofit.

RELATED EXPERIENCE

Young Athletes Foundation, Stamford, CT, 2008

HEAD OF SPEAKER'S BUREAU (6-month interim/consulting assignment)
Rapidly mastered new field without prior sports knowledge or experience. Identified, approached, secured, negotiated, and coordinated speaking engagements at events and at colleges, nonprofits, and large corporations for prominent young athletes. Developed fund-raising events.

- **Pioneered speakers training for young athletes to increase foundation's revenues:**
  - Trained athletes one-on-one and in groups to speak effectively in front of large audiences of up to hundreds of people. Authored parts of presentations.
- **Sold speaking engagements** for athletes to large nonprofit organizations, capturing 300% revenue increase.
- **Continued to attract and sign high-profile athletes despite downward industry trend** following Merrill Lynch's shift from external to internal sourcing for motivational speakers:
  - Targeted and booked athletes considered "unobtainable" by peers and supervisor.
- Streamlined operations: implemented structure and categorized speakers (amateur/professional).

Career Change: *From talent manager to communications trainer.*

Strategy: *Group communications and training-related experience at the front of the resume, following a strong summary that includes a distinguishing branding statement.*

PATRICK J. KELLY

C: 203.911.9073 ▪ pkelly@kelly.com ▪ Page 2 of 2

ADDITIONAL PROFESSIONAL EXPERIENCE

Patrick Kelly Productions, Danbury, CT, 2004 to 2010
TALENT MANAGER & PRODUCER
Founded and operated consulting firm specializing in career development and job/project placement for cabaret artists. Organized career fairs.

- Managed all public relations, publicity, and funding for individual clients.
- **Obtained bookings, negotiated contracts, and prepared clients for performances,** achieving success rate 60% above peer average.

Susan Bergman, Producer and Composer, New York, NY, 2002 to 2003
CO-PRODUCER
Managed fund-raising and publicity. Coordinated production staff for "Hairspray," "Into the Woods," and "Jekyll & Hyde."

- Streamlined fund-raising and publicity efforts, improving efficiency and outreach.
- Independently identified and capitalized on market base expansion in Florida.

Green Apple Barter Services, New York, NY, 2000 to 2001
ACCOUNT EXECUTIVE
Sold bartering memberships to private business owners in New York.

- **Doubled territory and business revenues in 6 to 8 months** by opening new market in Rockland County.
- **Delivered sales training** for peers to boost sales results.

Jill McNulty & Associates, New York, NY, 1998 to 2000
CO-DIRECTOR OF ADVERTISING
Hired to research radio advertising and sell drive-time ads for major NY radio station.

- **Achieved substantial press coverage and exceeded expectations** by targeting persons and organizations previously not considered, successfully raising the bar.

EDUCATION

M.A. degree in Speech and Theater, graduated with honors, GPA: 3.8
B.A. degree in Speech, English, and Media Arts, graduated with honors, GPA: 3.9
BARUCH COLLEGE, New York, NY

RESUME 60: BY MAJORIE SUSSMAN, ACRW, MRW, CPRW

Tina S. Parker

219-444-4887 • tsparker@gmail.com
24 Circle Court, Chicago, IL 60604

Qualified for position as…

Manager – Human Resources / Organizational Development

Staff Development • Process Improvement • Talent Recruitment

Eight years of progressive advancement in management with Fortune 50 Wells Fargo—developing talented teams, optimizing productivity, coaching high-potential individuals for upward mobility, and streamlining processes and workflow for measurable results. Talented public speaker and group presenter. Fluent in Spanish.

OPERATIONS:	HUMAN CAPITAL:	BUSINESS GROWTH:
Strategic Planning	Team Building & Training	Revenue Growth
Organizational Change	Program & Project Management	Cross-Cultural Communications
Policy Development	Recruitment & Retention	Customer Relationships
Continuous Process Improvement	One-on-One Coaching	Profitability Optimization

Professional Experience & Achievements

WELLS FARGO FINANCIAL, Highland Park, IL   2002–Present

SALES MANAGER II

Promoted within first year to management roles in 3 locations. Built first-rate organizations (total staff 42) infused with a team-based work culture by immediately zeroing in on talent recruitment, training, and leadership development as well as cost reduction, process improvement, and customer satisfaction.

Organizational Leadership Highlights:
- Developed 2 employees for promotions to Regional Leader and District Manager.
- Grew Highland Park location to top performer—from **$30M to $60M** net receivables—in 4 years.
- Delivered **350%** growth to **$45M** at Schererville branch—in 3 years.

Personal Recognitions & Honors:
- Top Performer in District Hires, 5 years
- First Quarter Top Performer, 4 years
- Top Coach, 2004 & 2008
- Rookie Manager of the Year, 2002

Earlier:

Paid 100% college tuition by working full-time as an Assistant Manager at Crunch Fitness, Inc., while attending St. Xavier University, 1998–2002.

Community Involvement

Participant in United Way and MS annual drives, 2002–2008
Sponsored marathon competitor, raising funds for child abuse victims, 2007 & 2008

Education & Professional Development

BS, Business Administration, Minor in Spanish, St. Xavier University, Chicago, IL, 2002
- Summa cum laude (GPA: 3.95)
- Semester in Oaxaca City, Mexico

Career Change: *From sales manager to human resources generalist.*

Strategy: *Start with a "qualified for" headline and incorporate relevant keywords into a rich summary. In describing work experience, pull out HR-related highlights and downplay sales activities.*

JASON THUNE

654 Tonnelle Avenue • Jersey City, New Jersey 07305
201.725.3078 • thunejason3078@comcast.net

CORPORATE TRAINING & MANAGEMENT DEVELOPMENT

Finance ~ Banking ~ Insurance ~ Securities ~ Foreign Exchange

Highly accomplished financial professional with an extensive Wall Street trading history. Track record of success instructing executives on details of foreign exchange and securities markets. Adept at analyzing market conditions and facilitating trades in high-yield, distressed, and crossover bonds as well as other financial instruments. Excellent communication skills with aptitude for establishing and cultivating relationships with domestic, Asian, and European clients/partners.

Areas of expertise include:

- Strategic Planning
- Presentations
- Relationship Management
- Regulatory Compliance
- Financial Analysis
- Client/Partner Liaison
- Business Development
- Training & Mentoring
- Arbitrage Identification

PROFESSIONAL EXPERIENCE

—FIMAT (FORMERLY COWEN & CO., LLC/SG COWEN), NEW YORK, NEW YORK 1983–2010
U.S. investment bank acquired by Fimat parent Société Générale in 1998.

Special Limited Partner & Inter-Dealer Broker
Hired as Broker Assistant and navigated career through NYSE Floor Clerk to positions as Broker/Trader on U.S. Convertible and Eurobond Desk and Trader for Japanese and European securities. Promoted to Inter-Dealer Broker in 1989 and to Special Limited Partner in 1995.

Key Achievements:

- Forged relationships with high-profile clientele, including Merrill Lynch, Lehman Bros., Goldman Sachs, and other financial institutions.

- Prepared and delivered comprehensive presentations and mentoring sessions on European and Japanese markets to U.S.-based Fimat executives.

- Harnessed new opportunities in emerging Eurobond market with initial European Texaco bond issue, cultivating partnerships with Barclays, Credit Suisse, Barings Bank, and other international players.

- Bridged clients and dealers to secure orders for Japanese warrant market.

- Captured nearly 3-fold increase in trading desk revenues to earn promotion to Special Limited Partner.

EDUCATION & CREDENTIALS

Bachelor of Science in Business Administration/Finance
New Jersey City University, Jersey City, New Jersey

Active NASD/FINRA Series 7 & 55 Licenses

Career Change: *From securities broker to corporate trainer.*

Strategy: *Start with a profile that helps readers understand his vast experience in the securities industry to qualify him for training roles in this industry.*

RESUME 62: BY SHARON MCCORMICK, MS, MCC, NCC, NCCC, CPRW

MATTHEW BENSON

1234 5ᵗʰ Street   Indianapolis, Indiana 46240   (317) 555-6789   E-mail: MBenson@hotmail.com

CAREER PROFILE

ACCOMPLISHED HUMAN RELATIONS PROFESSIONAL with 6+ years of experience in marketing, clinical counseling, investigation and case management, human services, curriculum development, program facilitation, and training. Proven track record of success in the education, medical, insurance, and human services fields. Comprehensive experience with a top-ranked research university, a Level-1 trauma medical center, a **Fortune 1000** insurance company, and 2 highly respected human services agencies.

Passionate professional driven by a desire to see clients advance and develop personally and professionally. Consistently achieve excellent performance evaluations. Honors student with an extensive history of community involvement, public speaking, and volunteerism.

PROFESSIONAL OBJECTIVE

Seeking to contribute to a company's training and development function in the human services, human resources, and/or workforce development field.

EDUCATION

INDIANA UNIVERSITY, Bloomington, IN
M.S., ADULT EDUCATION, Department of Education (anticipated 2010)
CERTIFICATE, MANAGEMENT & SUPERVISION, School of Continuing Education (2009)
❖ Concentration in *Staff Training & Development.*
❖ Work full-time while in school full-time.
❖ Financing **100%** of education.

B.S.W., SOCIAL WORK (2005)
❖ **G.P.A.: 3.4 / 4.0**
❖ Worked part-time as an Indiana University Ambassador, giving tours to hundreds of prospective students.
❖ Successfully completed an intensive internship with Wishard Hospital in Indianapolis, IN (2005).
❖ Member, Golden Key National Honor Society.
❖ Member, Phi Alpha Honor Society, School of Social Work.

THE UNIVERSITY OF MIAMI, Coral Gables, FL (2001–2003)
❖ Completed 2 years of coursework toward a Bachelor of Science degree in *International Relations.*
❖ Participated in College Work-Study program as a Referee for Basketball, Football, and Soccer Intramurals.
❖ Transferred to **IU** to target the respected **B.S.W.** degree program.

Career Change: *From prevention counselor to training and development professional.*

Strategy: *"Repackage" him as a soon-to-graduate student with recent and relevant education and position prior experience as added value rather than the primary qualification.*

MATTHEW BENSON ❖ MBenson@hotmail.com   **Page Two**

PROFESSIONAL EXPERIENCE

CROSSROADS, INDIANAPOLIS, IN
Prevention Counselor, New Directions (2008–Present)
Crisis Counselor (2007–2008)
- ❖ Enthusiastically provide individual/group on-site clinical counseling services for teenagers at 3 local high schools. Address substance abuse prevention and treatment topics, including academic achievement, anger identification & management, family & peer relationships, problem-solving, and self-esteem.
- ❖ Implemented the ***Parenting Wisely*** program in the home for families at risk to strengthen communication. Utilize cutting-edge technology to present vignettes that depict commonplace situations.
- ❖ Facilitate family members role-playing and discussing possible solutions for the scenarios.
- ❖ Participate in ongoing staffing meetings to review the family's progress.
- ❖ Coordinate continuity of care case-management services with school personnel, Department of Children & Families caseworkers, and other professionals relevant to the client's achievement.
- ❖ Researched various topics and helped develop the curriculum for parenting and substance-abuse topics.
- ❖ Completed extensive documentation within tight deadlines.
- ❖ Speak to other interested community groups about substance abuse prevention in Marion County.
- ❖ Consistently earn praise for curriculum development, motivational speaking, and enthusiastic training style.
- ❖ Began working part-time as a Crisis Counselor; promoted to Prevention Counselor.

THE TEEN SCENE, INDIANAPOLIS, IN
Residential Counselor (2006–2007)
- ❖ Coordinated admissions, treatment plans, progress reports, and discharges for highly respected children's home.
- ❖ Provided crisis intervention and individual, family, and group counseling to residents ages 5–17.
- ❖ Received consistently high performance evaluations for counseling and documentation skills.

FIRST PLACE INSURANCE, DANVERS, MA
Automobile Claims Adjustor (2005–2006)
- ❖ Successfully case-managed hundreds of automobile claims totaling hundreds of thousands of dollars for this **Fortune 1000** insurance company.
- ❖ Contacted and established rapport with all appropriate personnel to determine coverage, exposure, and liability.
- ❖ Consistently earned praise for defusing difficult customer situations, expediting claims, and preparing thorough documentation.

WISHARD HOSPITAL, INDIANAPOLIS, IN
Social Work Intern (2004)
- ❖ Provided extensive social work education and intervention services for up to **120** patients and their families in a **700**-bed *Level-1 Trauma Center* hospital psychiatric unit.
- ❖ Gained experience with culturally diverse patients and their various diagnoses.

COMMUNITY / VOLUNTEER ACTIVITIES

*Completed the **Toastmasters International Communication & Leadership Program**, Indianapolis, IN (2009)*
*Volunteer, **The Great American Teach-In**, North Central High School, Indianapolis, IN (2009)*
***SERVE Volunteer**, Delaware Trails Elementary School, Indianapolis, IN (2008)*
***Guest Lecturer, "Teambuilding,"** Butler University, Indianapolis, IN (2007)*

RESUME 63: BY SHARON GREEN, MA, CPRW, LPC

RITA M. BAYLOR

 2500 East Shea • Phoenix, AZ 85028 • baylorrita@cox.net • **602.222.4444**

TARGET POSITION: EMPLOYEE RELATIONS / RECRUITMENT

AREAS OF EFFECTIVENESS

<u>*COACHING:*</u> Developing individual plans and conveying feedback to facilitate behavioral change. Delivering orientation programs and articulating critical information to guide program participants. Negotiating difficult situations between conflicting parties. Training new hires to expedite transition to new environment.

<u>*LEGAL AWARENESS:*</u> Ensuring strict compliance with government regulations and remaining current on related information through continuous training. Collaborating effectively with attorneys / judges in preparation for and during court proceedings. Maintaining confidentiality of sensitive records.

<u>*LEADERSHIP:*</u> Hiring, training, mentoring, and evaluating performance of support staff. Leading retreats and monthly meetings to drive departmental planning and issue resolution while advancing team-building efforts. Maximizing productivity and performance within office. Interfacing effectively with management.

<u>*RECRUITMENT:*</u> Executing targeted and general-recruitment strategies, including dissemination of information and conducting large-group presentations at community events. Interviewing individuals to discern relevant information and matching parties according to guidelines. Representing agency on television and radio spots.

SKILLS / STRENGTHS

Mediation ♦ Information Dissemination ♦ Public Speaking ♦ Conflict Resolution ♦ Networking
Organized ♦ Self-directed ♦ Compassionate ♦ Poised

PROFESSIONAL EXPERIENCE

Family Specialist / Recruiter, *Adoption Services*, Phoenix, AZ, 2007–Present
- License adoptions and manage up to 22 cases simultaneously, guiding families through all phases of process.
- Execute targeted and general-recruitment activities to build program awareness and increase referrals and prospects.
- Increase market presence for programs through television and radio appearances as well as newspaper articles and public-speaking engagements.
- Distribute materials to hundreds of individuals while working information booths to promote program.
- Design and maintain flowchart outlining adoption process to distribute to prospects during recruitment within community.
- Train new employees on policies and procedures.

Continued…

Career Change: *From adoption specialist to employee relations and recruitment professional.*

Strategy: *Highlight core capabilities within four skill sets that are relevant to her goal.*

– RITA M. BAYLOR –

Professional Experience continued…

Social Worker, *Mesa Health Systems*, Mesa, AZ, 2006–2007
- Maintained ongoing caseload of more than 45 clients with varied needs, including completing thorough needs assessment and collaborating with partner agencies.
- Functioned as client advocate to address grievances and determine viable solutions.
- Thoroughly investigated and maintained detailed records pertaining to case families.
- Consistently received positive feedback from clients and managers acknowledging outstanding dedication and performance.

Case Assistant, *The Carey Support Program*, Tucson, AZ, 2005–2006
- Hired, oriented, trained, scheduled, and conducted performance reviews for 12-person team.
- Charged with development, design, editing, and distribution of multi-page, visually appealing newsletter targeted to families.
- Played integral role in planning major conference to promote new adoption-support system.
- Quickly received increased responsibilities, including case management, after initially being hired to manage records of long-term cases.

Case Worker, *Department of Economic Security*, Tucson, AZ, 2003–2005
- Served as legal guardian and advocate for up to 52 children.
- Collaborated with Attorney General's office to strategize on cases.
- Gained broad-based understanding of individuals in need of rehabilitation programs.
- Orchestrated case meetings to bring together all parties to share cases and solutions.

EDUCATION / COMPUTER SKILLS

Bachelor of Arts in Sociology, University of Arizona, Tucson, AZ, 2002
Intermediate PowerPoint skills; Proficient in Word, Excel, Outlook, and Publisher

RESUME 64: BY JAN HOLLIDAY, NCRW

Kathleen Hunt

453 Roth Drive ◆ Souderton, PA 18964 ◆ 215-660-5498 ◆ khunt@dotresume.com

Goal

Recruiting position that will utilize my strengths in employee matching, sales, and customer relations to deliver top-notch service to candidates and customers.

Qualifications Summary

- ◆ Creative problem solver; proven ability to match people to jobs and products to customers utilizing active listening and persuasive presentation skills.
- ◆ Self-starter; demonstrated talent for building sales and providing high-quality service.
- ◆ Excellent interpersonal skills; easily develop rapport with people from diverse backgrounds; experience working with individuals in broad range of occupations.
- ◆ Highly organized; facility for multitasking and prioritizing in fast-paced environment.
- ◆ Computer literate and Internet savvy; knowledge of Microsoft Office.

Experience

Career Coaching

OPTIONS FOR WOMEN, Lansdale, PA, 2005–2009

Helped clients discover skills and personal strengths, match qualifications to occupations, and find employment.

Sales/Customer Service

FABRIC CITY, Quakertown, PA, 2006
SILK IMPORTS, INC., Doylestown, PA, 2005–2006
BUSINESS OWNER/OPERATOR (Faux Painting), Souderton, PA, 1997–2005
CEDARBROOK SCHOOL, Souderton, PA, 1995–2006

As business owner/operator, grew client base through networking and relationship building, direct calling, and flyer distribution. Sold products for Silk Imports and Fabric City to designers and consumers, evaluating customers' needs—spoken and unspoken—and matching with company products. In all positions, won customers' appreciation with respectful attitude and fast, friendly service. At Cedarbrook School, developed network as committee/event chairperson and informally championed school to increase enrollment.

Administration

A. JAMESON ASSOCIATES, CENTRAL MONTGOMERY HOSPITAL, Lansdale, PA, 2009–present
MONTGOMERY COUNTY TECHNOLOGY COUNCIL, Norristown, PA, 2006–2007

Researched member companies and industry trends for sales representatives, provided input for event planning, attended events, and managed office functions for organization serving 500 member companies doing business in high-tech arena. Currently serve as point of contact for busy medical practice serving 600+ cardiac patients per month. Screen, prioritize, and schedule patients, negotiating to obtain appointments with outside providers when necessary. Help maintain calm, professional atmosphere in high-stress environment.

Education

M.A., University of Pittsburgh, Pittsburgh, PA
B.A., Indiana University of Pennsylvania, Indiana, PA

Career Change: *From office administrator to recruiter.*

Strategy: *Group experience into categories in order of relevance to her target position, rather than chronologically. The most prominent experience (career coaching) was as a volunteer.*

Margaret Lemeshaw

414 Acorn Court, Lawrenceville, NJ 08648
(609) 771-5555 ▪ marlem@earthlink.net

Spanish Teacher at the Middle or High School Level

EDUCATION & CERTIFICATION

New Jersey Teacher's Certification, Spanish K–12

BA, Spanish Language & Civilization / Teaching (cum laude), Rutgers University, New Brunswick, NJ
Two semesters at University of Valencia, Spain. Summer study at University of Madrid.
MBA, International Business / Marketing, Columbia University, New York, NY

PROFILE

☑ Fluent Spanish. Basic conversational Portuguese and good reading ability. Familiar with French.
☑ Experienced Spanish teacher with demonstrated track record of obtaining outstanding results by utilizing highly effective interpersonal and communications skills.
☑ Detail-oriented, analytical professional with proven organizational and problem-solving abilities.
☑ Computer literate: MS Windows, Word, Excel, Outlook, and Internet Explorer; Broderbund Print Shop.

PROFESSIONAL EXPERIENCE

TEACHING / COMMUNICATIONS
- Designed Spanish-language curriculum and taught one 2½-hour class weekly for The Princeton Community School. Used text, multimedia, and visual aids to make classroom learning relevant to adults. Resulted in high re-registration rate for following semesters.

- Trained small groups of end users on computerized banking services for Mercantile Banking and Trust Company. Conducted product presentations and consultative interviews with clients and prospects. Created and implemented marketing plans for corporate clients in Latin America.

- Consulted with clients of International Research Corporation to determine specifications for customized market / opinion research projects. Wrote proposals and translated textbook chapters and questionnaires from Spanish to English. Developed marketing collaterals and account relationship management techniques to ensure top-notch company image and service.

ORGANIZATION / PROJECT MANAGEMENT
- Coordinated complex, comprehensive multinational research projects for Research Analysis Corporation and International Research Corporation. Ensured timely completion of projects within budget.

- Coordinated translations from Spanish to English for scholarly magazine, obtaining and evaluating board-member input on editorial content, all while meeting strict publication deadlines. Streamlined procedures for foreign-language advertisement and order fulfillment (Medical Learning Systems).

EMPLOYMENT HISTORY

Director of International Marketing	International Research Corp., Somerset, NJ	2004–2010
Spanish I Teacher	Princeton Community School, Princeton, NJ	2004–2009
Field Administrator	Research Analysis Corp., Skillman, NJ	2003–2004
Coordinator—Latin American Services	Medical Learning Systems, Skillman, NJ	2001–2002
Community Volunteer Activities and Family Child Care	Lawrenceville, NJ	1995–2001
Senior Marketing & Sales Rep.	Mercantile Banking and Trust Co., New York, NY	previously

Career Change: *From marketing professional to teacher.*

Strategy: *Margaret discovered her passion for teaching while conducting Spanish classes at a community school. Her resume relates her professional and volunteer experiences to her new target.*

BRYCE CARLSON

265 Charlotte Street
Asheville, NC 28801

(828) 555-7893 *home*
(828) 254-7893 *cell*
gatehous@aol.com

HISTORY TEACHER
North Carolina License, Social Studies 9–12

PROFILE

Proactive, uncompromising advocate of improving critical reading, writing, and thinking skills. Use creativity, flexibility, resourcefulness, and organizational and interpersonal skills to facilitate learning through positive, encouraging environment.

Strengths

"A page of history is worth a volume of logic." —Oliver Wendell Holmes

- Capable teacher thoroughly grounded in U.S., Middle Eastern, World, and European History.
- Rapport builder with parents (they think they're all alone out there), able to gain their positive involvement, trust, and respect in creating a participative environment.
- Adept, available, and adaptable classroom manager—combine discipline plan with effective procedures and varied lessons to attract the inattentive and enforce student accountability.
- Student motivator—can use cooperative learning, jigsaw, and other student-directed, process learning techniques to incorporate diverse students, foster a team spirit and inclusive group identity, and build teamwork and goal-setting skills.
- Develop useful daily lesson plans and instructional resources.
- Friendly, interactive, and dependable.
- Some fluency in Spanish (can read Spanish newspaper).

EDUCATION

B.A., History, Magna Cum Laude, December 2009
University of North Carolina at Asheville

Coursework

- U.S. History, Medieval Europe, Politics of the Middle East, Political Science, Chinese History (Revolutionary China), Afro-American History, Human Rights & International Politics, Humanities. Dean's List every eligible semester.

Student Teaching

"I teach skill in asking questions through my skill in asking the right question...."

- Charl High School, Spring and Fall 2009—rotating 11th-grade college-prep classes in U.S. History. Selected to teach AP U.S. History class due to knowledge of material.

  - Contributions included judging senior projects, proctoring end-of-course tests, and sponsoring the fledgling debate club.

  - Because my co-op supervisor was on the school improvement team, was able to observe planning and goal-setting functions in the effort to meet constantly changing requirements. Participated positively in parent-teacher conferences.

Honors & Affiliations

Cited by department faculty for original, critical thinking....

- Selected for Phi Alpha Theta History National Honor Society (high GPA and faculty recommendation).

- Selected by History Department faculty for the Moses Lowe History Scholarship as most promising student in the field of history, despite being on an education track.

- Participant, UNCA History Association.

- Alpha Phi Omega National Service Fraternity—Chapter President. As Vice President of Service, initiated projects involving Boys and Girls Clubs; fund raising for Ride for Kids 2008 (pediatric brain tumors); highway beautification; hunger food bank (packing); and RiverLife (river clean-up).

Career Change: *From boiler operator to teacher.*

RESUME 66, CONTINUED

gatehous@aol.com • (828) 555-7893 *home* • (828) 254-7893 *cell*   **BRYCE CARLSON**

Prior Education	**Diploma, Welding** (one-year program), 1987 Carolina Technical Community College Coursework in Anthropology, Biology, and Spanish, 1980 University of Massachusetts—Boston
PRIOR EXPERIENCE	BOILER OPERATOR: Crawford Plant Works, Summerville, NC—1987–2004 Operated steam- and electric-generating utility for largest textile mill of its kind in the world, on 10 acres, with its own waste-treatment and water-filtration system. Member of 2-man team: managed electrical control room, maintenance, welding, machinery repair, and pipefitting. ENGINEER: 100-foot *Lad In Blue* fishing boat, Gloucester, MA—1978–1987 MACHINIST MATE: United States Navy—1974–1978 Served on the U.S.S. *Georgetown* (spy ship—traveled to Mozambique Civil War; the Indian Ocean; and Havana, Cuba) and U.S.S. *Severn* (oil tanker refueling ships at sea in the Mediterranean). Trained Navy personnel (including firemen and 3rd class petty officers) to work with tools and operate equipment.
COMMUNITY REINVESTMENT	▪ Coached Roller Hockey for Boys and Girls Clubs, ages 13–18, in league competition. ▪ Tutor, Afterschool Club, Salvation Army. ▪ Big Brothers/Big Sisters, 1988–1990. Mentored 7-year-old boy (gardening, movies, sports, homework). ▪ Member of Church Inquiry Committee—answer questions to assist one in deciding whether to join the church; prepare lesson plans and curriculum for those interested in doing so.

Strategy: *Emphasize teaching and academic skills, adding quotes and a graphic to make the resume stand out. Briefly summarize experience on page 2 and add a strong community involvement section to show a trend of working with youth.*

JOHN BRYAN ATKINS

345 Evergreen Terrace
Milton Mills, NH 03852

jbatkins@aol.com

Home: (603) 222-9871
Mobile: (603) 393-7610

PROGRAM SPECIALIST

Dedicated to the development and education of all students

Highly skilled professional dedicated to making a positive impact on students' lives by creating an atmosphere conducive to learning. Cater to diverse modalities of learning to promote and enhance individual student strengths, instilling in youth a love of knowledge and the desire to meet and exceed expectations. Skilled use of positive reinforcement, communication, and problem solving to establish outstanding rapport with students. Exceptional team-builder and leader, creating a strong sense of community for students and staff.

- ☑ Progress Monitoring
- ☑ Classroom Management
- ☑ Curriculum Design & Development
- ☑ Visual & Tactile Learning Methods
- ☑ Individual Education Plans (IEPs)

- ☑ Budget Planning
- ☑ Student Motivation
- ☑ Parental Involvement
- ☑ Vocational Development
- ☑ Team-Building Techniques

QUALIFICATIONS

Bachelor of Science, Special Education
UNIVERSITY OF SOUTHERN MAINE

2010

Bachelor of Science, Vocational/Occupational Education
UNIVERSITY OF SOUTHERN MAINE

2008

EDUCATIONAL EXPERIENCE

GABE FOUNDATION SCHOOL—*Maine*

2003 to PRESENT

Program Specialist (Volunteer)

Report to Director of Special Education for this private school developing educational programs. Research and develop curriculum, write IEPs, attend meetings in accordance with IDEA, teach integrated curriculum, interact with school districts, and manage classrooms.

Program/Curriculum Development

- Initiated and implemented three educational programs for at-risk youth, actively engaging students and creating programs to satisfy the school's growing referral base.
- Independently developed curriculum for elk farming program, enabling students to run the day-to-day operation of the elk herd, including TB testing, worming, and cutting velvet.
- Taught an integrated curriculum in all content areas by adapting curriculum to accommodate vastly diverse functioning levels, and accelerating achievement of educational objectives.
- Expanded programs to serve more students and promote active learning; started programs on new sites by adding new themes on current sites, including aquaculture, scuba diving, and boat building.
- Researched and developed curriculum requirements, ensuring programs were within curriculum frameworks and state content standards and benchmarks.

Student Learning/Interaction

- Encourage student involvement in their local community by having students complete community project each year. This year's project involved building offices in a community center. Past projects have included developing a park, building a bandstand, and roofing town buildings.
- Collaborated with students in resolving fish and wildlife concerns about contamination of local fish populations with the importation of tilapia. After persisting for 2 years to resolve issues, students received permits to import and raise tilapia.
- Provided a more structured and intense program that increased student interest and learning in reading.
- Directed the foundation's Fertile Farm Program, providing tutoring for up to 14 students diagnosed with AD/HD, ADD, and Bipolar disorder.

Career Change: *From farmer/rancher to teacher.*

Strategy: *Focus on educational experiences related to a volunteer position he has held for several years.*

JOHN BRYAN ATKINS ▪ jbatkins@aol.com   **Page 2**

Educational Experience, Continued

Communication/Relationship Building
- Develop and maintain professional business relationships with district administrators to ensure adherence to IDEA by attending meetings and interacting with directors and superintendents in 7 school districts and 2 states.
- Collaborate with parents, fellow teachers, and school-based support team members to develop Individual Education Plans (IEPs), enabling all students to progress toward individual goals.

RIVERTON SCHOOL—*Maine*   1998 to 2003
Substitute Teacher—Special Education Aide
        Shop Teacher
- Substituted all grades K–8 in art, music, and gym, creating and implementing lessons in the absence of lesson plans or daily schedules to support student academic, social, and personal development.
- Provided tutoring to special-needs students to enhance student learning and understanding of subject matter. Ensured effective behavior management by incorporating motivational activities and positive reinforcement strategies.
- Instrumental in developing middle school woodworking shop program, creating educational activities to make learning enjoyable and exciting.

PROFESSIONAL EXPERIENCE

ATKINS ELK FARM—*Maine*   1983 to PRESENT
Business Owner/Manager
- Engage special-needs students in educational activities to make learning enjoyable and exciting; transport students to and from the elk farm, allowing them to interact with animals.
- Manage and execute all operational processes for 20-head elk farm, including managing aquaculture hatching and grow-out facility.
- Appointed as manager by the State of Maine to operate the abused farm animal facility, ensuring the proper care and well being of the animals.
- Astutely control all budget forecasting and management, performing statistical analysis relative to expense control, planning, and forecasting.

MAINE NAVAL SHIPYARD—*Maine*   1984 to 1994
Nuclear Crane Electrician/Chief Steward

CERTIFICATIONS

Vocational Special Needs
Vocational Electrical
Vocational Electrical/Electronics

PROFESSIONAL AFFILIATIONS

Member, North American Riding for the Handicapped Association (NARHA)
Member, Aircraft Owners & Pilots Association (AOPA)
Member, Civil Air Patrol (CAP)

REFERENCES AVAILABLE UPON REQUEST

Michael J. Butterworth

HIGH SCHOOL MATH TEACHER

Explaining Math in Plain English

*"I never thought I'd see the day when my son told me
how much he enjoyed Math. Thank you, Mr. Butterworth!"*
M.G., Parent, 2008

Enthusiastic, dedicated educator with a gift for teaching complex concepts using imaginative examples related to daily life. Ability to engage students' curiosity and develop their analytical skills through hands-on activities. Expertise with up-to-date instructional methodologies and educational technologies to spur student creativity and learning. Proficient in Mathematica, PowerTeacher, and MS Office.

HIGHLIGHTS OF QUALIFICATIONS

- Curriculum & Lesson Development
- Learning Styles
- Student Assessment
- Classroom & Behavior Management

- Motivational Program Design
- Instructional Strategies
- Educational Technology & Manipulatives
- Student-Parent Relations

EDUCATION

Master of Science Candidate in Mathematics, expected December 2010
UNIVERSITY OF CALIFORNIA, Los Angeles, CA

Professional Clear Single Subject Credential in Mathematics, 2008
NATIONAL UNIVERSITY, Sherman Oaks, CA

Bachelor of Arts in Mathematics, *summa cum laude,* 1994
STANFORD UNIVERSITY, Palo Alto, CA

STUDENT TEACHING

Redondo Shores High School
Redondo Beach, CA, 2007–2008
STUDENT MATH TEACHER, Eighth Through Tenth Grade

Developed curricula to meet California Standards and Frameworks, taught lessons, and graded assignments for 30+ students. Taught Algebra, Geometry, and Trigonometry.

- Engaged and motivated students by using demonstrations and group projects that applied math concepts learned in class.
- Evaluated student progress and assigned remedial activities based on individual need.
- Involved parents in their children's education through parent-teacher conferences.

---

498 S. Pacific Coast Highway • Redondo Beach, CA 90277 • mbflyer@gmail.com • (310) 555-5555

Career Change: *From technical writer to teacher.*

Strategy: *Devote all of page 1 to skills, knowledge, and experience related to teaching and place past work history on page 2.*

mbflyer@gmail.com
(310) 555-5555

MICHAEL J. BUTTERWORTH
Page 2

———————————— PROFESSIONAL EXPERIENCE ————————————

Ultimate Motorcycling Magazine (formerly Robb Report), Malibu, CA

STAFF WRITER, 2004–2007

Toyota Motor Sales, U.S.A., Inc., Torrance, CA

SENIOR TECHNICAL WRITER/EDITOR, 1997–2004
PRODUCT QUALITY ANALYST, 1994–1997

———————————— HONORS & AFFILIATIONS ————————————

Member of South Bay Toastmasters, Torrance, CA, 2002–Present

Member of Experimental Aircraft Association, 1995–Present

Recipient of Young Eagles Horizon Award by Experimental Aircraft Association in 2006 for significant contributions to the overall success of the Young Eagles program. Introduced 204 children to general aviation by providing introductory airplane rides.

RESUME 69: BY BONNIE KURKA, CPRW, JCTC, FJST

Julia Flowers

15204 Caribou Road ◇ Staunton, Virginia 22587 ◇ 540.487.9586

*"Enhancing learning and providing an extraordinary environment
for students to recognize their full potential"*

Summary of Qualifications

Enthusiastic, dedicated, and adaptable; willing to experiment and adjust plans to the situation. Love to learn and make a difference in children's lives. Adept at finding root of problem and trying many options to help children reach potential.

Core Strengths

Problem-solving skills	Communication skills—verbal and written
Curriculum development	Community outreach and relations
Higher-level critical-thinking skills	Cultural diversity awareness

Education

- Accepted into **Master of Education** program, Radford University, Summer 2009
- **Initial Teacher Licensure Program,** Maryland University, College Park, Maryland, 2008
- **Bachelor of Arts,** History, College of William and Mary, Williamsburg, Virginia, 1997
- **Associate of Arts,** Education, Northern Virginia Community College, Fairfax, Virginia, 1994

Professional Experience

Yorktown Elementary, Richmond, Virginia, April–June 2008
Student Teacher

Taught 1st grade. Observed children for clues as to their needs and learning styles; adapted teaching methods to accommodate their needs. Identified a struggling reader and after consulting with parent, issued personal challenge for student. The child met challenge over summer and is doing well in 2nd grade this year.

- Parents related positive feedback from children.
- Received *A* for course.

Hecht's Department Stores, Fairfax, Virginia
Customer Service Representative 2004–Present
Personnel Manager 1999–2004
Cash Office Supervisor 1997–1999

Began in cash office; promoted to Personnel Manager; requested step-down to customer service position while completing education degree.

Extensive experience in **training, customer service,** and **management.** Good rapport with team members. Exceptional interpersonal skills. Use active listening, paraphrase problem to customer, remain calm, and provide options to resolve customer complaints and other issues. Interviewed and hired staff; recruited seasonal hires. Conducted three-hour new-employee training orientation. Encouraged questions and feedback from new hires. Practiced open-door policy.

- Instrumental in helping customer service desk receive rare score of 100 in internal audit.
- Received various awards and positive comments from customers.
- Developed creative merchandising methods; received positive comments from regional manager.

Career Change: *From retail salesperson and manager to teacher.*

Strategy: *Carefully match qualifications with the mission statement of the school district. Focus on her relevant people skills, customer service experience, and management and training background.*

STEPHANIE MCCALL

Page 1 of 2

8 Monahan Avenue ▪ Staten Island, NY 10308 ▪ Home: (718) 209-1129 ▪ Cellular: (646) 692-2298

FOCUS AND QUALIFICATIONS

FOCUS: Career in college or university environment teaching graduate and undergraduate students. Qualified to teach Criminal Justice, Political Science, Urban Affairs, History, and Public Administration.

QUALIFICATIONS: NYPD Sergeant with experience teaching graduate-level Criminal Justice and Public Administration courses at Baruch College, New York. Exemplary 20-year NYPD record, holding multiple awards. Talented instructor with New York State Police Instructor Certification (MOI) and a 10-year record of cross-level police instruction. Recognized by NYPD and educational institutions for outstanding academic performance, instructional skills, and community contributions. Extensive exposure to multicultural environments. Bilingual (English-German) with conversational skills in Spanish. Master's degree in Political Science.

EDUCATION, TRAINING, AND CERTIFICATION

- **MASTER OF ARTS DEGREE—2009**
  Major: **Political Science**
  Baruch College—New York, NY
  Graduated magna cum laude; G.P.A.: 3.90
  Recipient of Herbert Bienstock Research Award

- **BACHELOR OF SCIENCE DEGREE—2002**
  Major: **History**
  The College of Staten Island—Staten Island, NY
  Graduated magna cum laude—G.P.A.: 3.89

- **CERTIFIED SIMMUNITION TRAINING AND SAFETY SUPERVISOR—2008**
  Simmunition Division SNC Technologies, Inc.
  New York, NY

- **CERTIFIED VERBAL JUDO INSTRUCTOR—2003**
  Verbal Judo Institute—New York, NY

- **METHODS OF INSTRUCTION—1999**
  Division of Criminal Justice—New York State

PROFESSIONAL EXPERIENCE

TEACHING/INSTRUCTING

Solid 10 years of experience instructing recruits, in-service Police Officers, Sergeants, Lieutenants, and Captains. Selected in 2000 by Professor of Criminal Justice and Public Administration at Baruch College to serve as substitute lecturer while working toward master's degree. Average class size comprised 20 to 35 graduate and undergraduate students. Authored lesson plans, selected textbook readings, and assigned and graded homework. Received highly positive student feedback regarding methodology, professionalism, and personality.

- Authoring lesson plans for INTAC (In-Service Tactical Training Unit)—scenario-based training in a "live-fire" environment to reinforce proper tactics and firearms restraint to minimize escalation of incidents. Result: Sharp decline in shooting incidents since program's inception in 2003.
- Instructing NYPD Counter-Terrorism Program for INTAC Unit, teaching up to 30 people at a time.
- Transforming inexperienced recruits into street-ready Police Officers as Police Science Instructor, preparing recruits for NYPD career through familiarization with police administration and legal procedures.

Continued..

Career Change: From police officer to teacher.

STEPHANIE MCCALL

Page 2 of 2

Home: (718) 209-1129

- Using outstanding classroom management skills and an interactive, animated teaching style, generated high level of student enthusiasm.
- Applying advanced communication and foreign-language skills to effectively interact with cross-cultural college students and international communities in New York City.

LAW ENFORCEMENT

Broad and successful background as Sergeant and Police Instructor. Challenged to patrol and supervise high-crime precincts, relying heavily on superior listening, communication, and negotiation skills to thwart potentially harmful incidents. Strongly committed to well-being of all parties involved.

- Special training in OSHA and hazmat regulations, suicide awareness.
- Consistent performance reviews ranking 4.5 to 5 out of 5 for excellence and professionalism.

CHRONOLOGY

Baruch College, New York, NY   2008 to 2010
Substitute Lecturer in Criminal Justice and Public Administration

New York Police Department (NYPD)   1990 to 2010
Retired March 2010

- INTAC Supervisor—In-Service Tactical Training Unit, Brooklyn/Queens   2003 to 2010
- Borough-based Training—Uniformed In-Service, Brooklyn   2001
- Recruit Instructor, Police Science—Police Academy, Manhattan   1999 to 2001
- Sergeant, Patrol Supervisor, and Desk Sergeant—Queens   1996 to 1999
- Police Officer—Brooklyn North   1990 to 1996

AWARDS AND HONORS

- **Education Achievement Citation**—NYPD, NY—2009
  Awarded for successfully balancing full-time work and six years of education.
- **Perfect Attendance Recognition Certificate**—NYPD, NY—2007
- **Herbert Bienstock Research Award**—Baruch College, New York, NY—2006
- **Greenpoint Community Service Award**—Greenpoint, NY—1995
  Awarded by community in recognition of effective volunteer youth efforts.
- **Commended for investigatory skills leading to homicide confession**—NYPD, NY—1994
- **EPD—Medal** (Excellent Police Duty)—NYPD, NY—1991
  Awarded for verbally disarming mentally disturbed person armed with knife.

Strategy: *Focus on her relevant teaching/training experience in her full-time job. Feature education prominently because it is recent and gives her an essential qualification for teaching at the college level.*

Curriculum Vitae

Martin R. Kronfeld, B.A., M.S. (Statistics), M.B.A., PMP

2020 Northbeach Circle, Jefferson, Illinois 64100
mkr10000@jefflink.net ■ 630.765.5985

WHAT I OFFER **NORTON COMMUNITY COLLEGE** AS YOUR NEWEST INSTRUCTOR IN INFORMATION SCIENCES

- **Passion** to lead students to *want* to excel

- **Dedication** to help build interdisciplinary curricula

- **Skill** to "build in" quality measures my students and I use every day to maximize learning

- **Flexibility** to tailor media selection and teaching style to individual learners — on the fly, if necessary

- **Commitment** to continuing self-development so that what I teach has lasting value

- **Subject-matter expertise** to make courses "come alive" in the classroom

EDUCATION:

- M.B.A., University of Concord, Concord, Illinois   1998
  Earned this degree while working 40 hours a week. Funded by my employer. GPA 3.84.

- M.S., Statistics, Carlton Tech, Smithson, Illinois   1985
  Paid my own way. GPA 3.20.

- B.A., Psychology, Martin College, Shenleyville, South Carolina   1982

RECENT AND RELEVANT WORK HISTORY WITH SELECTED EXAMPLES OF SUCCESS AS AN EDUCATOR:

- Owner and **Practicing IT Consultant,** Kronsight Consulting, Jefferson, IL   2006–Present

  My company specializes in subcontract work touching on IT solutions for the telecommunications and e-mail industries. Companies engage me to analyze not only their business systems, but the data that underlies the information they need to prosper.

  EDUCATING TO EQUIP PEOPLE TO HANDLE PROBLEMS NOW AND IN THE FUTURE

  Completed a comprehensive "needs analysis" for a company that had to master new concepts to help it grow. Not only educated demanding, well-informed senior leadership, but gave their team members the skills they needed to educate their customers as well. *Outcomes:* Client's customer base grew significantly.

Career Change: *From IT consultant to college instructor.*

Strategy: *Show his performance as a teacher rather than from an IT perspective. An integral part of the strategy was a cover letter closely attuned to the needs of his target employer.*

Curriculum Vitæ (continued)

| Martin R. Kronfeld | **Instructor in Information Sciences** | 630.765.5985 |

■ *Hired away by the General Manager to be* **Senior Consulting Engineer,** Arista Technologies, Centerville, IL   2002 to 2008

This firm manufactured a line of high-speed data communications products. With sales approaching $200M, it served customers worldwide.

Served as a reporting official for five senior software and consulting engineers.

USING NEEDS ANALYSIS AS A FOUNDATION FOR LEARNING AND GROWTH

Transformed a group of well-intentioned strangers into a "learning machine" that got the answers to vital questions efficiently and effectively. Our customers and our engineers had "talked past each other" for 18 months when management called me in to troubleshoot. Used seminar techniques to help team members develop a clear vision of what they needed to learn to work together and value the process. *Outcomes:* Excellent solution in just six months.

■ **Director, Network Systems & Protocols,** Kronos Corp., Centerville, IL   2000 to 2002

This small, regional company provided data communications consulting.

Served as a reporting official for four programmers.

USING TECHNICAL SUBJECT MATTER EXPERTISE TO TEACH EFFECTIVE OUTCOMES

Gently guided a customer whose business model contained a faulty assumption. Did my homework to master the appropriate technologies and then asked the right questions of the right people. Using what we learned, I helped the customer develop a new business model. My instruction led him to adopt my suggestions as his own good ideas. *Outcomes:* Company had greater confidence in where to invest scarce resources and had trusted ways to estimate return on investment.

■ *Hired away by the Director to serve as* **Advisory Programmer,** Prodigy Services Company, White Plains, NY   1995 to 2000

PROVIDING DURABLE INSTRUCTION TO HELP LEARNERS BEYOND THE "CLASSROOM"

Showed a customer how to attack a complex problem—getting the most from three incompatible systems—in a consistent, logical fashion. Quickly found the native strengths of each team member; then used those strengths as a basis for mentoring. By documenting our approach, I built the "lesson plans" the company would later use to educate new employees. *Outcomes:* Went beyond solving the problem at hand to show employees how rigorous inquiry leads to excellence now and in the future.

■ Additional experience as a private consultant and **principal member of technical staffs** in software and network development groups for Unimation, Inc., and ITT.

Curriculum Vitæ (continued)

Martin R. Kronfeld　　　**Instructor in Information Sciences**　　　630.765.5985

CERTIFICATION:

- Project Management Professional, Project Management Institute　　　2009

COMPUTER LITERACY:

- **Networks and operating systems:**

    Expert: UNIX, Solaris, ESCON, Ethernet, and Giga-bit Ethernet

    Proficient: Windows 7/Server 2008/NT/Vista/XP/2000, MVS, VM, DB 2, Linux SCSI, Fibre Channel, FICON, ATM, T1/E1, SONET, and ISDN

- **Programming languages:**

    Expert: C and SNMP
    Proficient: C++, MASM, Java, XML, MFC, WMI, SQL, CICS, and HTML
    Working knowledge: .NET, COM, IMS, IDMS, VTAM, PL/1, COBOL, CICS EXEC, Assembler, and ASP

- **Middleware:**

    Proficient: IBM MQ (Websphere)
    Working knowledge: TIBCO Rendezvous and MSMQ

- **Embedded systems development:**

    Proficient: CE and NT, RTX, C-EXEC, and VRTX
    Working knowledge: P-SOS

- **Protocols:**

    Expert: TCP/IP (sockets)
    Proficient: RS232 and RS422
    Working knowledge: NetBIOS, Novell IPX/SPX, ISO, and SS7

- **Wireless data protocols:**

    Working knowledge: GPRS, GSM, CDMA, TDMA, WAP, ANSI-41, and IS-2000

- **Other:**

    Expert: Network device drivers and hardware support
    Proficient: Object-oriented design and programming (OOD/OOP), LAN/WAN installation and management, data networking protocols, telecommunications equipment ISO-9000, and computer-based project management

MEMBERSHIP IN PROFESSIONAL ORGANIZATION:

- Member, Project Management Institute　　　Since 2009

Page 3 of 3

JOHN P. DALTON

897 Airborne Inn, Room 432
Fort Bragg, North Carolina 28314

(910) 958-8656
jdalton@cox.net

University Program Director / Advisor / Training & Development Leader
Strategist and Management Leader—Greek Life Director—Related University Roles

Strong management experience in a wide variety of roles within multiple high-pressure settings with skills that can be utilized to positively add value to programs/processes at the university administration level. Skill base summary includes but is not limited to the following:

- *Program Development/Facilitation*
- *Training Development*
- *Team Leadership*
- *Materials/Facility Management*

- *Operations Management*
- *Teaching, Mentoring, and Motivation*
- *Multi-Task Project Management*
- *Budget Management*

Education / Awards

NORTH CAROLINA STATE UNIVERSITY
Raleigh, NC
BS in Political Science, May 2002
- *ROTC Scholarship Winner*
- *Distinguished Military Graduate*
- *Who's Who Among Students in American Universities*
- *Inter-Fraternity*
- *Kappa Alpha Order, President*
- *Student Government Association*

UNIVERSITY OF GEORGIA
Athens, GA
- *Pursued MA in Counseling/Student Personnel Administration (2000–2003)*
- *Assistantship/Graduate Advisor, Men's Fraternities*

UNITED STATES ARMY/NATIONAL GUARD

Security Clearance
- *Top Secret Security Clearance*

Recognition
- *5 Army Commendation Medals—Operation Enduring Freedom*
- *Army Achievement Medal*
- *The National Defense Medal*
- *The Southwest Asia Service Medal*
- *Army Service Medal*
- *Airborne/Air Assault Schools, Maintenance Officer Course*
- *Officer Basic Leadership Course*

Summary of Qualifications

- Proven track record working with all levels of personnel and on projects in materials management, inventory control, shipping, logistics, and multiple distribution areas as well as highly disciplined military training through the U.S. Army, U.S. Army Reserves, and National Guard.
- Regarded by industry peers as a fair, knowledgeable, consistent, and trustworthy leader who strives for a high level of quality while meeting and exceeding quantity objectives.
- Excellent verbal and written communication skills; able to organize and present training or other materials to a group.
- Reputation as a team player and achiever who applies leadership skills to advanced managerial tasks.
- Team-based leadership philosophy and supervisory style; proven ability to successfully direct the integration of cross-functional teams, internal departments, and personnel to build organizations, develop ongoing training programs, and execute on-campus organizational plans.

Career Change: *From military officer to university administrator.*

Strategy: *Emphasize direct experience from positions in the military; emphasize advanced education.*

JOHN P. DALTON

jdalton@cox.net

Professional Experience

UNITED STATES ARMY, Fort Bragg, NC
Plans & Operation Officer, United States Army Special Forces Command (Airborne) (12/2007–Present)

> From Recent Evaluations: *CPT Dalton is one of the best Captains I have served with in my 18 years of service...CPT Dalton has been my point man on my staff for Special Forces operations in Afghanistan, Uzbekistan, and Kuwait in support of Operation Enduring Freedom.*

- Position has included short international tours in addition to mission-critical responsibilities in support of Operation Enduring Freedom and PENTCOM AOR.
- Serve as National Guard Advisor—Plans and Operations Officer, Army National Guard at the U.S. Army Special Forces Command at Fort Bragg, NC. This critical coordination and high-profile position reports directly to senior/general staff and coordinates directly with the theater Special Operations Command, The National Guard Bureau, and others for planning and execution of exercises and major regional contingents.
- Selected key projects have included planning and operational support for the deployment of 1,600 Special Forces National Guard Personnel.
- Total responsibility for planning, supervising, and coordinating all actions for all Special Forces soldiers within the 79th and 89th Special Forces Group/Airborne Worldwide.
- Analyze and ensure logistics, strategic plans, training, and operational issues are coordinated and supported by the appropriate organization and resources.

CREE RESEARCH, Research Triangle Park, NC
Production Manager (6/2004–11/2007)
- In production management role, maintained readiness in a high-level, high-intensity production environment; responsibilities included setting, training, and enforcing quality standards within department.
- Supervised the production of chicken per production and safety specifications/standards.
- Provided daily scheduling and supervision of production employees; oversaw changing and proper functionality of production-line parts and materials.

PLANNING PARTNERS, Athens, GA
Sales Representative (6/2002–6/2004)
- Executed strategic marketing and sales plans; effectively utilized high levels of customer contact to drive sales and direct customer accountability as well as indirect through their sales managers and sales representatives.
- Managed existing customer relationships and developed new customer relationships in existing and new markets.
- Provided sales forecasts in company's regions and closely monitored the attainment of the goals under its management.
- Developed tactical plans to ensure attainment of sales and profit goals for company's customers and regions; attained gross margin and expense budget objectives to ensure that the budgeted profit was attained.

CHAPTER 9

Resumes for Career Changers Seeking Sports and Recreation, Cultural, and Creative and Performing Arts Positions

Many of the resumes in this chapter were written for people who wanted to make their avocation their vocation. Because these candidates are so passionate about their fields, they often have relevant (although perhaps unpaid) experience that they can highlight. You will also see some examples of personal statements and vision statements that convey the intangible yet important qualities that make these positions a great fit. The career transitions represented in this chapter include the following:

- Warehouse manager to sports/recreation director

- College teacher to manager of recreation programs in the hospitality industry

- Salesperson to professional sport fisher

- Military operations to fitness trainer

- Press-relations manager to wine and food promoter

- Telecommunications operator to broadcasting professional

- Landscaper to audio/video production assistant

- Fuels specialist in the military to film production apprentice

- College professor to interior designer

- Intelligence analyst in the U.S. military to architectural designer

- Attorney to cultural arts director

RODNEY ALLEN

213 Ashburn Farm Drive ♦ Ashburn, VA 20147
(703) 555-9576 ♦ sportsmanager@earthlink.net

GOAL

To advance 18+ years of management experience and an educational background in Recreation Administration and Intramural Sports into the career arena of sports administration, recreation programming, or facilities management.

♦ Senior manager offering extensive experience in purchasing and materials management; personnel training and supervision; and organizational development in both start-up and high-growth operations.

♦ Proven leadership and interpersonal skills; flexible in working with people of all ages and socioeconomic backgrounds.

♦ Performance-focused, intuitive coach; astute in recognizing individuals' strengths and assigning the right person for the right job.

♦ Highly effective in managing multiple priorities, with a propensity for minimizing problems through effective daily planning and scheduling.

♦ Noted by customers, management, and staff as ethical, intelligent, and hardworking.

♦ Committed to personal lifelong learning and creating opportunities for individuals and teams to attain desired goals.

EDUCATION

Master of Intramural Sports and Recreation—Miami University, Oxford, OH
Bachelor of Arts, Recreation Administration—University of Maryland, College Park, MD

PROFESSIONAL RECORD

INDEPENDENT GLASS DISTRIBUTORS, Alexandria, VA   2003–present
(A full-service wholesale distributor of current-model and vintage automotive replacement glass)

Facility Manager
Recruited to launch and manage a Baltimore-area start-up operation. Tasked with personnel recruitment, inventory stocking, and operations policy development. Oversee the day-to-day operation of an 18,500-sq.-ft. warehouse with annual gross sales of $2.5M. Direct the daily activities of a cross-functional team of sales representatives, warehouse workers, and delivery drivers servicing 75 customer accounts. Orchestrate long-range planning for operations, sales, and customer service.

♦ Established a formal materials management function to gain control of inventory and ensure purchasing of the best products at the most reasonable cost.

♦ Built and maintain a diverse and loyal customer base in a price-conscious, competitive consumer-products industry.

♦ Captured first-place standing for company-wide gross annual sales by strategically planning and executing targeted market development, maintaining comprehensive and up-to-date inventory, and enforcing dependable delivery schedules.

♦ Reduced employee turnover and improved morale and productivity by initiating flexible work schedules and pay for performance, and by providing access to the best tools and resources available.

Career Change: *From warehouse manager to sports/recreation director.*

Strategy: *Highlight relevant degree along with transferable skills pulled from his unrelated experience as manager of warehouse operations.*

RODNEY ALLEN

(703) 555-9576 ♦ SPORTSMANAGER@EARTHLINK.NET

PAGE 2

PROFESSIONAL RECORD (continued)

SATELLITE GLASS, Bethesda, MD   1991–2003
  (An automotive glass retail installation company with 12 branches and an inventory warehouse)

Warehouse Manager

Managed a 15,000-sq.-ft. warehousing and distribution operation during a period of accelerated industry growth, locally and nationwide. Responsible for the purchasing, receipt, and subsequent distribution of more than $2M merchandise annually.

- Focused efforts on identifying quality suppliers, reducing net purchasing costs, and managing inventory volumes while maintaining adequate and current stock to keep pace with new model releases and changing customer needs.
- Maintained strong vendor and customer relations while responding to numerous demands and shifts in work priorities.
- Established daily service goals; scheduled and dispatched drivers to ensure on-time delivery.
- Developed and delivered a safety management and training program for warehouse personnel.

Prior Experience   1988–1990

Managed the intramural sports program for GMI Engineering and Management Institute, Flint, MI. Staffed and serviced a six-lane bowling alley; purchased and maintained all crib sporting equipment.

COMMUNITY INVOLVEMENT

ALEXANDRIA YOUTH ATHLETIC ASSOCIATION   2004–present

Youth Soccer Coach

Coach a team of youth, ages ten and under, developing and enhancing their individual and team skills and game strategies.

- Instrumental in drafting and implementing a Coaches Code of Conduct, which defines responsibilities and expectations for volunteer coaches and their interactions with players, parents, and other coaches.
- Plan and facilitate regular meetings to encourage parental involvement with the association and support of the Spectator Code of Conduct.

MIA ANDERSON

10/115 Constantine Avenue, Aspley Qld 4034 ♦ (04) 0233 3444 ♦ (07) 8888 9999 ♦ manderson@beonline.com

CAREER FOCUS

Hospitality Management…Recreation
Dynamic, results-driven manager seeking to capitalize on more than 9 years of sports and recreation experience utilizing exceptional leadership, customer relations, and sales and marketing skills.

"Mia has a deserved reputation as a positive leader who is skilled in leading teams to success in achieving organizational goals." (Current Employer)

PROFESSIONAL EXPERIENCE

Management and Administration
▶ Strategically planned, coordinated, and delivered multi-site sports and recreation training programs.
▶ Led team of 15 to achieve optimum results; hired, trained, motivated, and managed performance of staff.
▶ Oversaw development of effective policy and procedures for new department; implemented by deadline.
▶ Managed departmental budgets; consistently delivered initiatives on time and within budget.

Sales and Marketing
▶ Developed and implemented diverse range of innovative and highly customer-focused programs.
▶ Marketed services using cost-effective strategies; designed all advertising and promotional material.
▶ Coordinated events for 450+ people; secured nationally recognized guests and local media coverage.
▶ Delivered presentations to potential customers; displayed strong public speaking and networking skills.

Interpersonal and Communication
▶ Actively fostered relationships with existing and potential customers in industry and the wider community.
▶ Provided quick resolution to customer complaints; delivered win-win solutions and personalized service.
▶ Cultivated positive "can-do" spirit and culture of participation among diverse customers and staff.
▶ Multilingual; possess written and verbal fluency in English, Spanish, and Italian.

CAREER HIGHLIGHTS

♦ Built number of program participants from zero to 250 during initial 12 months; numbers now exceed 350 and still growing quarterly.
♦ Initiated quality improvement program for department; selected as winner of 2009 "Outstanding Individual Award" for contributions to continuous improvement.
♦ Secured senior management approval for numerous sports and recreation training programs; earned reputation for implementing "the right ideas at the right time."
♦ Set up, from scratch, two new fitness centers, including designing layout, ordering equipment, and training staff.
♦ Oversaw design and construction of new sports facilities for tennis, squash, and football.

EDUCATION & TRAINING

▶ **Certificate in Business Studies (Hospitality Management),** Cairns Technical College, Cairns, 2009
▶ **Bachelor of Applied Science (Human Movement),** University of Northern Queensland, Cairns, 2000
▶ **Advanced Open Water Diver and Rescue Diver,** Professional Association of Diving Instructors, Cairns
▶ **High Ropes Course Instructor,** YWCA, Townsville

EMPLOYMENT HISTORY

Manager (Sports, Recreation, and Fitness), Allanstown Private College, Allanstown, 2007–Current
Coordinator (Sports), North Sutherland Girls' School, North Sutherland, 2005–2007
Secondary Teacher (Sports), Sunshine Coast Girls' School, Buderim, 2001–2004

Career Change: *From college teacher to manager of recreation programs in the hospitality industry.*

Strategy: *Minimize references to teaching and play up ability to develop and implement sports and recreation programs, manage staff and budgets, develop sales and marketing strategies, and provide an exceptional level of customer service.*

BRENDON J. WALKER
AWARD-WINNING BASS FISHER

213 W. Belcrest ▶ Kewanee, IL 61614 ▶ (309) 852-0714 ▶ bassfish@aol.com

VISION STATEMENT

To utilize my professional sales and high-profile competition experience in effectively creating greater market exposure for my sponsors and their products / services; to provide vital sponsor support in penetrating new markets and expanding existing accounts; and to effectively use my sponsorships to catapult my professional competitor success to higher levels.

QUALIFICATIONS SUMMARY

Highly accomplished and enthusiastic professional bass fisher and sales professional with a proven track record of winning top-level competitions and increasing revenues by effectively promoting products. Polished communication, presentation, networking, and problem-solving skills; able to relate comfortably and effectively to people at all levels and develop long-term, professional, trusting relationships for repeat and referral business.

RECENT COMPETITIONS & AWARDS

CHAMPIONSHIP COMPETITION / CROSS LAKE—Shreveport, LA (September 11, 2009)
Placed 13th / Won $2,000

- ▶ **Placed 2nd / Won $20,000:** LAKE CHAMPLAIN—Plattsburgh, NY (July 19, 2009)
- ▶ **Placed 39th / Won $600:** LAKE WHEELER—Rogersville, AL (February 15, 2009)
- ▶ **Placed 50th / Won $500:** LAKE OUACHITA—Mt. Ida, AR (March 15, 2009)
- ▶ **Placed 64th / Won $400:** LAKE OKEECHOBEE—Clewiston, FL (January 23, 2009)
- ▶ **Placed 101st:** BEAVER LAKE—Rogers, AR (April 17, 2009)

PROFESSIONAL EMPLOYMENT

NORTHWEST WOOD PRODUCTS—Jefferson, IL   2001 to Present
Fast-track promotion through the following positions:

Sales Representative (2008 to Present): Recruited to promote a wide range of company fencing and deck products for the largest cedar fence and deck company in the state. Manage advertising, create flyers, directly pursue leads, utilize aggressive follow-up methods, design estimates, secure proposals, schedule jobs, and provide customer service.
- ▶ Successfully sold $600,000 of cedar fencing within a 6-month period.
- ▶ Recognized as 1 of the company's top 3 sales representatives.

Supervisor (2002 to 2008): Directed, hired, trained, mentored, and motivated a staff of up to 4 workers in managing all aspects of fence installations for residential and commercial clients. Tracked footage installed weekly. Served as the central point of contact and client liaison in providing information and resolving issues at all levels.
- ▶ Reputation for providing excellent quality work with 100% of the jobs requiring no follow-up or additional repair.
- ▶ Routinely installed a record amount of fence footage weekly.
- ▶ Started as an installer and quickly was promoted to supervisory position.

RUSTIC PINES COMPANY—Madison Heights, IL   1996 to 2001

Foreman: Oversaw fence installations and supervised / trained crew members.
- ▶ Promoted from general laborer to foreman due to skill level and dedication.

EDUCATION AND TRAINING

Diploma, VICTOR J. MADISON HIGH SCHOOL—Fairview, IL

Career Change: *From salesperson to professional sport fisher.*

Strategy: *Emphasize related experience and accomplishments from unpaid experience and part-time positions to support his goal of securing sponsorships and assuming a professional career in sport fishing.*

Fred Adams
316 Old Milford Road
Milford, KS 66514
Home: 785-237-1548
Work: 785-235-7200
adamsf@hotmail.com

OBJECTIVE	Position as a physical fitness trainer helping others to improve their personal well-being, health, and physical fitness.
SUMMARY OF QUALIFICATIONS	**Fitness Trainer Certification—International Sports Sciences Association.** Well-conditioned athlete who has followed a rigorous personal fitness program for the past 15 years. Interviewed individuals to determine their interests in improving their physical condition. Helped others to develop personalized programs suited for their needs. Used diet planning, conditioning, aerobics, anaerobics, and supplemental programs. Familiar with various types of weight conditioning equipment.
FITNESS AWARDS	• 1st Place in Body Building, Lightweight Classification, Camp Red Cloud, South Korea • Top 10, All-Services Fitness Competition, Osan, Korea • Lightweight Wrestling Champion (3 years), Fort Hood, TX • Army Physical Fitness Testing: minimum scores of 290 (out of 300) on all tests
INTERVIEWING	Met with prospective clients and discussed their interests in improving their physical condition. Secured information regarding their medical history, current state of physical conditioning, family medical history, and eating and sleeping habits. Also determined whether they were taking any medications that might have an adverse effect on training. Ascertained the extent of their commitment to goals for self-improvement.
DIET PLANNING	Asked individuals their personal likes and dislikes for beverages and food. Determined whether they had any particular adverse reactions to food and beverages. Identified their eating habits, schedules, and current weight. Established individualized goals for weight loss or gain. Created unique dietary plans that coincided with their training plans. Periodically checked their progress and altered plans as necessary.
CONDITIONING	Mapped out plans for phase training from beginning to advanced levels. Combined weight training with aerobics and anaerobics. Selected the right machines to develop each individual's program and conducted training in their proper use. Established cycle training with free weights and time schedules for aerobics combined with rest cycles. Also looked for long-term schedule changes concerning progress and relapse.

Career Change: *From military operations to fitness trainer.*

Strategy: *Use brief anecdotes to describe experiences that perfectly match the role he is seeking— even though these were secondary to his full-time job in the military.*

Fred Adams • adamsf@hotmail.com   Page 2

SUPPLEMENTAL PROGRAMS	Developed programs and time schedules for vitamin intake and liquid supplements. Determined current status of each client before beginning planning for personal intake. Scheduled vitamin intakes and liquids to complement each training phase. Recommended general and specific content levels for each vitamin and liquid. Closely monitored each individual's attitudes, habits, and physical reactions.
CPR/FIRST AID AND SAFETY	Trained and certified in CPR and first aid. Attended basic health, safety, and physical fitness courses. Trained others how to make triage decisions for evacuation and treatment of personnel. Also taught the proper use of various types of weight training and aerobic equipment.
INTERPERSONAL SKILLS	Effectively communicated with people, demonstrating skill in assisting individuals to identify personal and professional goals. Quickly and easily adjusted to policies of many different supervisors of mixed racial, cultural, religious, and geographical backgrounds. Work well on my own with little or no supervision or as an effective member of a team. Seek added responsibility whenever possible. Frequently called upon by my superiors for special projects because they had the confidence in my ability to complete these projects correctly and on time.

EMPLOYMENT HISTORY

- Physical Fitness Trainer, U.S. Army, Fort Hood, TX, and Fort Riley, KS, January 2006–December 2009
- Chemical Operations Supervisor, U.S. Army, Camp Red Cloud, South Korea, and Fort Hood, TX, January 2002–December 2005
- Chemical Operations Specialist, U.S. Army, Fort Bragg, NC, April 1999–December 2001
- Dental Assistant, U.S. Army, Fort Carson, CO, and Heidelberg, Germany, September 1994–December 1998

EDUCATION

- Certificate, Fitness Trainer, International Sports Sciences Association, Santa Barbara, CA, 2007
- Honor Graduate, Chemical Operations Specialist Course, 13 weeks, U.S. Army, Fort McClellan, AL, 1999
- Commandant's List, Primary Leadership Development Course, 4 weeks, U.S. Army, Fort Bragg, NC, 2001
- Diploma, Washington-Jefferson High School, Atlanta, GA, 1994

CHERI R. PIERRE

1434 Madison Boulevard
Orlando, FL 38917

pierre2010@aol.com

Residence: 954-555-1212
Mobile: 954-555-1111

CAREER OBJECTIVE & SUMMARY

Passionate epicure seeking to transition to a career dedicated to the appreciation and promotion of wine and food. Particular interest and experience in the regional culinary and wine traditions of France. Able to write and speak expressively about the aesthetics that emerge at the nexus of wine, food, and culture.

Competencies in writing, editing, public relations, communications, management, strategy development, and marketing. Broad range of skills honed during a fast-track, 10-year public relations / communications career at industry-leading firms in the U.S. and France. Talented evangelist for products and concepts.

- **Lived, Traveled, and Worked in France / Toured 50+ French Vineyards / Fluent French Speaker.**
- **Earned a Diploma at Ecole Ritz Escoffier, School of French Gastronomy, Paris, France.**
- **Authored Article: "From the Heart of France: The Undiscovered Culinary Traditions of Auvergne."**
- **Studied Principles of Vinification, Appellation, Winetasting, and Wine Serving.**
- **Completed Coursework in Food Writing, Wines of France, and Wines of Bordeaux.**

TRANSFERABLE SKILL SET & SELECTED ACHIEVEMENTS

Writing—Wrote bylined magazine and newspaper articles, press releases, proposals, and presentations.

Editing—Established and maintained high standards for all written materials.

Public Relations & Communications—Achieved positive press coverage in top media in the U.S., the U.K., and France, including the *Wall Street Journal* and the *New York Times*.

Relationship Building—Gained access to and forged positive relationships with influential industry players.

Management—Coordinated and directed international teams to achieve consistent messaging.

Marketing—Strategy Development, Positioning, Branding, Promotion—Successfully managed a multimillion-dollar corporate positioning program for Big Four accounting firm and drove corporate image-building within the upper echelons of a Top-40 French company.

Events Management—Designed a seminar on new media attended by 300 people, including CEOs of top media companies and 30 key journalists.

PROFESSIONAL EXPERIENCE

SANTETECHNOLOGIE, Paris, France
Multibillion-dollar medical software company. One of the top 40 companies in France.

Senior Manager, International Press Relations (2006–2009)

Managed business and trade press relations with U.S., U.K., and English-speaking media in Paris. Directed international media activities. Provided strategy-development consulting to senior executives. Coordinated and approved activities of 10 North American staff. Authorized to approve press materials and external communications for 6 divisions. Managed PR agencies in New York and London.

Career Change: *From press-relations manager to wine and food promoter.*

Strategy: *Describe unusual background and clearly relate to new goal; include a strong set of transferable skills along with the achievements to prove them.*

CHERI R. PIERRE (PAGE 2)

954-555-1111   pierre2010@aol.com

Professional Experience—(Continued)

- Secured positive press coverage on CNN and in the *Wall Street Journal,* the *New York Times, International Herald Tribune, Forbes, Fortune, Institutional Investor, Financial Times, Times of London,* and trade publications.
- Introduced American public relations standards, improving the company's ability to target U.S. markets with high growth potential.
- Introduced company to 100 key media targets, including 15 top-tier business publications.
- In a "first for the company," instituted policies and procedures to ensure that messaging was consistent company-wide. Incorporated personnel from communications, investor relations, and industry-analyst relations more fully into the PR process.
- Worked closely with the company's Secretary General and the Director of Government Affairs to achieve recognition for the company's CEO as a "player" in a global technology study group.
- Edited all announcements and print materials for high-profile events such as the *Fortune* Global Forum.
- Conceived, recommended, and sold a community outreach program to encourage grassroots innovation on the part of local Internet entrepreneurs.

BOWDITCH PUBLIC RELATIONS WORLDWIDE, New York, NY
Hired in as VP at one of the world's largest independent PR agencies with 25 offices and $170 million in revenues.

Vice President, Corporate Affairs Group (2001–2006)

Managed major account relationships. Worked with the Executive Vice President and agency CEO to strategize and implement new-business initiatives. Liaised with senior executives in client organizations. Managed up to 10 direct reports. Supervised global account teams on the larger accounts. Managed crisis communications.

- Managed $3.2 million global positioning program for a Big Four accounting and consulting firm. Developed all strategic initiatives, including media activities; roundtables; high-level global seminars on financial transparency; and a book promotion in the U.S., Europe, and Asia.
- Played a key role in creating a Professional Services Group that tripled the number of clients for the firm. Assisted with the hiring of 20 cross-functional mid- and senior-level professionals.
- Credited by a *Wall Street Journal* reporter with rescuing a potentially damaging story about a client company by exercising skills in diplomacy, communication, and analysis.
- Instrumental in securing multimillion-dollar accounts and in developing and implementing global PR programs. High-profile clients included industry leaders in global management consulting, international law, financial services, human resources consulting, and corporate travel management.

PAINE & JONES, New York, NY
One of the top 60 law firms with 250 lawyers in 6 international offices.

Communications Manager (1998–2001)

Implemented marketing and communications program. Worked with partners and all 12 practice groups.

- Created all communication materials, including brochures for 12 practice areas.
- Instrumental in organizing a major 3-day conference on energy with 200+ industry executives attending.

CHERI R. PIERRE (PAGE 3)

954-555-1111   pierre2010@aol.com

EDUCATION, AFFILIATIONS, AND SKILLS

UNIVERSITY OF CALIFORNIA AT BERKELEY
B.A. in English—Emphasis on literature and writing (1995)
Junior Year Abroad studying at the **British and European Studies Group, London, England**

NEW YORK UNIVERSITY, New York, NY
- International Business and Finance (1999)
- International Public Relations (1998)

ECOLE RITZ ESCOFFIER, SCHOOL OF FRENCH GASTRONOMY, PARIS, France (2008)
Diploma—Practical and Theoretical Training
  Foundations of the French Culinary Tradition
- Techniques of food and pastry preparation
- Product selection
- Time management and organization
- Presentation and service
- History of French gastronomy
- Regional culinary customs and traditions

  Foundations of French Wine
- Degustation (winetasting)
- Appellation (classification)
- Vinification (winemaking)
- Wine serving

BOSTON UNIVERSITY, Boston, MA
- Food Writing Seminar (2009)
- Careers in Food (2008)

THE NEW SCHOOL, New York, NY
- Basics of Wine Tasting (2004)
- Wines of France (2003)
- Wines of Bordeaux (2002)

PROFESSIONAL MEMBERSHIPS
- The Culinary Guild of the Southeast
- The French-American Chamber of Commerce
- The American Institute of Food and Wine

LANGUAGES: Fluent French speaker, proficient writer in the French language

COMPUTER SKILLS: Microsoft Word, Excel, PowerPoint; Internet research

Willing to relocate within the U.S. or internationally / Available to travel

RESUME 78: BY **BILL KINSER,** MRW, CPRW, JCTC, CEIP, CCM

GLENDA GULLIVER

1245 Corcoran Street NW, Apt. 15A, Washington, DC 20036
Home: (202) 833-4582, E-mail: glendagull@onlineamerica.com

GOAL	**Radio or Television Broadcaster / Announcer / On-Air Personality**
BROADCAST EXPERIENCE	**Producer,** *Daily Literary Theatre,* WWOW Radio, Washington, DC

➤ Collaborated with a six-person team to coordinate daily on-air performances of classic literature readings.

➤ Selected the works for the show, oversaw casting of roles, conducted rehearsals, and edited content of books selected.

➤ Received the following industry awards:

- **American Association of Female Broadcasters (AAFB) Broadcast Award** for the *Daily Literary Theatre*'s presentation of *The Howard Women* by Sally Skylar.

- **International Reading Organization Award for Broadcasting.**

- **National Radio Commission Broadcast Entertainment Award** for the *Daily Literary Theatre*'s presentation of *Long Road Traveled* by Mary Stephanie Stevens.

Producer, *Critic's Selections,* WWOW Radio, Washington, DC
Reader, *Permission to Dream,* WWOW Radio, Washington, DC

STAGE WORK

Performed dramatic and comedic roles in numerous productions at the following theatres: Washington Area Performing Arts Center, Impromptu Performance Theatre, and Broadway View Theatre.

Role	Production
Alison	*The Long Journey* by David T. Worley
Vera	*Abundance* by Thomas Shriver
Professor Callaghan	*The Course of Life* by Allen Griswold
Sarah Roberts	*Sarah Roberts* by Henri Connors
Judy Austin	*Weddings* by Alicia Sanders

POETRY READINGS

➤ *One Woman Show,* Community Spotlight Theatre, Washington, DC

➤ Black History Month presentation, U.S. Department of Labor, Washington, DC

➤ *Special Programs Featuring Young Producers,* Written Word Bookstore, Washington, DC

➤ *The Saturday Morning Series,* The Warner Theatre, Washington, DC

➤ *The Children's Literary Hour,* Novel Books, Washington, DC

➤ *Marathon Interpretive Reading of Epic Works,* Krandall Books & Café, Washington, DC

EDUCATION

BA, **Performing Arts & Children's Literature,** Howard University, Washington, DC

Career Change: *From telecommunications operator to broadcasting professional.*

Strategy: *Focus on diverse work in the performing arts, which she had pursued on a part-time and unpaid basis for many years. Dates are excluded to camouflage the exact number of years and thus disguise her age. Her unrelated work experience in telecom is not even mentioned.*

Alex Standish

4429 Del Mar Avenue, Chula Vista, CA 91915
Home 619-451-0904 ▶ Mobile 619-204-1121
audio-alex@aol.com

GOAL	**Audio/Video Production Assistant**

QUALIFICATION HIGHLIGHTS	▶ Current training in traditional and state-of-the-art audio and video production. ▶ History of bringing projects to successful conclusion, on time and on budget. ▶ Track record of leadership and achievement in customer-focused jobs. ▶ Proven ability to quickly learn and train others in new processes and systems. ▶ Positive attitude and strong work ethic.

EDUCATION	**Associate of Applied Science, Audio/Video Production** COASTAL COLLEGE OF TECHNOLOGY, San Diego, CA, 2010

SKILLS	**Production Management** ▶ Script breakdowns ▶ Schedules ▶ Budgets ▶ Shot logs **Production** ▶ DVC and DVCPro cameras ▶ AVID editing system ▶ Production aesthetics **Lighting** ▶ Studio, chroma-key & product lighting ▶ 3-point lighting ▶ Diffusion **Audio** ▶ Microphone setup ▶ Location audio ▶ Pro Tools audio tools ▶ Analog recording ▶ Foley miking ▶ Foley editing ▶ Signal flow and patching on audio ▶ 24-track linear tape ▶ Non-linear Digital Audio Workstation

PROJECTS	Repeatedly elected as **Production Manager** of 5–8 person project teams because of excellent organizational skills. Brought all projects in on time and within assigned budget without compromising quality. Highlights include ▶ **6 start-to-finish commercial filming projects.** Participated in hands-on project work (planning and setup of audio, camera, and microphones; studio filming; extensive editing). Prepared scripts, budgets, and timing sheets. ▶ **3 audio recording projects.** Prepared demo/marketing tapes for local bands via live studio sessions. Participated in studio hook-up, track mixing, level setting, CD burning. ▶ **Lighting, analog recording, Foley editing projects**—all facets of audio/video work.

ADDITIONAL EXPERIENCE	**Project Manager/Landscaper:** BAYSIDE NURSERIES, San Diego, CA, 2005–2009 ▶ Independently managed assigned accounts, both residential and commercial; designed, installed, and maintained visually appealing landscape projects. ▶ Managed equipment, tools, and project schedules; quickly resolved on-site problems. ▶ Based on reliability and performance, selected to remain for year-round greenhouse position when seasonal work ended. **Customer Service Representative:** AL'S GARDEN CENTER, Chula Vista, CA, 2004–2005 ▶ Hired as first cashier prior to new store opening; rapidly promoted to customer service desk based on ability to quickly and resourcefully resolve customer questions. ▶ Used computerized inventory program. ▶ Chosen to train new employees in store procedures and customer service skills.

COMPUTER SKILLS	▶ Microsoft Word, Excel, and Publisher. ▶ Solid foundation of computer knowledge gained during 13 months of full-time studies in Computer Science (University of California at San Diego, 2005–2007).

Career Change: *From landscaper to audio/video production assistant.*

Strategy: *Highlight, in some detail, recent training, skills, and knowledge related to the field of audio/video production. Use the Additional Experience section as a differentiator from other new graduates.*

LaVonne J. Washington

123 Bayside Place, Middletown, RI 02840
401-235-1234 • ljwashington@earthlink.net

OBJECTIVE:	Television, Video, and Motion Picture Production		

Equipment:	Fill Lights	Boom Microphones	Lapel Microphones
	VMS Editor	Graphics Creator	Sound Generator
	Switchboard	CD Rewrite	VHS Camera
	Camcorder	Studio Camera	

Software:	MS PowerPoint	MS Word	MS Excel
	Internet communications	Studio 7	QuarkXPress

EXPERIENCE:

- Directed "The Last Man," semifinalist in The Universal Studios High School Competition, 2005.
- Directed and coordinated the production of television programs.
- As Producer, budgeted, procured equipment, cast talent, and composed and recorded music soundtracks.
- Coordinated production details to produce live television programs from locations distant from the station.
- Coordinated audio work, music, camera work, and script to produce show.
- Edited videos of television shows, music videos, commercials, documentaries, and short movies.
- Copied and edited graphics, voice, and music onto videotape.
- Read, interpreted, and edited script. Conducted rehearsals. Directed cast and technical crew.
- Auditioned and interviewed performers for specific parts, considering such factors as physical size and appearance, quality of voice, expressiveness, and experience.
- Scheduled sequences of scenes to be filmed for each day of shooting, grouping scenes together according to set and cast of characters to meet timeline requirements.
- Obtained costumes, props, music, or other equipment or personnel to complete production.
- Operated cameras, sound mixer, and videotape deck.
- Conferred with co-editor to ensure that music, sets, scenic effects, and costumes conformed to script.
- Conferred with cameramen to explain details of scene to be photographed. Utilized inserts, transparencies, backgrounds, and trick shots.
- Informed technicians of scenery, lights, props, and cameras required.
- Rehearsed live feed, music and commercials, and cast to elicit best possible performance.
- Met with directors, screenwriters, and other staff members to discuss production progress and results.
- Reviewed audiotape recordings. Verified that program, script, and sound effects conformed to broadcast standards.

TRAINING:

Television Production, Middletown High School, Middletown, RI, 2002–2005

Studies Included:	Beginning Studio	Basic Equipment	Studio Setup
	Editing	Graphics	Sound Setup
	Creating Talent	Audio Music	Switchboard Operations
	Light Placement	Camera Operations	Computer Video Making

Laptop Computer Training	2005	
Advanced Laptop Computer Training	2006	

Career Change: *From fuels specialist in the military to film production apprentice.*

Strategy: *Ignore military experience and focus resume on real training and experience gained in high school.*

ANNE FITZPATRICK

PROFILE

- Highly motivated, creative, collaborative professional with diverse design credits.
- Gifted artist and skilled craftsperson, both imaginative and technically proficient.
- Strong leader with team spirit; organized, efficient, detail-oriented, and calm under pressure.
- Loyal, articulate, enthusiastic, supportive individual with good sense of humor.

DESIGN AND RELATED SKILLS

- Uniquely expressive in the manipulation of color, form, light, and texture.
- Sensitive to the interactive nature of space and flow as well as spatial relationships.
- Knowledgeable in historical periods/styles of architecture, art, and décor.
- Adept at eliciting concept and practical needs of client/director.
- Experienced in computer-aided drafting.
- Proficient at carpentry; technical drawing; painting; faux finishes; sewing; patterning; cutting; draping; and creation of window treatments, slipcovers, pillows, bedspreads, and shams.

TYPES OF DESIGN PROJECTS

- Decorated residential interiors.
- Remodeled historic homes.
- Created theatre costume shop with makeup/dressing rooms, laundry/dye facilities, and wardrobe storage.
- Designed and built theatrical scenery (professional and educational): commercial and residential interiors, hospitals, hotels, courtrooms, and exteriors that represented varied historical periods and social milieu.
- Fashioned stage costumes for dance, drama, musical theatre, and opera.
- Designed and executed stage lighting for dance, drama, musical theatre, and opera.

PERSONAL AND INTERPERSONAL SKILLS

- Proven leadership skills with capacity to empower individuals and promote teamwork.
- Excellent troubleshooting, problem-solving abilities.
- Aptitude for multitasking.
- Ability to create effective working relationship with client/director.
- Capacity for working independently or as part of group.
- Organized, disciplined, thorough, and reliable.
- Amiable, positive, and aware of needs of others.

489 Stratford Street ▪ New York, New York 10015 ▪ 212.987.1212 ▪ 212.689.3636 (cell) ▪ fitz205@the-spa.com

Career Change: *From college professor to interior designer.*

Strategy: *Emphasize design and related skills on page 1 but also include management experience and other facets of her academic background on page 2 to strengthen her overall credentials.*

ANNE FITZPATRICK—Page 2

EXPERIENCE

Interior designer/decorator and design consultant (freelance) 1996–Present

New York University, New York, NY
Chair of Theatre Department 1997–2009
- Recruited and evaluated students, faculty, and staff.
- Allocated and managed fiscal resources.
- Developed curriculum, scheduled courses, and reviewed academic programs.
- Managed theatre facilities.
- Coordinated/scheduled dance, drama, and music events.

SoHo Community Theatre, New York, NY
Production Manager 2006–Present
- Hire all technicians.
- Manage all production budgets.
- Create/maintain master calendar.
- Maintain costumes/properties/scenery during show runs.

EDUCATION

Yale University, New Haven, CT
Master of Fine Arts in Theatrical Design
Graduate Fellowship

University of Michigan, Ann Arbor, MI
Bachelor of Arts
Major: Theatre
Minor: Art

489 Stratford Street ▪ New York, New York 10015 ▪ 212.987.1212 ▪ 212.689.3636 (cell) ▪ fitz205@the-spa.com

DONALD D. CARPENTER

2307 Hillsborough Lane, Bradenton, FL 33901
(813) 671-1234 • doncarpenter@msn.com

Knowledge & Experience

Model Types:
- Architectural models of single-family homes, apartment complexes, and commercial buildings.
- Diorama scale models, with historic accuracy and to appropriate scale with topographic detail:

Industrial construction projects	Furniture and cabinetry	Automobiles
Model railroad accessories	Dollhouses	Aircraft

Materials:
- Plastic, glass, balsa wood, foam, metal, paper, and papier-mâché.
- Cutting and gluing; painting and coloring with oil, acrylic, and enamel paint to produce finishing, weathering, and detailing.

Tools:
- In addition to the standard shop tools, such as table saws, bandsaws, and routers, utilize the following for working in miniature:

Scroll saws	Sanders
Lathes, both woodworking and metal	Miniature drills and drill presses
Miniature welding and silver soldering equipment	Airbrush to produce realistic finishes

Memberships • Exhibitions • Education • Recognition

Associations / Memberships:

Cincinnati Railroad Club	Plastic Modeler's Society	Victorian Society
Louisville & Nashville Historical Society	Surface Warship Association	Mid-America Modelers

Published in:

How to Build Dioramas	Wooden Villages: Designs for 18 Miniature Buildings
How to Use an Airbrush	Encyclopedia of Military Modeling

Exhibitions:

North American Model Engineering	Exposition Beaufort Ships Museum
Mystic Seaport	Cumberland Toy and Model Museum

Education:
Bachelor of Science in Mechanical Engineering, U.S. Naval Academy, Annapolis, MD, 1990

Computer-Aided Design	2003	Instructor Training	2007
Architectural Modeling	2004	Residential and Commercial Modeling	2008
From Idea to Blueprint	2004	Leadership / Management	2008

Recognition:
- Recognized as **"Modelmaker of the Year,"** Mid-America Modelers   2007
- **Navy Achievement Medal** for CAD Design Project   2009

Career Change: *From intelligence analyst in the U.S. military to architectural designer.*

Strategy: *Load the resume with diverse experiences that demonstrate his lifelong interest and extensive (although unpaid) experience.*

Richard French

198 Jamison Boulevard
Orlando, Florida 32801

(407) 471-5195
rfrench@msn.com

ASSISTANT DIRECTOR OF CULTURAL AFFAIRS

QUALIFICATIONS SUMMARY

- Over 20 years of experience building and managing professional service organizations including Financial Planning / Staffing / Technology / Marketing / Planning & Forecasting / Administrative Management / Problem Resolution / Legal Affairs

- Experience in local government operations, systems, and legal compliance—accustomed to dealing with government policies, issues, and officials

- Accomplished public speaker: lecturer, seminar presenter, and radio and television talk-show host

- Strong cultural background inspired through family member, Graham French, a renowned American Abstract Expressionist displayed in museums worldwide

PROFESSIONAL EXPERIENCE

President	French Law Offices, CHTD; Lewiston, Florida	2002–Present
Managing Partner	Green, Hatfield & French, CHTD; Orlando, Florida Rated AV; Martindale-Hubbell Law Directory	1998–2002
Partner	French and Simon, P.A.; Orlando, Florida	1994–1998
Sole Practitioner	Richard French, Attorney at Law; Orlando, Florida	1988–1994

Established a general law practice in 1988; formed a partnership in 1994; merged with a larger firm in 1998; and returned to sole practitioner and business owner in 2002.

- Managed all phases of each practice, including financial management, administrative operations, staffing, technology, marketing, case management, and client relations. Built and managed a client base of 6,000+ clients encompassing a diverse range of industries.

- Created, produced, directed, and hosted an hour-long informative weekly talk-radio show, *French's Legal Line* (1993–2008), responding to callers' legal questions. Periodically invited guests included governors, mayors, Supreme Court justices, and other attorneys.

- Appointed by Lewiston City Mayor to Board of Directors of TVTV Channel 11 (2007). Worked as liaison between Lewiston City Council and TVTV. Assisted TVTV in obtaining funding/grants from Lewiston City Council 2007, 2008, and 2009. Managed yearly budget of more than $300,000; assisted with purchase of studio/office building, station management, program quality, and content.

- Created, produced, directed, and hosted weekly half-hour TV talk show. Oversaw production staff of 9 people. Produced 3 hours of live programming every Monday night.

- Presented lectures and seminars on estate and financial planning for more than 15 years.

- Assisted in teaching a court-ordered bimonthly DUI school for offenders for 18 years.

Career Change: *From attorney to cultural arts director.*

Strategy: *Highlight relevant key strengths, skills, experience, and accomplishments. Pull out arts- and culture-related activities he participated in during his many years as an attorney.*

Richard French   rfrench@msn.com • Page 2

- As Managing Partner of Green, Hatfield & French, restructured operating, financial, and legal infrastructure for a group of 6 attorneys and 8 staff members. Negotiated/renegotiated strategic partnerships, forged profitable new alliances, expanded market channels, and standardized contracts and business documentation. Achieved and honored with highest rating, AV, in Martindale-Hubbell law directory.

- Represented thousands of cases from initial interview through final hearing/judgment. Argued, petitioned, and tried cases in Magistrates Court, District Court, Florida Court of Appeals, Florida Supreme Court, and United States Supreme Court. Attended more than 1,500 pretrial conferences.

  – City Attorney, Downey, Florida, representing city in all legal matters. Attended all City Council meetings, providing advice and counsel on all matters. Provided civil representation for the city as well as prosecuting misdemeanor criminal cases.

  – Co-counsel for state of Florida United States presidential campaigns. Provided representation in state of Florida for 2 presidential elections.

  – As legal counsel to Textile Processors, AFL-CIO, negotiated contracts, assisted in employer/employee relations, and participated in collective-bargaining process.

  – Provided representation from trial through various appellate levels; argued, drafted, and prepared briefs for 2 published cases: Smith v. Hatter (Case No. 14721) and The State of Florida v. John Sherman (Case No. 15832).

  – Successfully defended a real estate developer/building contractor (High Ridge, Florida) in a high-profile, multimillion-dollar case.

Intake Counselor   Health and Rehabilitative Services, District 8, Orlando, Florida   1987 to 1988

As Intake Counselor/Child Advocate, represented the child in neglect and abuse cases. Participated in all court proceedings, including detention, emergency shelter placements, arraignments, adjudication, and disposition. Prepared reports and recommendations to the court.

EDUCATION

J.D.—South Texas College of Law, Houston, Texas

B.S.—University of Florida College of Journalism and Communications, Gainesville, Florida
        Major: Advertising—Minor: Theatre

Theatre—London Program, Florida State University

COMMUNITY WORK

Principal Civitan Club member since 1990 (a coed civic organization that assists in funding the Special Olympics)—Treasurer, 1991; Vice President, 1992; President, 1993; Judge Advocate for the 7-state Southeast District, 1994–1995

Lewiston Chamber of Commerce member 1989–2006—participated in leadership training program

CHAPTER 10

Resumes for Career Changers Seeking Legal, Law Enforcement, Public Safety, and Investigator Positions

In response to changing world conditions, the growing field of public safety and security attracts people from all walks of life. To make their case, they must emphasize related skills drawn from their past experience, whether or not the experience is related directly to their new field. The resumes in this chapter focus on the following career transitions:

- Salesperson to public safety and security officer

- Correctional officer to police officer

- Electrician/contractor to U.S. Marshal

- Police officer to corporate security professional

- Bank officer to fraud investigator

RESUME 84: BY KIRSTEN DIXSON, CPBS

SEAN MACBAIN

sbm67@rogers.com

895 King Street West, Apt. 1213
Toronto, Ontario, Canada M5V 3S1

home (416) 326-4109
mobile (647) 829-0426

"The world is a dangerous place to live, not because of the people who are evil, but because of the people who do not do anything about it." — Albert Einstein

OBJECTIVE

Public Safety and Security position where I can contribute my experience and education in health care, international relations, immigration, psychology, and creative problem solving. Areas of interest include community safety, crime prevention, emergency management, and counterterrorism.

RELEVANT AREAS OF EXPERTISE

Problem Solving

- Reduced hospital re-admittance rates and increased resources for new patients by instituting follow-up care processes for both patients and caregivers.
- Observed need for more communication after patient discharge and persuaded senior management to provide social workers with incentives for additional home visits.
- Initiated product line and service training for technicians who visited customer sites that led to increased profits.
- Investigated overseas shipping options and secured deals to minimize expenses.
- Successfully navigated through government bureaucracy to legally emigrate to the United States and then Canada.

Communication

- Built a productive network of contacts and cultivated relationships using presentation, delivery, cross-cultural, and interpersonal skills.
- Saved thousands of dollars through effective negotiation of supplier contracts and prices.
- Bilingual: English & Portuguese.

Administration

- Managed RTR's New Jersey office and prepared detailed and timely reports for parent company that justified investment.
- Seamlessly expedited international sales process from acquisition to export.
- Incorporated RTR Import & Export, Inc., in the State of New Jersey.

Computer Applications

- Proficient with Windows applications: Microsoft Word, Excel, PowerPoint, Internet Explorer, and Outlook.

Career Change: *From salesperson to public safety and security officer.*

SEAN MACBAIN PAGE TWO

(416) 326-4109

PROFESSIONAL EXPERIENCE

General Manager 2002–2010
RTR Import & Export, Inc., New Jersey, United States

Served as the sole United States territory representative for a large medical equipment supplier in Brazil. Challenged to establish U.S. market presence and broaden the sales portfolio by researching and pursuing profitable purchasing opportunities.

Sales General Supervisor 2000–2002
RTR Electronica Ltda., Uberlandia, Brazil

Recruited from medical school, for medical industry and product knowledge and fluency in English, to work for this major importer of critical-care medical equipment.

Medical Intern 1998–2000
Guadalupe Hospital, Uberlandia, Brazil

Successfully completed three internships with exposure to various specialties, including psychiatry, psychology, general clinics, social work, and emergency care. Worked directly with 15–17 patients at a time to explain therapy and provide family support.

After learning and analyzing operations of various departments, took initiative to develop and propose new action plans that enhanced the effectiveness of the system for the community. Served as a resource to diverse groups and collaborated in teams to realize positive outcomes.

EDUCATION

Medical Degree, State of Para Medical School, Uberlandia, Brazil 2000

PROFESSIONAL MEMBERSHIPS

Canadian Association for Security Intelligence Studies Present

Strategy: *Use an objective statement to make the target clear and communicate how well the candidate's background and interests relate to his current goal. The functional approach on page 1 emphasizes relevant skills and achievements before revealing an unconnected work history on page 2.*

Peter M. Quinn

7509 Maple Drive
East Haven, Connecticut 06555
203-467-8585   peterquinn@snet.net

Law Enforcement Officer

- Graduate of Connecticut Police Officer Training; certified 2010.
- Proven ability to deal effectively with prisoners, establishing respect for authority while treating individuals fairly.
- Thorough, hardworking, disciplined, and reliable, with a serious attitude and a career commitment to law enforcement.

Professional Experience

NEW HAVEN COUNTY SHERIFF'S DEPARTMENT   2009–Present
Corrections Officer • County Correctional Facility

Maintain inmate control over 100-plus prisoners in a dormitory-style jail. Supervise inmate behavior and respond to infractions. Count and lead prisoners to meals and recreation. Maintain detailed hourly logs and records of inmate transfers and other activities. Transport felons to higher-security jails. Assume responsibility in other areas of the jail on an occasional basis.

- Developed skills in dealing with individuals of all types.
- Gained experience in effectively handling tense situations.
- Consistently achieved excellent performance evaluations.
- Member of Sheriff's Power Lifting Team; hold an American record in bench press.

Other Experience

RYDER'S, New Haven, CT   2008–2009
Doorman/Bouncer

GRANT ASSOCIATES, New Haven, CT   2006–2008
Field Representative

Negotiated and sold the services of a collection firm to business clients such as mortgage companies, doctors, and other health-care providers.

Education

Connecticut Police Officer Training and Certification (2010), CONNECTICUT POLICE OFFICERS ACADEMY, Storrs, CT

Criminal Justice Degree Program (2009–Present), QUINNIPIAC COLLEGE, Hamden, CT

Graduate (2006), NORTH HAVEN HIGH SCHOOL, North Haven, CT
- Member of Wrestling Team

Career Change: *From correctional officer to police officer.*

Strategy: *Emphasize related experience from current job as a prison officer along with recent and ongoing education in the field of law enforcement.*

PATRICK K. LANGLEY 1006 Elm Street • Woodbridge, VA 22191

Phone: (703) 930-0381 • E-mail: pklangley@comcast.net

CAREER GOAL: DEPUTY U.S. MARSHAL

Top-performing business leader with 15 years of experience in the construction industry. Analytical problem-solver who employs strong managerial, decision-making, and communication skills to optimize performance and safety of personnel and systems. Holder of **Top Secret** and **Secret Security Clearances** and **certification in Firearm Safety.**

LEADERSHIP
Project Management
Relationship Management
Problem Resolution
Performance Development

OPERATIONS
Efficiency Improvement
Job Task Analysis
Multisite Management
Quality Assurance

SAFETY
OSHA Standards
Policies & Procedures
Regulatory Compliance
Safety Training

QUALIFICATIONS SUMMARY

- Encourage open-door leadership style, building and maintaining valuable partnerships with clients, employees, and vendors.
- Direct and lead weekly meetings with Associate Managers, ensuring work is completed within budget and to code.
- Deliver problem-solving solutions that achieve targeted goals.

- Handle administrative functions, including vendor selection, price negotiations, material acquisition, and inventory management.
- Manage, supervise, and train 12 employees, overseeing workmanship, quality, and safety measures.
- Optimize processes, systems, and procedures to maximize efficiency and output.

- Investigate hazardous situations, analyze underlying causes, and implement preventive measures to secure public safety.
- Collaborate with local, state, and federal inspectors and agencies to comply with government regulations and standards.
- Facilitate and lead operational safety meetings at multiple job sites on bi-monthly basis.

PROFESSIONAL EXPERIENCE

Langley Contracting, Woodbridge, VA 2000–Present
Contractor / Owner
Provide subcontracting services for electrical installations within Top Secret government facilities. Direct 12 company employees, facilitating compliance with government regulations through technical guidance and resource planning.

- Prevent public access to restricted areas by installing security devices including fire alarms, security cameras, key lock devices, wired barricades, and lighting.
- Consult with clients and supervise construction projects from design to completion ($50K–$1.3M).
- Create cost-effective budgets by accurately evaluating job costs of equipment, material, and manpower. Reduced cost overruns 12% annually.
- Train employees to understand and read technical blueprints and specifications to improve quality control and customer satisfaction.

Career Change: *From electrician/contractor to U.S. Marshal.*

Strategy: *Highlight specific areas where Patrick's experience overlaps with core qualifications for a U.S. Marshal: leadership, operations, and safety.*

PATRICK K. LANGLEY   E-mail: pklangley@comcast.net   **Page Two**

N.K. Electrical Designs, Alexandria, VA   1998–2000
Journeyman Electrician
- Collaborated with engineers, consultants, and suppliers on designs, systems, and upgrades for 5 separate projects.
- Tested and inspected electrical systems, equipment, and components. Repaired hazardous materials and conditions in compliance with Electrical Safety Code.
- Supervised, trained, and coordinated daily work schedules for electricians, apprentices, and laborers on 4 different work sites.
- Maintained accurate safety records and reports for company and government review.

Durman Contracting, Inc., Annandale, VA   1995–1998
Electrician
- Installed all types of main service distributions for lighting, electrical heating, motor control centers, and power loads.
- Accurately estimated costs of new installations and repairs, meeting project deadlines and budgets 93% of time.
- Followed up completed assignments, verifying adherence to quality assurance and customer satisfaction standards.

EDUCATION / LICENSURE / AFFILIATIONS

Completed 90 credit hours, Northern Virginia Community College, Annandale, VA, 1996
- Proficient with Mac and PC hardware; MS Word, Excel, PowerPoint, Access, and Outlook software; and Internet

Licensure

Journeyman Electrical License, 1998–Present
Contractor's Business License, State of Virginia, 2000–Present
Certified in Firearm Safety, 2008–Present
Top Secret and Secret Security Clearance (active)

Coursework

Journeyman License Review—Code Requirement Training, 2008
Motor Control Training, 2007
Worker's Compensation Resource Standards, 2007
Plintum Rated Fire Alarm Cabling, 2006
Hunter Safety Course, 1999

Volunteer Affiliations

Board Member / Coach, Woodbridge Little League, 1999–Present
Member, Featherstone Civic Association, 2003–Present
Board President, Featherstone Civic Association, 2003 and 2004

ALLEN JURGENS

3605 Red Barn Road
Agua Dulce, CA 91350

661-859-3157
ajurgens@netzero.net

SECURITY PROFESSIONAL

More than 10 years of increasingly responsible management experience as **Field Supervisor, Criminal Investigator,** and **Administrator.** Combination of strong field experience with excellent qualifications in departmental management, budgeting, resource allocation, reporting, and technology. Excellent performance in liaison affairs; negotiations; problem-solving, crisis management, and relationship management skills; investigations; and data analysis. Expert in law enforcement training and interagency relations. Good presentation and communication skills.

A dependable team player; relate well and work cooperatively with diverse personalities. Work well under pressure without losing control and with all levels of management in a professional, diplomatic, and tactful manner. Able to coordinate and focus efforts of others. Positive motivator, mentor, and delegator. Hardworking and dependable with a **strong work ethic.** Entrepreneurial attitude, energy, and style.

Well-versed in the use of advanced technologies for research, reporting / documentation, customer tracking, competitive intelligence, information management, and other applications. Knowledge of Internet search methods and online data sources. Hold direct responsibility for

- Asset and Personnel Protection
- Emergency Planning and Preparedness
- Crisis Response and Crowd Control
- Community Outreach and Education

- Interviewing and Investigations
- Fraud Investigation and Documentation
- Tactical Field Operations
- Discreet Surveillance

Appearances as **Expert Witness** in state and federal courts. Experience with special events: logistics, security, budget allocation, vendor sourcing, and contract negotiations.

AWARDS

- Unit Supervisor, **Team of the Quarter,** 2006
- **Employee of the Quarter,** 2004
- City of Torrance Proclamation for **Actions Above and Beyond the Call of Duty** (rescued people from fire), 1994
- City of Torrance Proclamation for **Actions Above and Beyond the Call of Duty,** 1991

PROFESSIONAL EXPERIENCE

LAGUNA NIGUEL POLICE DEPARTMENT, Oceanside, CA   1996–2010

Field Supervisor (2005–2010)
Watch Commander (1999–2005)
Field Training Officer (1996–1998)
Officer-in-Charge, Special Events (2001–2010 concurrently)

Rapidly promoted through a series of increasingly responsible law enforcement and management positions in this 125,000-resident community. Earned several commendations for outstanding service to the department and local residents.

Career Change: *From police officer to corporate security professional.*

Strategy: *Spotlight safety expertise, knowledge of the law, and interpersonal skills.*

213

ALLEN JURGENS–Page 2

661-859-3157   ajurgens@netzero.net

LAGUNA NIGUEL POLICE DEPARTMENT   continued

- As **Field Supervisor,** held total responsibility for all tactical actions and daily activities. Directed management of personnel actions for 30 line officers. Ensured adherence to schedules in various projects. Executed major cost-reduction projects. Effectively listened and addressed citizens' complaints. Acted as community liaison: Designed, developed, and instructed a series of community outreach programs designed to increase resident knowledge of safety and security. Led multiple presentations to fraternal groups, business groups, schools, and nonprofit organizations.

- As **Watch Commander,** handled all administrative work, ensured accuracy of reports, and resolved citizens' complaints. Mentored junior officers; provided remedial training for deficient officers and in-service training for field units.

- As **Field Training Officer,** trained, mentored, and evaluated rookies. Wrote performance reviews. Oversaw basic police patrol functions.

- The scope of responsibility as **Officer-in-Charge** was varied and encompassed staffing of auxiliary facility (scheduled shifts and served as **Consultant** on performance issues, among many other functions) and coordination of special events (such as the Employee of the Year Banquet), which entailed determining logistics and security, negotiating contracts, sourcing vendors, retaining master of ceremonies, selling tickets, and staying within budget.

- **Certified Drug Recognition Expert, Certified Drug Recognition Expert Instructor, Primary Response Team Member (SWAT):** Taught defensive tactics, instructed and trained new academy recruits, and monitored / evaluated unit performance. Administered drug tests.

- As **Unit Supervisor in Community Policing,** conducted surveys; analyzed results; and listened, dealt with, and resolved complaints.

TORRANCE POLICE DEPARTMENT, Torrance, CA   1990–1998

Narcotics Detective / Senior Officer / Police Officer
Provided patrol / undercover surveillance in this 75,000-resident community and regional drug trafficking center. Designed and led training for narcotics and the tactical unit. Initiated and coordinated narcotic investigations; selected and mentored new detectives for this special unit. Provided expert testimony in state and federal courts.

PROFESSIONAL AFFILIATIONS
Member, Board of Directors, Torrance Police Officers Association
California Narcotics Officers Association (CNOA)
Toastmasters

EDUCATION and CONTINUAL TRAINING

Master of Arts, Human Resources Management, California State University, Northridge, CA
Bachelor of Science, Criminal Justice Administration, Burlington State University, Burlington, SC

- 40-hour Basic Narcotics Investigator Course
- 40-hour Field Training Officer Course
- Various courses in narcotics investigations and drug recognition

- California POST, Advanced
- Drug Recognition Expert Course
- Drug Recognition Instructor's Course
- CPR

RESUME 88: BY ANNEMARIE CROSS, CPRW, CEIP, CRW, CCM, CERW, CEIC, CMRW

JANET BERENDS

5678 North Avenue ♦ Los Angeles, CA 92009 ♦ 619.222.9874 ♦ jberends@hotmail.com

INVESTIGATOR / FRAUD & LOSS MINIMIZATION SPECIALIST

Credit Card/Check Fraud ♦ Loss Aversion ♦ Fund Protection & Recovery ♦ Problem Resolution

15-year veteran in the banking & finance industry.

QUALIFICATIONS PROFILE

High-performance, results-focused professional with exceptional insight and experience into the investigation of credit card/check fraud, implementing initiatives to minimize loss while optimizing the recovery and protection of funds for bank and clientele. Possess extensive experience and outstanding accomplishments within the banking and finance industry, delivering customer service excellence to drive revenues, market growth, and overall bottom-line performance. Comprehensive insight into, and full compliance with, Code of Banking Practice, Privacy Act, and Discrimination and Harassment. Sound knowledge of banking products, policies, and procedures.

- ♦ Investigation & Arbitration Excellence
- ♦ Loss & Fraud Minimization
- ♦ Procedural Design & Execution
- ♦ Research & Analytical Excellence
- ♦ Credit Card Fraud Prevention
- ♦ Guideline & Protocol Compliance

QUALIFICATIONS & TRAINING

Code of Banking Practice ♦ Privacy Act ♦ Discrimination & Harassment
♦ Introduction to Legal Aspects of Banking ♦ Consumer Affairs & Trade Practices

Bachelor's Degree in Law ♦ Northeastern University, Massachusetts

SELECTED CAREER HIGHLIGHTS

Circumvented ombudsman/media involvement and averted losses through incisive investigative, negotiation, and arbitration competencies. Insightful in distinguishing genuine from fraudulent claims while executing strategic initiatives to secure successful outcomes without incident.

- ♦ Isolated and impeded numerous inaccurate claims for compensation against credit cards, merchant customers, and the bank by unscrupulous and often re-offending parties; investigated and interfaced with various departments/organizations to ascertain accurate occurrences; and executed strategic resolutions with full compliance to set guidelines and protocols.
- ♦ Prevented cashing of stolen checks; optimized bank's profile with large corporate client.
- ♦ Five years of experience in Fraud & Forgeries Department in a banking environment; gained exceptional understanding into operational methodologies/protocols and the establishment and maintenance of profiles for suspicious customers and account transactions.

Developed key alliances with law enforcement authorities, local community representatives, and cross-functional internal/external banking departments to facilitate achievement of goals and objectives in the prevention of fraudulent activities.

- ♦ Interfaced with local crime-prevention groups in the establishment and coordination of fraud profiles on suspicious entities, patterns, and behavior, with meticulous input into comprehensive database while remaining abreast of fraud activity trends.
- ♦ Provided pertinent credit card and other information to police to facilitate investigations and subsequent arrest of fraudulent credit card suspects.
- ♦ Collaborated with law enforcement authorities to ascertain and document associated crime statistics, enhancing and optimizing crime prevention within the local community.

Continued…

Career Change: *From bank officer to fraud investigator.*

Strategy: *Highlight transferable skills and experience to "repackage" her in line with her new goal.*

JANET BERENDS ◆ jberends@hotmail.com **Page 2**

Problem-solved and defused numerous customer complaints and concerns without incident, executing strategic customer relationship management techniques to secure client satisfaction, retention, and repeat business; upheld the bank's reputation and professional profile.

◆ Arbitrated diverse cases, minimizing loss/claims through tactical investigation, sound judgment, and ability to devise and implement mutually acceptable solutions; renowned for expertise in resolving issues fairly, often being called by clients to mediate and offer advice concerning arising banking issues.

◆ Researched, advised, and arranged suitable banking products for customers unaware of best options to suit their needs; established rapport, trust, and recognition for banking products knowledge and expertise.

◆ Placated displeased client after they discovered double insurance premiums being deducted from their account over a two-year period; investigated and implemented corrective actions that successfully appeased and prevented customer from taking further action.

PROFESSIONAL EXPERIENCE

US BANKING CORPORATION   1997–Present
National Customer Liaison Officer (2002–Present)
Restore relationships with disgruntled customers over products/services or unresolved long-term issues to circumvent ombudsman involvement. Establish and maintain strategic alliances with cross-functional departments to facilitate speedy resolution of client complaints. Maintain scrupulous records and detailed accounts of customer contact, conversations, and reactions to impede possible future claims alleging improper handling of concerns. Minimize and reduce risks for customers and the bank by remaining current with credit risk procedures in order to identify trends in fraudulent activity and subsequently expedite necessary steps.

◆ Achieved stringent weekly targets of finalizing 24 cases requiring outstanding research, analysis, and resolution competencies to achieve realistic win-win outcomes, thus circumventing potential costly legal action.

◆ Frequently awarded Certificates of Recognition for exceeding 100% of targets.

◆ Distinguished from peers by receiving the majority of formal customer compliments for going above and beyond the call of duty.

◆ Entrusted by management to present induction training programs to new recruits due to extensive retail banking and credit card knowledge. Coaching encompassed standard protocols, role expectations, and methods to balance the art of customer service with diplomatic conflict resolution.

Customer Service Officer, Head Office Contact Center (1997–2002)
Fast-track appointment to Acting Team Leader role; supervised, trained, and mentored 30 staff to maximize team performance within a complex, high-pressure customer service environment.

◆ Recognized for outstanding performance, possessing a record of achievement that remains unbeaten to present day for exceeding call targets and selling most banking products.

◆ Enhanced and revitalized call center staff performance through provision of on-the-job training in product sales and customer needs analysis; crafted scripts of suggested responses to "brick walls" or rejection. Created environment that encouraged staff's continual knowledge growth.

◆ Pioneered comprehensive list of "*dos and don'ts*" to standardize telephone protocols, improve workflows, and drive revenues and market growth.

UNITED BANKERS NOMINEES   1995–1997
Data Entry Operator—Settlements Department
Meticulous data entry into computerized mainframe system, rapidly delivering output to achieve time-critical deadlines.

◆ Instrumental in capturing significant reduction in error rates, with virtual elimination of rekeying labor and overtime costs.

CHAPTER 11

Resumes for Career Changers Seeking Positions with Nonprofit Organizations

Whether fueled by passion for a cause or the desire to give back, there is a trend for experienced professionals to transition to nonprofit organizations. To show themselves as strong candidates for positions with these organizations, their resumes demonstrate both relevant skills/experience and some less-tangible but equally important assets that are highly pertinent to their target organizations. The resumes in this chapter represent the following transitions to nonprofit careers:

- Corporate administrative assistant to nonprofit researcher and administrator
- Clergy to nonprofit association manager
- Newspaper/magazine sales agent to university fund-raiser
- Engineering technician to Peace Corps volunteer
- Sales manager to town manager
- International consultant to association manager
- Attorney to association director

RESUME 89: BY NORINE DAGLIANO, CPRW

Annette Stiles Ollry

P.O. Box 52 ◆ Hagerstown, MD 21740   240.555.1815 ◆ aso@mindspring.com

Profile

Highly committed, intelligent career professional seeking to transfer 15+ years of corporate operational support experience to the nonprofit arena.

Background exemplifies a proactive customer service orientation, computer proficiency, and exceptional written and verbal skills.

Recognized for strong reading comprehension and editorial abilities; excellent at synthesizing complex information to provide concise, streamlined responses to operational issues.

Naturally inquisitive; organized; detail oriented.

Exemplify a blend of creative and analytical abilities, which combine efficiency with innovation to produce bottom-line results.

Educational Background

BA, Interdisciplinary Studies, THE COLLEGE OF WILLIAM AND MARY, Williamsburg, VA   2004

  Scholarship recipient for a summer study abroad, England

  Knowledge of French, Spanish, German, and Italian

  MAC and PC software applications and troubleshooting

  Photography; graphics composition and layout

Professional Background

ABX GLOBAL EXPRESS, INC., Rockville, MD   1994–Present
(Internal transfers to Richmond, Springfield, and Vienna, VA)

Global market leader of the international air express industry serving more than 120,000 destinations in 228 countries and territories. Acquired a breadth of diverse experience within the company, which attests to ability to fully utilize resources and effect results that are profitable to the company and beneficial to the customer.

Positions Held

STATION ASSISTANT / SATURDAY OPERATIONS LEAD / COURIER / AIRFREIGHT ASSISTANT

- ◆ Demonstrate a thorough understanding of the complexities of international shipping and customs regulations; recognized as a key resource for compliance issues.
- ◆ Implement a consultative approach in assessing delivery problems and negotiating win-win resolutions with customers and staff.
- ◆ Utilize a worldwide corporate email, telephone, and fax network to communicate with customers and staff in processing international shipments.
- ◆ Assist in coordinating and planning most economical and efficient transport for bulk freight shipments.
- ◆ Plan and execute delivery and pick-up routes for time-sensitive materials.
- ◆ Consistently provide a level of service that meets or exceeds customer expectations.

Career Change: *From corporate administrative assistant to nonprofit researcher and administrator.*

Strategy: *Identify and showcase skills in grant development and global affairs.*

Annette Stiles Ollry
240.555.1815
aso@mindspring.com
Page 2

Professional Background (continued)

Highlights

- Assumed responsibility for supervising Saturday courier operations, delegating assignments to 6 employees, and providing oversight for the timely arrival and departure of shipments.

- Made key contributions to the successful implementation of a new computerized performance analysis system, conducting qualitative data assessment, analyzing reports, and making recommendations for performance improvements.

- Assisted in resolving complex handling of an international shipment; identified corporate, customer, and regulatory needs and requirements, and identified the appropriate existing guidelines and procedures to be followed to achieve the goal.

- Set up a company-standard email tracing system for the local office.

- Received numerous awards for service, innovation, and safety compliance.

RESEARCH ASSISTANT, SEARCH CORPORATION, Great Falls, VA   1991–1994

- Conducted research of American medical and technology companies and their products to provide information to international companies interested in investing in American high technology.

- Prepared comprehensive reports of findings and forwarded to client companies.

Technical Skills

MS Office (Word, Excel, PowerPoint, Outlook)	HTML Internet

Working knowledge of Adobe Photoshop, Illustrator, Java, JavaScript, and UNIX

Special Interests

COMPETITIVE HORSES, Middletown, VA   1976–Present
STABLE MANAGER / AMATEUR RIDER / TRAINER / INSTRUCTOR (personally and professionally)

- Manage stable operations for 5 farms in and around Great Falls, including budgeting; inventory; and employee supervision, training, and scheduling.

- Serve as a liaison between the owners and boarders, including clarifying business policies and procedures to mediate management and client misunderstandings.

- Provide comprehensive care to the horses; assist with veterinary care and follow-up.

- Established proficiency goals and training objectives for instruction; give one-on-one riding lessons to youth, ages 4 to 10.

- Work as an assistant and groom to riders and trainers before and during competitions.

Tony J. Willows

7777 Altos Hill
Spokane, WA 99201

(509) 776-4560
email: tjw@email.com

PROFILE

Extensive **ADMINISTRATIVE** and **MANAGEMENT** experience with demonstrated strengths in **GUIDANCE** and **LEADERSHIP.**

Excellent presentation and communication skills—very good at bringing out the best in people.

Highly ethical, analytical, conscientious, diligent, and adaptable, with a great sense of humor and sense of drama.

Strong background in adult education and teaching, public relations, finance, and human resources management.

Successful consultant and trainer.

Proficient in program development and implementation.

Skilled in research and computer technology.

Willing to travel.

"...interactions with people from diverse backgrounds and various ages are a definite advantage... sets goals, missions; knows how to attain them...stays current in methods of efficiency...."

"...his energy, his expertise, and his people skills are of the highest caliber...."

"...unusually bright, imaginative, possesses an orderly and logical mind, is both a critical thinker and curious, has excellent interpersonal skills, and is a 'natural' teacher...."

quotes from evaluators

AREAS OF EXPERTISE

- Human Resources/Finance/ Real Estate Management
- Policies and Procedures Development and Implementation
- Volunteer Recruitment and Coordination
- Public Relations—Communication with Civic and Religious Leaders in Local and State Communities
- Public Speaking/Presentations—27 Years of Experience Presenting to Large Audiences
- Training Workshops—Office Personnel, Administrators, and Executives
- Teaching—Children and Adults
- Counseling—Premarital/Marital/Crisis/ Addiction Intervention/Bereavement
- Organist/Musician

"This instructor was the best teacher I have had...he made class fun and everyone understood what he was trying to teach...."

"...professor was always upbeat and knew his material...."

"...he is genuinely interested in the students' learning...can tell he is doing something he enjoys, which makes the best teacher...."

"Tony Willows is an excellent teacher, and I consider my time in his class invaluable...."

quotes from students

Career Change: *From clergy to nonprofit association manager.*

Strategy: *Downplay clergy title but highlight specific areas of expertise drawn from that background. Add punch with pertinent, positive endorsements.*

Tony J. Willows

page two of two   (509) 776-4560 · tjw@email.com

CAREER SUMMARY

Professor of Philosophy, 12/2007–present
Interdisciplinary Studies Department
Spokane Community College, Spokane, WA

- Instruct courses in Symbolic Logic.

Professor of Logic and Biomedical Ethics, 1996–2007
Arts and Sciences Department
Albuquerque Technical Institute, Albuquerque, NM

- Instructed courses in Biomedical Ethics and Philosophy to students of diverse cultural backgrounds. Tailored course materials and class activities to the context of students' life experiences and goals. Available for individual tutoring during and after office hours.

Organist, ongoing

- Provide service music and accompany congregational singing and professional vocal soloists. Prior to and following each service, perform concerts of recognized organ literature. Acted as Curator for the Allen Digital Organ. Elected to Board of Directors of American Guild of Organists (Albuquerque Chapter).

Pastor, 1978–1994 (retired)
Diocese of Halls, CA

- Performed ministry functions, public speaking, counseling, training, child and adult education, staff hiring and supervision, building maintenance, and budget management. Communicated with civic and religious leaders in local and statewide communities.
- Managed and oversaw design, construction, and repair of all corporate real estate holdings and buildings through Southern California—$100 million responsibility. Secured financial stability and debt reduction through member involvement.

Hospital Chaplain, 1996–2004
Bon Secours–St. Francis Xavier Hospital

- Provided spiritual care and counseling to patients, family members, and hospital staff.

Director of Recruitment, 1986–1990

- Supervised recruitment and training of candidates for religious leadership.

Judicial Vicar and Presiding Judge, 1979–1990

- Supervised and managed operations of judicial branch of Diocese of Charleston.

Chairperson, Personnel Commission, 1985–1986

- Advised CEO in placement of executive personnel.

EDUCATION AND CERTIFICATIONS

J.C.L.
University of St. Paul
Canon Law

M.C.L.
University of Ottawa
Canon Law

M.Ch.A.
Catholic University of America
Church Administration

M.A.
Catholic University of America
Theology

S.T.B.
Catholic University of America
Theology

B.A.
St. Mary's College
English, History, Philosophy

CPE, Certificate
Clinical Pastoral Education

JCL, Licensed Canon Lawyer,
European Civil Code

RESUME 91: BY CATHY ALFANDRE, CCMC, MRW, ACRW

HANNAH OSBORNE

337 North Billings Road, Fairfield, CT 06824 • 203-366-7382 • hosborne@gmail.com

CAREER OVERVIEW

- More than 20 years of **fund-raising, sales, and marketing** experience and expertise.
- Exceptional track record of outstanding results in diverse settings.
- Reputation for uniquely skilled leadership, combining courage, business savvy, strategic thinking, effective team building, and thoughtful development of individual team members.
- Innate ability to build enduring, trusting relationships, evidenced by broad and deep network of lifelong connections and contacts.
- Ideal position: Senior-level development role in university setting.

VOLUNTEER FUND-RAISING AND LEADERSHIP EXPERIENCE

ST. PAUL'S EPISCOPAL CHURCH, Fairfield, CT, 2001–present
- Member of finance advisory committee (2007–present), developing and implementing strategies to close budget shortfall.
- Vestry member (2006–present); adult and youth education committee member (2001–present); senior high youth group leader (2002–present); confirmation mentor (2007–2008).

WHEATON COLLEGE, Norton, MA, 1982–2005
- Secretary of Alumni Board (2002–2005); worked with Board of Trustees to develop Wheaton 2010 long-term strategic plan.
- Class President (1997–2002); class fund agent (1982–1997); contributed actively to $95 million Capital Campaign.

GREENS FARMS ACADEMY PARENT ASSOCIATION, Greens Farms, CT, 2000–2007
- Co-chaired "Java Jam," major concert fund-raiser for Faculty Development.

ROGER LUDLOWE MIDDLE SCHOOL, Fairfield, CT, 2000–2002
- Co-President of new school PTA; liaison between Administration, faculty, and parents.
- Recruited, developed, and trained more than 100 volunteers for 23 new standing committees.

OSBORN HILL ELEMENTARY SCHOOL, Fairfield, CT, 1999–2000
- Conceived and designed all aspects of first fund-raising vehicle for newly reopened school; wrote manual that is still in use today.

JUNIOR WOMAN'S CLUB OF FAIRFIELD, Fairfield, CT, 1988–1998
- Vice-President (1996–1998); co-chaired "Santa's House," doubling revenue in 1 year and developing first corporate sponsorships.

PROFESSIONAL EXPERIENCE

DIRECTOR OF ADVERTISING, County Kids Magazines, Westport, CT, 2004–present
- Selected as first full-time Director of Advertising.
- Designed, developed, and implemented sales procedures and systems.
- Identify and secure new business, selling 90%–95% of all advertising monthly.
- Create/implement sales strategy to achieve monthly goals by coaching and motivating part-time sales staff.
- Analyze market conditions and formulate monthly budgets.
- Created 2 new sales products in 2008; achieved 5% increase in down market, exceeding industry standard.

Career Change: *From newspaper/magazine sales agent to university fund-raiser.*

Strategy: *Position extensive volunteer fund-raising experience up front and highlight sales, relationship-building, and team-management capabilities.*

HANNAH OSBORNE, Page 2
203-366-7382 • hosborne@gmail.com

PROFESSIONAL EXPERIENCE (continued)

ADVERTISING ACCOUNT REPRESENTATIVE, Minuteman Newspapers, Westport, CT, 2001–2004
- Revitalized and rebuilt neglected territory, selling $250,000 in first year.
- Reestablished positive client relationships, securing old business and developing new business, delivering 3.5% average increase yearly.
- Promoted to Director of Advertising for sister publication, based on exceptional management, organizational, and turnaround results.

TEAM MANAGER, Mary Kay Cosmetics, Inc., Fairfield, CT, 1990–Present
- Identified and recruited 20+ independent contractors to form sales team.
- After 2 years, achieved Team Manager position and won free Mary Kay car, sustained by team inventory sales for 24 months.
- Continue to receive monthly team commissions after 18 years.

ASSISTANT TRAINER AND SALES SUPERVISOR, JCPenney, Inc., Stamford, CT, 1983–1989
- Promoted 4 times from Sales Associate to Management.
- Trained, supervised, mentored, and scheduled more than 100 sales associates.
- Handled senior-level responsibilities, including evening store closings, sales monitoring, and computer tallies.

OFFICE MANAGER AND REALTOR, Century 21, Trumbull and Greenwich, CT, 1980–1983
- Selected to manage Trumbull office after 2 years of outstanding performance.
- Pioneered Century 21 selling techniques in Greenwich market.

EDUCATION

UNIVERSITY OF THE SOUTH, Sewanee, TN
Education for Ministry; current studies in accredited 4-year program.

FAIRFIELD UNIVERSITY, Fairfield, CT
Additional religious course work.

YALE DIVINITY SCHOOL, New Haven, CT
Graduate courses toward Master of Divinity.

WHEATON COLLEGE, Norton, MA
Bachelor of Arts

Mark Kejanian

6 Wentworth Drive
Middleton, MA 01949

(978) 372-7779   mkej@yahoo.com

PEACE CORPS / SOCIAL ACTION / NGO OR INTERNATIONAL ASSISTANCE PROGRAMS

Experienced, highly motivated engineer with a strong desire to help people and make a difference. Combine social action with engineering and management skills to support sustainable projects in developing countries. Able to create and manage programs that generate a focused commitment to measurable results. Successfully built relationships, established effective interaction among diverse communities, and developed a high degree of mutual loyalty and trust at all levels. Socially active, interacting directly to help people function the best that they can in their environment.

Excellent record of positive outcomes and attention to cost with sensitivity to the complexities in meeting the needs of multiple constituencies. Recognized talent in balancing conflicting priorities and creating a clear direction to improve people's lives.

- Direct Service
- Operations Management
- Client Advocacy
- Communication
- ESL Training

- Program Planning/Implementation
- Community Outreach
- Needs Assessment
- Community Resources Integration
- Alliance and Team Building

SUMMARY OF ACCOMPLISHMENTS

- Collaborated on major engineering contributions for the development of products in medical instrumentation, surgical technology, and genome research.

- Awarded six patents.

- Managed numerous multi-discipline technical teams challenged to create state-of-the-art products with fixed budgets and critical schedules.

- Applied engineering skills pro bono to several municipal projects involving facilities construction, qualification of vendors, lobbying for funding, site selection, and project oversight.

- Provided ongoing assistance to immigrant coworkers and their families with immigration assistance administration, ESL and GED prep training, house hunting, and home-construction projects.

- Assisted family business in managing environmental compliance.

- Assisted Tanzanian students via the Internet in obtaining books and other materials for a local college, developed Internet content material for a Tanzanian-owned tour company, and tutored students in computer use and Internet search skills.

- Taught beginning through advanced snowboarding techniques to children and adults, 22 hours per week during the winter.

- Provided help and inspiration over many years to a person afflicted with Muscular Dystrophy.

Career Change: *From engineering technician to Peace Corps volunteer.*

Strategy: *Emphasize public-service activities that have been largely voluntary but are substantial and relevant.*

Mark Kejanian • mkej@yahoo.com   Page 2

PROFESSIONAL EXPERIENCE

Farmington Technologies, Dover, MA   2007–Present
Project Manager
Responsible for managing the mechanical/optical development of an advanced technology compact laser-marker system. Additional responsibility for delivery of custom-design solutions for laser scanner systems.

Dorchester Products, Medfield, MA   2003–2006
Manufacturing Engineering/Facilities Manager
Responsible for product design transitioning to manufacturing, budgeting, tooling, supplies, and facilities maintenance for a metal-fabrication job shop that manufactures made-to-order retail display fixtures. Managed 7 professionals and staff.

American Controls, Newbury, MA   2001–2003
Product Development Engineer
Responsible for integrating mechanical and industrial airflow control systems and clean-room HVAC valves for critical environments (e.g., temperature, moisture, cleanliness).

TKG, Franklin, NH   2000–2001
Principal Mechanical/Industrial Design Engineer
Collaborated on a multidisciplinary engineering team to develop affordable electronic fingerprint-acquisition technology.

International Transfer Technologies, Billerica, MA   1997–2000
Mechanical/Industrial Design Engineer
Design engineer developing 3-D laparoscopic technology for increased surgical accuracy.

Museum of Arts and Science, Beijing, China   1996–1997
Mechanical Engineer
Contract position designing 31 unique interactive museum displays to exhibit scientific principles. The project was completed on time and within budget.

EDUCATION

MS, Finance—Boston University, Boston, MA
BS, Mechanical Engineering—University of Michigan, Ann Arbor, MI
Entrepreneurship and Intrapreneurship Program—Worcester Polytechnic Institute, Worcester, MA
Fine Arts Studies—New Boston School of Arts, Boston, MA
Alternative Energy Opportunities Forum, Lowell, MA

FRED ANDERSON

89 Lawrence Street • North Granby, CT 06060 • (860) 595-2091 • fredanderson@aol.com

TOWN MANAGER

Ten+ years of leadership experience in town government as an elected chief administrative and fiscal officer. Key contributor impacting operational, budgetary, staffing, and resource needs throughout the municipality.

Extensive human resources and public speaking background. Effective communicator and team builder with planning, organizational, and negotiation strengths, as well as the ability to lead, reach consensus, establish goals, and attain results. Additional business management experience in the private sector. Competencies include

- Management/Administration
- Fiscal Management/Budgeting
- Project/Program Management
- Public/Private Sector Alliances
- Economic Development
- Staff Development/Empowerment

PROFESSIONAL QUALIFICATIONS

TOWN OF NORTH GRANBY, North Granby, CT   1999 to Present
SELECTMAN (part-time elected position)

Administration/Management—Proactive executive providing strategic planning and leadership direction to diverse municipal departments as one of 3 elected board members governing the Town of North Granby. As board member, direct multiple open town meetings, develop and oversee $10 million budget, and administer various projects. Experience includes chairing Board of Selectmen for 3 years. Serve as a Police Commissioner.

Human Resources—Authority for recruitment, promotion, and supervision of town administrator and 10 department heads with up to 214 full- and part-time staff, as well as Department of Public Works and Police Department. Personnel functions also encompass recruitment, contract negotiations, benefits administration, employee relations, and policy development and implementation.

Economic Development—Support strong public/private partnership toward diversified growth and prosperity. Source and negotiate with businesses, as well as secure agreements to retain and attract new businesses. Develop financial vehicles for public improvements.

Regulatory Affairs—Develop and manage relationships, as well as advocate for municipal affairs, with federal and state regulatory agencies, local business executives, congressional members, and other legislators.

Public/Community Relations—Instrumental in enhancing Town's image and building consensus with all boards. Active participant in numerous annual community events; act as spokesperson with the media.

Contributions

- Turned around employee morale and productivity, instituted training and employee recognition programs, and fostered interdepartmental cooperation, creating a positive work environment while restoring accountability and confidence in the administration. Municipality is recognized for having the "most responsive and best-managed administration statewide."

- Leader in the execution of several town revitalization projects following failed attempts by prior boards:
  - $2.9 million renovations to Town Hall, Senior Center, and Council on Aging
  - $5 million public safety complex
  - $1.3 million public library project with state library grant of $200,000
  - $15 million sewer project with more than $5 million secured in federal grant funding

- Personally negotiated Tax Incentive Financing (TIF) Agreements to retain and attract businesses.

- Effectively negotiated with the presidents of local companies to relocate their businesses back to North Granby. Results led to construction of new manufacturing facility for 4 companies employing 550 people and an agreement to expand employee base.

- Spearheaded search for new providers and negotiated improved employee benefits program while avoiding any rate increase.

Career Change: From sales manager to town manager.

Strategy: Focus on his 10 years of municipal leadership experience and accomplishments rather than his "real" job as a district sales manager.

FRED ANDERSON - Page 2

BUSINESS MANAGEMENT EXPERIENCE

MONROE & COMPANY, New York, NY   1998 to present
(Global multibillion-dollar manufacturer)

    District Manager   2005 to present
    Account Manager   1999 to 2005

Promoted to develop business plan and manage $23 million district that extends from the Northeast to Florida. Supervise 5 broker sales organizations.

Manage budgets; oversee and motivate the sales team; deliver sales presentations; and provide training on sales strategies, product knowledge, marketing programs, and administrative policies/procedures.

Develop and implement sales and marketing programs. Interface with executives of multimillion-dollar corporations. Manage $3 million annual marketing/advertising budget, providing support to major customers.

Contributions

- Implemented successful sales/marketing programs that contributed to the district's growth and exceeded sales plan during last two trimesters in 2009 despite declining sales trend company-wide.

- Singlehandedly transitioned the district from a direct sales force to a successful food broker network; efforts represent an entirely new direction for the company.

- Elected to the Leadership Club in 2005 for consistently ranking among the top 10% in overall sales performance throughout company.

- Renegotiated marketing programs with major customers that increased sales and profits while achieving acceptable dollar spends.

- Succeeded in securing new authorizations and expanding existing accounts while opening key accounts generating substantial business volume.

EDUCATION / PROFESSIONAL DEVELOPMENT

BENTLEY COLLEGE, Bentley, VT
M.B.A., Finance, 2005
B.S., Business Administration, 2001

Additional: Several seminars on municipal administration sponsored by Connecticut Municipal Association and Selectmen's Association

COMMUNITY AFFILIATIONS / LEADERSHIP

Selectmen's Association
Vice President, North Granby Rotary Club
Chairman, Conservation Commission

RESUME 94: BY GEORGE DUTCH, BA, CMF, CCM, JCTC

MONIQUE OUTREMOUNT

6821 rue Agincourt
Orléans, Ontario, Canada K1P 4R9
Tel.: (613) 286-9648 (day) / 286-6735 (evening)
Fax: (613) 286-3370
mfco@internet.ca

"Integrity, purpose, and the right to opportunity"

Dedicated professional committed to strengthening institutional capacity to design and implement policies and programs that reflect the needs, interests, and aspirations of the poor and marginalized groups in developing countries. More than 20 years of experience providing strategic direction and optimizing organisational and human resources. Highly effective working within international environments. Specialized in good governance, social responsibility, poverty reduction, and gender equality. Skilled cross-cultural negotiator with excellent interpersonal, problem-solving, and communication skills in French, English, and Spanish. Additional capabilities include

- Leadership & Team Management
- Strategic Planning
- Policy Analysis & Development
- Social Auditing, Reporting & Accounting
- Coaching
- Program/Project Design, Implementation, Monitoring & Evaluation

- Civil Society & Government Linkages
- Community Development & Outreach
- Capacity Building & Institutional Strengthening
- Gender Mainstreaming
- Facilitation
- Results-Based Management & Outcome Mapping

PROFESSIONAL ACCOMPLISHMENTS

- Championed improved access to and use of social services for the poor through $6M capacity development initiative in social communication (CIDA—Pakistan).

- Set strategic direction for $5.5M capacity-building project to mainstream gender equality considerations in the policies and programs of the Government of Bangladesh and sectors of civil society.

- Implemented complex analytical needs assessment of CIDA/partners' capacity to integrate gender equality considerations within 20 new/ongoing projects through review of concept papers, PADs, PIPs, AWPs, and RBM frameworks (The Commonwealth Caribbean/Canada).

- Designed evaluation methodology/survey instruments to analyse perceptions for Inter-American Development Bank (IDB). Results utilised to revise gender training program.

- Designed methodology and led impact evaluation of a rural water supply and sanitation project.

- Led review of South American and Central American Gender Equity funds evaluating institutional development, HRD, sustainability, and gender equality strategies.

- Set organisational policy direction impacting overall management of firm, human/financial administration, implementation of all assignments, and launch of corporate marketing plans.

EMPLOYMENT HISTORY

MFCO Consulting, Inc., 2008–Present
President/Management & International Development Consultant

Colabour International, 2003–2008
Vice President, Social Development Group and Corporate Marketing, 2005–2008
Project Manager/Gender Equality and Institutional Specialist, 2003–2005

- 1 -

Career Change: *From international consultant to association manager.*

Strategy: *Highlight her relevant professional accomplishments while clearly conveying her passion and commitment to nonprofit causes.*

Service-Growth Consultants, 1999–2001

Management Consultant

WATCH International Centre, 1996–1999

Executive Director, 1997–1999
Management Coordinator, 1996–1997

Conference Board of Canada, 1994–1996

Corporate Secretary, 1995–1996
Development Manager, 1994–1995

Berlitz Language Centers, 1982–1994

Director, 1985–1994
Language Instructor, 1982–1985

BOARDS OF DIRECTORS

Canadian Association of International Development Consultants, 2004–2006
Canadian Council for International Cooperation, 1996–1998
WATCH International Centre, 1995–1996

PROFESSIONAL AFFILIATIONS

Canadian Association of Management Consultants
Ethics Practitioners' Association of Canada
Association for Women's Rights in Development (AWID)
Society for International Development

EDUCATION/PROFESSIONAL DEVELOPMENT

Master of Business Administration (2004)
University of Ottawa, Ottawa, ON
International Strategy Certificate (2003)
École Supérieure de Commerce, Reims, France
Bachelor of Social Science—Political Science (1985)
University of Ottawa, Ottawa, ON

Various specialized training modules: Corporate Director Certificate (Schulich School of Business);
Social/Ethics Auditing, Reporting & Accounting, (EthicScan); Organisational Effectiveness (Universalia);
Outcome Mapping (IDRC); Results-Based Management Training (CIDA); Social Gender Analysis Training
(CIDA); Project Management Certification (Bates Project Management, Inc.); Media Training (Conference
Board of Canada)

PRESENTATIONS/PUBLICATIONS

Violence Against Women: A Human Rights & Development Issue—OECD DAC/WID Working
Group (1999)
Human Rights and Cultural Pluralism from a Gender Perspective—Canadian Foreign Service (1999)
Women's Rights as Human Rights—Presentation to Ford Foundation (1999)
Canadian Council for International Co-operation—Position paper to Foreign Affairs Parliamentary
Committee

EXPERIENCE IN & KNOWLEDGE OF DEVELOPING COUNTRIES

Commonwealth Caribbean, Costa Rica, El Salvador, Guatemala, Honduras, Nicaragua, Panama, Bolivia, Brazil,
Colombia, Ecuador, Paraguay, Peru, Rwanda, Tanzania, Zimbabwe, Bangladesh, Pakistan, and Vietnam.

- 2 -

Joseph M. Ramirez, Sr.

825 West Jackson #215 • Chicago, Illinois 60661
ramirezlawoffice@aol.com
Home: 312-466-5321 • Cell: 312-606-1112

EXECUTIVE DIRECTOR

▸ Proactive legal professional with 25+ years of day-to-day and strategic experience in entrepreneurial, public service, advertising, and general management positions. Accomplished public speaker with early acting career in local markets.

▸ Strong desire to transition a "gift of persuasion" and 30-year passion for motorcycles into a career building membership for the Indian Riders Group. Avid motorcycle enthusiast averaging 6,000–8,000 miles each year.

▸ Background working with boards of directors, fund-raising committees, legal teams, and a diverse public to ensure actions reflect organizational values and goals. Experience managing budgets up to $16 million.

▸ Technical skills include Microsoft Word and Excel and knowledge of records/membership database management.

Notable Skills:

Start-Up Ventures	Alliance Development	Board of Directors Interface	Budget Management
Fund-Raising Efforts	Organizational Development	Analytical/Financial Analysis	Advertising Production
Media Relations	Long-Range Planning	Customer-Driven Management	Persuasive Selling
Public Outreach	Strategic Planning/Leadership	P&L Management	Customer Loyalty

CAREER PATH

LAW OFFICE OF JOSEPH M. RAMIREZ, SR., Chicago, Illinois   1995–Present

Principal
Hold full P&L responsibility and manage strategic administration of day-to-day operations while practicing law as a Criminal Defense Attorney. Handle family law, real property law, collections, Uniform Commercial Code issues, and bankruptcy cases. Supervise a 3-member administrative team.

▸ Increased revenue 10%–15% year-over-year, with 75% of business built on referrals. Began business by relying on court appointments and quickly developed private clientele.

FRONT-TIER CORPORATION, Omaha, Nebraska   1994–1995

General Counsel/Board Secretary
Led 4-member legal team and held strategic responsibility for legal business concerns of time-share property/resort property corporation. Managed securities regulation, taxation, employee benefits, termination issues, real property concerns, and other corporate issues.

▸ Reported to 6-member Board of Directors and served as Board Secretary.

WOODBURY COUNTY, IOWA, Sioux City, Iowa   1993–1994

Interim County Attorney (7/94–11/94)
Managed $16 million budget and directed staff of 10 attorneys and 8 support/clerical personnel. Continued to maintain heavy caseload of trial work while advising various county entities on legal matters. Prepared and drafted legal documents pertinent to county suits.

▸ Selected from a pool of 5 applicants to serve out term of former County Attorney.

Assistant County Attorney (8/93–7/94)
Conducted in-depth research and prepared/drafted legal documents (motions, orders, and trial briefs) for felony prosecutions. Maintained heavy caseload with concomitant plea negotiations and other necessary tasks.

▸ Elevated status of position and office by prosecuting the first Class A felony in the county.

Page 1 of 2

Career Change: *From attorney to association director.*

Strategy: *Pull out accomplishments directly related to the position of executive director of a motorcycle association.*

Joseph M. Ramirez, Sr. *Page 2 of 2*

CAREER PATH *(continued)*

LAW OFFICES OF BAKER AND RAMIREZ, Des Moines, Iowa   1992–1993

Partner
Managed administrative and financial duties, including case and status updating. Represented clients in areas of family law, real property law, collections, and bankruptcy. Participated in court-appointed public service work.

UNION COUNTY, Cresco, Iowa   1990–1991

Assistant County Attorney
Managed a heavy caseload to provide legal counsel to county residents. Supervised a 4-member administrative support team.

EARLY CAREER

TRIAD STUDIOS INCORPORATED, Omaha, Nebraska

Advertising Promotion
Hired as a method actor for TV and radio commercials. Negotiated advertising contracts with small- to large-size companies, including Radio Shack, Bankers Trust, and Aetna. Prepared and presented promotional advertising copy.

▸ Won 11 Addie Acting Awards for interpretations of various characters. Played a key role in winning 2 additional Addie Awards for the company.

EDUCATION

DRAKE UNIVERSITY, Des Moines, IA

Doctor of Jurisprudence, Drake School of Law—1988
Bachelor of Arts, History & Political Science—1985

LEADERSHIP / MEMBERSHIPS

Memberships:
Illinois Bar Association
American Bar Association
Alpha Kappa Gamma Law Fraternity
Veterans of Foreign Wars

Leadership:
Boy Scouts of America:
Steering Committee, Mid-Iowa Council 2004–2005
Eagle Scout Leader / Scoutmaster, Boy Scouts of America 1992–2007
Fund-Raising Committee 2002–2007
(Solicited $40,000–$50,000 annually for Camp Mitigua)
Eagle Scout Aeronautical Achievement Committee
(Raised $210,000—best year in history)

825 West Jackson #215 • Chicago, Illinois 60661 • ramirezlawoffice@aol.com • Phone: 312-606-1112

CHAPTER 12

Resumes for Senior Executives Seeking Lower-Level Business Positions

The typical career progression is upward, from one position to a more challenging and responsible role. But sometimes, for a variety of reasons, business leaders who have reached the top decide to step back just a bit. They want to be involved in important business challenges but prefer not hold the most senior role in the company. Just as with other career-changer resumes, the key is to highlight just those skills and achievements that relate to the current goal without distracting or overwhelming the reader with career information that might be true but is not relevant at this career stage. The example transitions in this chapter include the following:

- Senior manager to mechanic

- IT manager to hands-on technologist

- Company president to sales/operations manager

- CEO to marketing executive

- CEO to human resources executive

TOM W. MURRAY

301-555-5616   103 Mason Place ♦ Cascade, MD 21719   twmurray@aol.com

PROFILE

- High-energy self-starter with a broad scope of experience in the manufacturing, purchasing, product development, and quality inspection of electromechanical and electronic devices.
- Committed to the continuous improvement process, with total team participation.
- Proven ability to meet all delivery, quality, and cost-savings objectives.
- Exceptional interpersonal skills; diplomatic and effective with customers, managers, and production teams.
- Detail oriented; competent in managing paperwork and written communication.
- Strong mechanical aptitude.
- Computer proficient with Word, Excel, and PowerPoint.

PROFESSIONAL EXPERIENCE

Electronics Corporation, Frederick, MD   1985–2010

Completed a successful career with a world leader in the design, manufacturing, marketing, and sales of power protection, thermal sensing, and electronic packaging products. Strong record of achievement in the following areas:

Technical & Mechanical Applications

- Developed an expertise in reading and interpreting blueprints and technical drawings.
- Established a CNC department, showing comprehensive knowledge of machine setup, operation, and SPC.
- Implemented a completely automatic assembly line that produced 30K subminiature thermostat units daily.
- Developed and implemented a scheduled preventative maintenance program that reduced breakdowns and improved equipment longevity.
- Led teams operating injection-molding machines, die-casting and screw machines, cut-off and band saws, vertical milling machines, vertical CNC machining centers, lathes, and high-speed drill presses.

Quality Assurance

- Skilled in the use of all precision-measuring instruments, including calipers, micrometers, and dial indicators.
- Monitored manufacturing processes and tested products for compliance with industry specifications; proficient in using SPC methods for process control.
- Involved in ISO 9001 certification process for Thermal Products Group Division; qualified as ISO auditor.

Inventory & People Management

- Planned and scheduled people and materials; shortened product flow distance through the manufacturing areas by more than 55%.
- Converted a manual MRP system to a fully automated system; directed the installation of MAPICS/DB.
- Excelled in organizing and coaching personnel to work effectively in teams.
- Oversaw team operations in Manufacturing Engineering, Facilities Engineering, Purchasing, Materials, Scheduling, and Shipping & Receiving.
- Diagnosed and rectified production needs and problems.

Purchasing

- More than 15 years of experience managing supplier relations, purchasing, cost control, and supplier quality; directed a +95% improvement in OTD.
- Developed a total working knowledge of indented bill of materials as well as shop-floor routings.
- Managed the bid process for all purchased materials/components, tooling orders, and MRO supplies; established a vendor rating system; negotiated contracts.
- Worked with engineering and QA to develop sources and track national/international marketing trends.
- Dealt in various commodities such as stampings, turned assemblies, molded plastics, magnets, die-cast components, and electronics components.

MECHANICAL HOBBY

Build custom Harley-Davidson motorcycles.

Career Change: *From senior manager to mechanic.*

Strategy: *Use a skills-based format and delete his high-powered job title.*

SASHA SAMPSON

1699 Hillsdale, San Jose, CA 95124
Ph: 408.333.2221 ▪ Cell: 408.999.2221
email: sasha@tech.net

SOFTWARE ENGINEER

➤ Hands-on project-management and software-development strengths.
➤ Solid record of contributions to project success, business growth, and technology advancement.
➤ Reputation for strong work ethic, commitment to customers, industry knowledge, and ability to thrive in challenging situations.

SALES & TECHNICAL EXPERTISE

▪ Relationship Building	▪ Startup / Turnaround	▪ Vendor Relations / Negotiations
▪ Customer Service / Support	▪ IT Needs Assessment	▪ Technical Training
▪ Technical Troubleshooting	▪ IT Infrastructure Development	▪ System Security / Disaster Planning
▪ Project Development	▪ Systems Implementation	▪ Productivity Improvement

CAREER & ACHIEVEMENT SUMMARY

ALPHORIM, INC.—Santa Clara, CA
(Startup technology company engaged in providing proprietary hardware/software solutions with capacity to deliver voice, data, and video over DSL, PONs, and regular POTs circuits)
MANAGER, INFORMATION TECHNOLOGY (2007 to Present)

Overview: Initially hired as company's sole IT staff member with responsibility for establishing internal 24×7 IT infrastructure to support community of more than 120 local/remote users over a 2-year period. Specifically responsible for all networking, data storage, remote access, and telephony operations, as well as installations, maintenance and upgrades, budgeting, purchasing, and negotiations for services and equipment. Charged with creating stable and scalable environment while maintaining low costs without compromising quality. Upgraded and maintained Windows networking and UNIX environments; ensured 100% backup of information; selected vendor for off-site storage; oversaw internal voice, data, and support contracts; and served as key contact for all software/hardware purchasing. Provided technical leadership, technical troubleshooting, and performance improvement for all IT operations. *Assumed greater responsibilities as company grew from initial staff of 20 to more than 120 employees.*

Key Projects & Contributions

- **Successfully led move of entire IT infrastructure,** including servers, networking, and telephony over single weekend with successful "opening" by start of business Monday.
- **Captured significant telecommunication savings** by selecting outsourced VoIP phone system with contract that included equipment, training, installation, and PRI circuits for 120+ users (initially 50, grew to 120). Consolidated bandwidth, local, and long-distance expenses.
- **Consistently boosted system functionality and performance** by upgrading backup system and implementing VPN (and enhancing when necessary). Performed ongoing monitoring of network and firewall, and closed performance issues with Network Appliance Filers.
- **Delivered $1,000 monthly savings while improving support and overhead** by researching/selecting new phone system for customer service group.
- **Saved more than $100K in IT equipment purchases in 2009** (recognized as "one of the lowest-spending departments in the company").
- **Sustained cost-effective IT operations** by cultivating excellent vendor relationships, expertly negotiating pricing, and utilizing alternative technologies to solve problems.
- **Impacted profitability results** by hiring one Desktop Support Administrator to support all IT efforts; work in tandem to ensure smooth operations and high productivity despite rapid growth of company.
- **Enhanced overall IT operations and productivity** by authoring and implementing formal security usage (policy and procedures) and IT disaster recovery plan.

Career Change: From IT manager to hands-on technologist.

Strategy: Emphasize strong technical experience and omit mention of senior-level leadership activities.

SASHA SAMPSON

Ph: 408.333.2221 ■ Cell: 408.999.2221
email: sasha@tech.net

JOURNEY TECH—Santa Clara, CA
(Technology company engaged in bringing video to home market via broadband [DSL] connection using proprietary hardware and video compression software)
SENIOR LAN ADMINISTRATOR (2006 to 2007)

Overview: Charged with managing network and client workstations and administering internal functions including email, adds, moves, and changes for voice and data operations. Supported users and managed backups and VPN usage. Provided research for new equipment, led purchasing decisions, and performed general system administration of all Windows 2000 servers. *Note: Company was not able to generate profits and closed shortly after launching.*

Key Projects & Contributions

- **Introduced productivity improvements,** including testing and documentation of bug-tracking system (DreamApps) and ERM (FirstWave).
- **Facilitated user training on several technology applications,** including new bug-tracking system.

SOLUTION CENTRAL—San Mateo, CA
(Startup web portal company; initial products included a database of technical training courses)
SITE ADMINISTRATOR (2005 to 2006)

Overview: Accountable for all systems administration and desktop support of Windows NT Network for ecommerce portal; essentially functioned as Information Architect. Assisted development staff with transfer of data to production environment and provided ongoing maintenance and troubleshooting.

- **Reduced monthly expenses** by leading transition from company mail with external hosting to in-house Exchange 2003 within one week (including all setup and user training).
- **Managed site transfer from in-house servers to off-site servers.** Created duplicate set of servers in-house that matched that of hosted production site and led staging/test area for code.
- **Improved security** by managing company firewall; halted unauthorized network infiltration.

NEW YORK UNIVERSITY—New York, NY
PROGRAMMER ANALYST (2003 to 2005)

Overview: Hired to support email and dial-up accounts for 10,000 end-users; quickly earned promotion to Programmer Analyst. Authored technical notes and procedure documents related to changes in network architecture, services, and software. Monitored system logs and backups. Performed troubleshooting for campus-wide networking and SMTP issues as well as individual accounts.

- **Developed numerous well-received classes, including** "You, Your Computer, and the Internet" and "E-mail Tips and Tricks for Windows."
- **Generated high levels of productivity for staff of 13;** trained new network operations staff members in troubleshooting methods and customer service while fielding all escalated calls.
- **Designed and implemented ACD system** to help route calls and generate reports related to hosted website that held training materials, scheduling, and software downloads.

EDUCATION & CERTIFICATION

BA, English Literature—New York University, New York, NY

UNIX Systems Administration Certification, valid through 2012—U.C. Extension
Numerous seminars, including USENIX and technical writing and editing

-2-

RYAN EDISON

Home 781-944-1063 • Mobile 781-709-2401
292 Pearl Street, Reading, MA 01867
ryan_edison@verizon.net

Sales & Operations Management Professional

Invigorating Growth • Improving Performance • Surpassing Expectations

Strategic and tactical leader of both sales and operations, with a track record of consistent growth, continuous improvement, and turnaround leadership. Effective manager of sales organizations, production teams, and key business initiatives, combining customer and process focus with authentic leadership style that creates a collaborative teamwork environment.

Sales Qualifications: Consultative/needs-based/solution sales expert. Repeatedly satisfied customers by developing solutions that save time, cut costs, and ensure consistent quality. Restored dormant accounts and gained preferred/exclusive provider status. Drove rapid sales growth.

Operations Expertise: Leader in introducing technologies, methodologies, and processes that streamline operations and achieve stringent quality, production, and profit goals. TQM/Production Cells/Quality Manuals/Performance Incentive Plans/Team Building/Cost Control.

Experience and Achievements

EASTERN RUBBER & PLASTICS, Lynn, MA   2007–Present
Distributor of industrial rubber products to MRO buyers in multiple diverse industries

BRANCH MANAGER, SOUTHERN NEW HAMPSHIRE, 2008–Present

Provided turnaround leadership for faltering branch suffering sliding revenues and 7 years of unprofitable performance. Developed and executed strategic plan for rapid improvement and sales growth.

Scope of responsibility is diverse and includes all operations as well as sales and business development for $1M+ branch. Hire, train, and manage sales associates in target markets; train and manage warehouse employees in compliance with company ISO 9002 procedures.

- Rejuvenated sales performance: Grew sales 30% in one year and was the only company branch to achieve sales growth in 2009.
- Successfully launched OEM sales for the company and grew to 20% of branch revenues. Secured the company's first OEM account ($50K annual sales) and created the operational and administrative processes for efficient management of this line of business.
- Transformed "order taking" to needs-based consultative selling/customer problem-solving that resulted in key wins with new and existing customers:
  - Became preferred supplier to a key target account and grew that business from zero to $20K.
  - Converted a product trial to $10K in new business with annual savings of $10K to the customer.
  - Rebuilt relationships with former accounts, translating their needs to product solutions that generated $20K sales revenue.

OPERATIONS MANAGER, HEADQUARTERS, 2007–2008

Created a high-performance organization—refocused and recharged the team, instilled customer orientation, and put in place metrics and benchmarks to guide continuous improvement. Brought on board to drive performance improvements and expand the business to new markets and sales channels. Managed operations team of 5, with full responsibility for timely, accurate, cost-effective shipments of 5 core product groups to customers nationwide.

- Led warehouse team from lackluster performance to consistent achievement of defined goals for productivity, inventory management, and housekeeping. Bonus attainment skyrocketed from 62% to 93%.
- Led a cost-cutting initiative, analyzing all operational expenses to find ways to drive cost from the operation without affecting quality, performance, or strategic growth:
  - Cut utility consumption by 60%.
  - Eliminated $8K annually in customer gifts that delivered little return on investment.

Career Change: From company president to sales/operations manager.

Strategy: Emphasize his recent interim role as branch manager without mentioning his concurrent title and responsibilities as president of the company.

RESUME *98,* CONTINUED

RYAN EDISON Home 781-944-1063 • Mobile 781-709-2401 • ryan_edison@verizon.net

- Created a collaborative work environment where customer service was the focus and the team knew precisely what was expected and how to achieve it. Initiated monthly team meetings and invited staff input.
- Improved efficiency by defining standards, developing operating procedures, and creating processes:
  - Matched product surplus with shipment status through inventory analysis.
  - Monitored orders through the entire workflow; pinpointed and eliminated bottlenecks.

EDISON CERTIFIED HOSE, Saugus, MA 2007
Start-up OEM supplier, acquired by Eastern Rubber & Plastics

GENERAL MANAGER

Launched start-up and, within 3 months, became an approved OEM supplier of certified hydraulic hose assemblies. Secured investment capital, developed business plan, put in place processes and equipment, wrote a quality manual, and gained production authorization.

- Negotiated profitable sale of the business to Eastern Rubber & Plastics; joined new organization as Operations Manager of its headquarters location.

BAY STATE INDUSTRIAL HOSE/REVERE RUBBER COMPANY, Revere, MA 1995–2007
Suppliers of certified industrial hoses through both OEM and distributor sales channels

GENERAL MANAGER/DIRECTOR OF SALES

Spearheaded both sales and operations for jointly owned industrial sales companies, one concentrating in the OEM market and the other in distributor sales; combined revenues exceeded $3M annually. Managed finance, P&L, human resources, production and shipping, purchasing/vendor relations, sales, and marketing. Used first-rate organizational and time-management skills to juggle diverse responsibilities for the 2 companies.

Operational Achievements

- Improved productivity 75% by introducing state-of-the-art methodologies (e.g., production cells).
- Instituted TQM meetings, wrote the firm's first quality manual, and built a culture of quality and teamwork.
- Eliminated $20K in unnecessary cost by analyzing expenditures and matching investment to ROI.
- Problem-solved customer production processes and recommended solutions that cut costs, streamlined production, and resulted in substantial sales opportunities.
  - Grew a $140K account to $700K by supplying quality (99%) and on-time delivery (99.99%) that could not be matched by the competition.
  - Gained exclusive account status with a key OEM customer by suggesting solutions that cut their costs and improved their profitability—while generating $250K in annual sales to our company.

Sales Performance

- Personally achieved 30% of company sales, topping 3 other producers while concurrently managing company operations.
- Realigned sales territories to better match resources with market opportunities. Equipped sales staff with technology to improve territory management and proposal processes.
- Developed and continuously refined marketing and sales strategies to drive profitable growth. Aligned sales initiatives with strategic growth opportunities; motivated and evaluated sales staff; performed sales/market analysis; created account plans; and trained sales staff in strategic, consultative selling.

Education

Bachelor of Business Administration/Major in Finance Salem State University, Salem, MA

Professional Development: Sandler Sales Institute and President's Club
University of Industrial Distribution: Key Account Selling and Territory Planning;
Selling and Building the Sales Team; Sales and Market Planning

RESUME 99: BY ROMONA CAMARATA, MS ED., ADM, GCDF, CPRW, CCC, CCMC

AMY M. CROW

812 Vermillion Street
La Porte, Indiana 46404

219-939-1415
E-mail: crow@insightbb.com

EXECUTIVE MARKETING MANAGEMENT ▪ STRATEGIC BUSINESS EXPANSION

Professional career reflects more than 15 years of results-oriented senior marketing expertise focused on enhancing comprehensive marketing strategies, developing advertising and public relations programs, and initiating brand recognition programs for established and start-up companies. Demonstrated history of creative problem solving in research and communications to develop and launch innovative campaigns earning recognition in mass media. Successful record of building, mentoring, and motivating teams to achieve goals and ensure full client satisfaction. These leadership abilities led to 45% revenue growth and substantial market-share increase over a 12-month period.

CREDENTIALS AND OBJECTIVES

In progress, **Master of Business** degree in **Marketing and Healthcare Administration.** Supported by **Bachelor of Science** degree in **Business** and **Bachelor of Arts** degree in **Psychology,** both from Purdue University. Have enhanced academic and professional credentials with additional training in leadership development, project management, corporate finance, healthcare management, and national and divisional accounts supervision.

These skills and experiences would enable me to serve your organization in a variety of leadership capacities. I believe my abilities could be maximized as **Vice President of Business Development, Vice President of Marketing, or Director of National Business Planning.** Given the opportunity to represent myself to you in person, I am confident you will find me to be a worthy addition to your marketing leadership team.

SELECTED ACCOMPLISHMENTS

Marketing

➢ Conducted daily competitive research and managed multiple ongoing projects, including corporate campaign development, company-wide product branding, national public relations, and presentation packets.
➢ Designed innovative visual aids impacting successful branding and campaign launch.
➢ Developed training manuals and documented new product designs using new troubleshooting processes.
➢ Created numerous media, investor, and marketing communications packages, including press releases for TV and radio announcement, ad copy, speeches, direct-mail campaigns, billboards, Web pages, PowerPoint presentations, and annual reports for Fortune 500 companies bringing in billions of dollars of revenues.
➢ Substantially improved internal communications by supplying clients with strong marketing displays for trade shows.
➢ Supplied clients with high-impact product branding to include packaging and launch services, logo and identity development, point-of-sale programs, and kiosks for national and international exposure.
➢ Authored how-to marketing articles for *Texas Lawyer* and *The Dallas Business Journal,* resulting in millions of dollars of increased revenues.

Business Management & Expansion

➢ Led teams in analyzing properties, developing competitive market forecasts, and creating expansion plans.
➢ Streamlined the market analysis methodology and efficiently managed multiple projects in tight time constraints.
➢ Implemented a successful acquisition group that yielded $40M in revenue and 82% increase in market share.
➢ Developed and implemented requirements, recommendations, and operations strategies for hundreds of customer-requested projects.

Career Change: *From CEO to marketing executive.*

Strategy: *Begin with a strong marketing-related positioning statement and support this with an extensive list of marketing-related career achievements.*

AMY M. CROW ▪ 219-939-1415 ▪ crow@insightbb.com   PAGE 2

CAREER HISTORY

CEO/Co-Owner   **Party & The Game Room**   **2008–Present**
- Took lead role in family-owned business and developed a marketing plan that increased revenue by 35%.
- Redesigned logo, Web site, and all marketing communications to create new brand image aligned with strategic business focus.

Vice President, Marketing   **E3M**   **5/2007–10/2007**
- Point person for subsidiary of Concentra Healthcare, focused on providing Internet software to Workers' Compensation industry. Developed the entire marketing and public relations plan and product branding from conception to launch.
- Implemented very successful marketing campaigns to capture business.
  - Collaborated with technical, product, and sales staffs.
  - Interacted with advertising agencies, printers, and other vendors to achieve goals and timelines.
  - Exhibited at domestic and international conventions.
  - Managed a five-member team consisting of a graphic designer, content manager, PR writer, field sales person, and marketing assistant.
- Negotiated distribution contracts with 200+ vendors.
- Established A1 credit lines with all suppliers within first year.

Executive Vice President   **JPI**   **1/2005–5/2007**
- Developed a market analysis to complete an in-depth assessment of key markets across 17 states for the nation's largest real estate investment (REIT) firm.
- Led three staff to finalize all communications and plans of conventional and student properties.
- Provided accurate assessment of current customers' emerging needs and predictions of overall market trends.
- Conducted national focus groups in each market over four-month period and presented results to board of directors and acquisition groups.
- Prepared extensive marketing materials, trade magazine ads, annual catalogs, and brochures for the California market.
- Organized and prepared an accurate assessment of current customers, emerging needs, and predictions, resulting in unprecedented new business developments with 20% increase in revenues.

Principal, President/CEO   **LedgeCOM/LedgeMARK**   **2001–2004**
- Founded and grew successful advertising, marketing, and public relations agency providing a wide range of services to Fortune 500 companies including Nokia, Cisco, and EmCare. Hired and managed team of six.

Product Consultant   **Nokia**   **1998–2001**
- Guided the product management group of a cellular phone manufacturer through a complex medical and technical information plan incorporating the Americans With Disabilities Act.

Director of Marketing   **Cardiovascular Physicians Resources**   **1995–1998**
- Directed the activities of 18 personnel to create an unprecedented marketing campaign and implementation program.

RESUME 100: BY WENDY ENELOW, CCM, MRW, JCTC, CPRW

JOHN GREGORY

gregoryjohnjr@mindspring.com
789 Craigmont Avenue, Duluth, MN 33383
(218) 333-3726

SENIOR EXECUTIVE PROFILE

Strategic Human Resources Leadership / Organizational Development / Change Management
Performance Optimization / Leadership Training & Development / P&L Management
Harvard MBA

Distinguished management career leading organizations through start-up, change, revitalization, turnaround, and accelerated growth. Cross-functional expertise with proven success in optimizing organizational growth, productivity, and efficiency. HR Generalist experience in benefits, compensation, recruitment, training, and HRIS technology. Expert team building, team leadership, communication, and interpersonal relations skills.

PROFESSIONAL EXPERIENCE

Chief Executive Officer / HR Director   2005 to Present
MED HEALTH SOLUTIONS, Duluth, Minnesota

CHALLENGE: *Lead the organization through a comprehensive organizational development and change management program to support corporate-wide diversification strategy.*

Senior Executive recruited to plan and orchestrate a complete redesign of strategic planning, HR/OD, administrative, information technology, marketing, and operating functions to increase revenues and bottom-line profitability. Manage within a tightly regulated and competitive industry.

- One of two senior executives credited with transitioning Med Health Solutions from 2005 revenues of $700,000 to current revenues of $1.8 million. Drove profit growth by more than 45%.
- Built a best-in-class HR organization; implemented advanced HRIS technology; designed benefit and compensation programs; established a formal salary structure; and introduced employee training, counseling, and coaching programs.
- Revitalized all core financial functions, implemented client/server architecture to optimize technology performance, and created a team-based/customer-based corporate culture.
- Negotiated $2.8 million acquisition of competitive company and facilitated seamless integration of personnel, technology, and product lines.

President / General Manager / HR Director   1996 to 2005
DYNAMIC SOLUTIONS, INC., Tampa, Florida

CHALLENGE: *Launch entrepreneurial venture in an intensely competitive consumer market and create strong infrastructure to support continued growth and market penetration.*

Senior Executive with full responsibility for strategic planning, business development, all HR functions (particular emphasis on staffing), operations, marketing, and P&L performance of an independent venture.

- Built new venture from concept to more than $1 million in annual sales with a 23% profit margin.
- Created performance-based training programs for all hourly and management personnel.
- Achieved and maintained a stable workforce with less than 5% turnover in an industry with average turnover of better than 20%.

Career Change: *From CEO to human resources executive.*

Strategy: *Emphasize only the challenges and results that relate to his target of human resources leadership.*

JOHN GREGORY – Page Two

gregoryjohnjr@mindspring.com
(218) 333-3726

Human Resources Director / CEO   1989 to 1996
LSI SOCIEDAD, S.A., Santo Domingo, Dominican Republic

CHALLENGE: *Orchestrate growth of new international venture within the financial services industry and transition through organizational change and market repositioning.*

Senior Management Executive and HR Director building a new professional services organization. Created organizational infrastructure, recruited/trained personnel, designed marketing and business development programs, and created all administrative and internal reporting systems.

- Built new company from concept into a $12 million annual revenue producer with EBIT of $1 million annually. Achieved/surpassed all corporate revenue and profit objectives.
- Led the organization through a successful internal transition and recreated core business processes to support massive change and recreate corporate image.
- Recruited and trained a team of more than 60. Introduced incentives linked to performance and focused on customer development, retention, and growth.
- Negotiated health and insurance benefit contracts for the corporation. Designed salary structures, incentive programs, and executive compensation plans.

Personal Assistant to CEO   1987 to 1989
BANCO DEL COMBRERO, Santo Domingo, Dominican Republic

CHALLENGE: *Facilitate market and revenue growth for a specialty import/export company.*

Recruited by CEO to assist with building a profitable international business venture. Scope of responsibility spanned all core executive functions, with particular emphasis on organizational design, policy/procedure development, recruitment and training, sales, and marketing.

- Instrumental in driving growth from $2.5 million to $5.5 million in annual revenues.
- Recruited former Procter & Gamble executive to the organization to provide critical industry and market leadership. Recruited sales producers from leading Latin American companies.
- Created organizational infrastructure and HR support to facilitate diversification and expansion into both emerging and established consumer markets.
- Designed HR policies, compensation plans, and performance review schedules.

EDUCATION

Executive MBA—Harvard University—1995 *(Distinguished Alumnus Award)*

BS—Business Administration—Lillymount University—1987

PROFESSIONAL AFFILIATIONS

Society for Human Resource Management (SHRM)

American Society for Training & Development (ASTD)

PART III

Cover Letters for Career Changers

CHAPTER **13**

Writing a Winning Cover Letter

Now that your resume is written, you might think that you're all set to launch your job search. If it were only that easy! Just as critical to the effectiveness and success of your job search campaign is your cover letter. To begin our discussion of this vital element in your search, let's start with a concise definition:

> **Cover Letter**: A document that accompanies your resume and is used to highlight your specific skills, qualifications, competencies, achievements, and more that *relate directly to the position for which you are applying.*

That's right: The best cover letters for every job seeker, particularly career changers, are letters that are targeted to specific positions (for example, a production management position with a local consumer products company, an accounting position with a nationwide management consulting firm, or a technology position with a regional supplier of wireless communications solutions). Targeted letters allow you to selectively include information about your past work experience, training and education, affiliations, professional activities, and more that directly support your candidacy for a particular position. In essence, you're taking everything about your career, laying it out on the table (so to speak), and then selecting only that information which is most important to your current career-change job objective to include in each cover letter.

Figure 13.1 is an example of a wonderfully written cover letter that is targeted to support this candidate's career change, from a police officer to an actuary (quite a remarkable career transition).

1854 Country Trail
Rochester, MN 55904

ROBERTA T. ELLIOTT

(507) 555-1166
bobbye@comcast.com

October 16, 2010

Watson Wyatt
Attention: Human Resources
8400 Normandale Lake Boulevard, Suite 1700
Minneapolis, MN 55437

RE: TheLadders.com Posting for Entry-Level Actuary

Dear Mr. Wyatt:

I've had an interest in—and have been good at—mathematics and science all my life. I'm also extremely curious, always trying to figure what makes things tick and why things happen the way they do. In fact, I rely on those inherent qualities whether I'm assessing a crime scene or generating an accident report. That's why I have the potential to be a great actuary: I possess the necessary analytical mindset blended with a perspective of reality gained from working on the streets every day.

When you take a look at my resume, you will see I recently returned to college to achieve my goal of becoming an actuary. Even though I was working full time and attending to my growing family, I was committed to earning the necessary credentials. In addition to completing a specialization in Actuarial Science to complement my earlier B.A., I have taken the "P" exam and earned VEE credits in Economics and Corporate Finance.

Through my work as a police officer, I have demonstrated that I can readily transition from working as a member of a team to taking command of a situation. Every day I must adapt my communication style to the diverse populations with whom I come in contact. Even being organized is a staple of the job. On a more personal note, I have been an interested investor for several years. All of these qualities and experience converge to make me just the right fit for an actuarial position.

What I can't adequately communicate on my resume is my eagerness to learn. Give me a project and I'll throw myself into it, seeking out whatever I might not know. Isn't this the kind of employee you are looking for? If so, I hope you will contact me so we can discuss my candidacy for an entry-level position. I can be reached at (507) 555-1166 or at bobbye@comcast.com. If I do not hear from you within a week's time, I will follow up to schedule an interview. Thank you for your consideration. I look forward to hearing from you.

Sincerely,

Roberta T. Elliott

Attachment

Figure 13.1: A targeted cover letter (submitted by Janet Beckstrom, ACRW, CPRW).

All too often, job search candidates write what we refer to as general cover letters—letters that can be used to apply for any position with any type of organization. In essence, these letters simply summarize information that is already included on your resume and tend not to be nearly as effective as targeted cover letters that are customized to each position to which you apply. This is particularly true for career changers who must focus both their resumes and their cover letters on the skills and qualifications they possess that are transferable to their new career objectives. When career changers write general cover letters without a specific position in mind, they are not able to highlight information that would be most essential in a particular situation. As such, we strongly urge that you stay away from general letters and devote the time that is necessary to develop targeted cover letters that will sell you into your next position.

Another real advantage to targeted cover letters is that the recipient will notice that you have taken the time to write an individual letter to him or her; and, of course, that leaves a great impression. When you are able to integrate specific information into your letter about the company to which you are applying, it clearly demonstrates your interest in the position and the organization, before you've ever had the opportunity to speak with anyone there. Just think how impressed a prospective employer will be when he or she realizes that you've spent the time and energy necessary to research and get to know their organization. This, in and of itself, will give you a distinct advantage over the competition.

Six Steps to Writing Better Cover Letters

To help guide you in writing and designing your own winning cover letters, we've created a step-by-step process and structure that will allow you to quickly and easily write letters that will get you and your resume noticed, not passed over:

1. Identify Your Key Selling Points
2. Preplan
3. Write the Opening Paragraph
4. Write the Body
5. Write the Closing
6. Polish, Proofread, and Finalize

Now, we're going to explore each of these steps in detail to provide you with an action plan to write your letters with ease and confidence. Our most detailed discussion will be of Step 1: Identify Your Key Selling Points, which is the entire foundation for your cover letter.

STEP 1: IDENTIFY YOUR KEY SELLING POINTS

What qualifications, experiences, achievements, and skills do you bring to a company? It's time to evaluate and quantify what makes you unique, valuable, and interesting to potential employers.

Know Your Objective

The best place to start is by clearly identifying *what* your job objective is now that you're changing careers. Do you want to be a sales associate, a purchasing agent, a chemical engineer, or a transportation planner? Or are you interested in opportunities as an accountant, an optician, a security officer, or a catering manager? Who do you want to be at this juncture in your career? It is critical that you be able to clearly and accurately define who you want to be in an instant. Remember, an instant is all that you have to capture your reader's attention, encouraging him not only to read your cover letter in full, but to read your resume and contact you for a personal interview.

Summarize Your Experience

Just as important, you must be able to clearly identify why an organization would be interested in interviewing and possibly hiring you. If you're a career changer, it will most likely be because of your transferable skills and qualifications and/or your newly acquired educational credentials. However, it might also be because of the companies you've worked for, the promotions you've earned, the accomplishments you've delivered, your technical expertise, your leadership performance, your foreign-language skills, or your international experience. Why would someone be interested in you?

Sell Your Achievements

Your achievements are what set you apart from others with a similar background. They answer the reader's all-important question, "What can you do for me?" because they tell precisely what you have done for someone else. Cover letters and resumes without achievements are simply dry compilations of position titles and responsibilities. They don't sell your unique attributes, and they don't compel readers to pick up the phone and invite you in for an interview.

In thinking about your achievements, ask yourself how you've benefited the organizations where you've worked and, most importantly, how those achievements support your current career-change objectives. In general terms, you can help an organization by doing the following:

- **Saving money** (cost reductions, streamlining, automating, efficiency improvements, manpower reductions)

- **Creating new things** (systems, processes, technologies, methodologies, metrics, techniques)

- **Improving existing things** (reengineering, redesigning, revitalizing, consolidating)

- **Improving personnel and/or organizational performance** (productivity, efficiency, quality, delivery, customer service)

- **Winning honors, awards, and commendations**

- **Making money** (revenues, profits, earnings)

In writing your achievements, think about the three key pieces of information you want to convey about each of your successes: what you did, how it benefited the organization, and how it relates to your current objectives. It is the combination of these three components that will make your achievements—and, in turn, you— shine.

Who you are, what you have achieved, and why an organization would want to hire you are critical questions you must ask yourself before you ever begin to write a cover letter. The answers to those questions will directly impact what you write in your cover letter and how you present that information. You must determine what you have to offer that relates to that organization's specific needs, what will be of interest to them, and what will entice them to read your resume and offer you the opportunity for an interview. That information then becomes the foundation for every cover letter that you write.

STEP 2: PREPLAN

Before you write a single word of your cover letter, you must determine the appropriate strategy for that particular letter. You're not ready to write until you can clearly answer the following questions:

- **Why am I writing this letter?** Am I writing in response to a print or online advertisement, sending a cold-call letter to companies or government agencies, contacting someone in my network, writing to an organization at the recommendation of someone else, or writing a follow-up letter to a company to which I already sent a resume? The answer to this question will significantly impact the content of your cover letter—the introduction in particular.

- **Have I researched the organization and the position?** There will be instances where you know, or can find, information about an organization you are writing to, the services and products it offers, the positions that are open, the types of candidates it hires, the hiring requirements, and so much more. Do your research! The more you know about each company and each position, the more on-target you can write your letters, relating your skills, qualifications, academic credentials, and experience to their identified needs. If you know a company is facing a serious budget crisis, focus on your success in cost-cutting and productivity improvement. If you know that the company is struggling with its technical support organization, focus on your success in building stronger help-desk operations and training technical support personnel. Your goal is to find common ground between you and the company and then leverage that to your advantage.

- Do I have a contact name? Have I double-checked the correct spelling of the name and the person's job title? Do I have the full mailing address or e-mail address? The fact is that if you write to a company's Human Resources department, you'll never quite know where your letter and resume have landed. However, if you write to a particular individual in a particular department with particular contact information, you not only know who has your resume and cover letter, you also know who to follow up with. This is critical for job search success in today's competitive market!

STEP 3: WRITE THE OPENING PARAGRAPH

The opening paragraph of your cover letter is your hook—your sales pitch—that tells your reader who you are and why you are of value to that specific organization. It should be written to entice the recipient to read your letter in its entirety and then take the time to closely review your resume. And, because it is so critical, the opening paragraph is often the section that will take you the longest to write.

> **TIP:** If you're having trouble writing the opening paragraph of your cover letter, leave it for the time being and move on to the body of the letter. Once you've written the rest, the opening paragraph will usually flow much more smoothly and quickly.

There are three specific questions you must address in the opening paragraph of your cover letter:

1. Who are you?

2. Why are you writing?

3. What message are you communicating?

Your answers to these questions, combined with the specific reason you are writing (for example, in response to an advertisement, on recommendation from a network contact, or because of an Internet job lead), will almost always dictate the type of opening you select. Review the introductory paragraphs in the sample cover letters in chapter 14 to help you get started developing your own introductions.

STEP 4: WRITE THE BODY

Now you're ready to tackle the real task at hand: writing the body of your cover letter—the substance, key qualifications, accomplishments, successes, technical expertise, and whatever other information you choose to highlight that will entice the reader to closely review your resume and offer you the opportunity for a personal interview. This can be a particularly challenging process for career changers, who must work extra hard to identify the skills and qualifications they possess that will entice and excite a prospective employer.

In order to sell yourself (or any product) as "the answer," you must highlight the attractive *features* and *benefits* of that product. Put yourself in the shoes of the buyer and ask yourself these questions:

- What will catch my attention?

- What's interesting about this candidate?

- What's innovative or unique about this candidate?

- Why is this candidate different from (or better than) other competitive candidates?

- Do I understand the value I'll get from this candidate?

- Do I need this candidate?

- Do I want this candidate to work for me?

Whether or not you're conscious of it, every time you buy something, you ask yourself these questions and others. It's the typical process that everyone proceeds through when they're deciding whether to make a purchase. It is imperative that you remember this as you begin to write your cover letters. Understand that you must clearly communicate the answers to these questions in order to get people to want to "buy" *you*.

> **TIP:** Your cover letter *should not* be written as "Here I am; give me a job," but *should be* written as, "Here I am; this is why I am so valuable; give me a chance to bring value to your organization and help solve your problems." Focusing on the value and benefits you have to offer is a good way to capture a reader's attention. Remember, the employer's most compelling question is "What can you do for me?" not "What do you want?"

Your challenge, then, is to convey your value in a short and concise document—your cover letter. Unfortunately, there are no rules to guide you in determining what to include in each specific cover letter that you write. It is entirely a judgment call based on the specific situation at hand—the position, the organization, and the required qualifications and experience. What you include in your letter is not necessarily based on what you consider to be your most significant responsibilities and achievements from throughout your career, but rather what is most relevant to the hiring company and its needs, and how those items relate to your specific career-change objectives.

Achievements, accomplishments, contributions, and successes are the cornerstone of any effective cover letter. It goes without saying that you want to demonstrate that you have the right skills, qualifications, and experience for a particular job. However, you do not want your letter to be a "job description"—a mere listing of job responsibilities. First of all, you've addressed a great deal of that information in the resume that you'll be sending along with your cover letter. You do *not* want your letter to simply reiterate what's in your resume. The challenge is to write a cover letter that complements the resume and brings the most notable information to the forefront.

Depending on the format of your letter, you can convey this information in a paragraph format, a bullet-point format, or a combination of both. Consider the fact that paragraphs are often used to "tell a story," whereas bullet points are often best used to highlight finite skills or accomplishments. Use whichever format you feel is most appropriate to convey the particular information about your career change that will position you as an enticing commodity to a prospective employer. If you decide to use full paragraphs, make sure that they are fairly short to promote readability. Edit and tighten your copy so that every word and phrase conveys information that relates to the employer's needs and your most relevant qualifications.

STEP 5: WRITE THE CLOSING

Now that you've written your introductory paragraph and the body of your cover letter, all you have left to do is the closing paragraph. Simple enough; in fact, this is generally the easiest section of your letter to write. To get started, ask yourself these two simple questions:

- What style of closing paragraph do I want to use?

- Is there any specific personal or salary information I want to include that was requested in the advertisement to which I am responding?

When it comes to choosing style, closing paragraphs are easy. There are basically only two styles—passive and assertive—and the distinction between the two styles is evident:

- **Passive:** A passive letter ends with a statement such as "I look forward to hearing from you." With this sentence, you are taking a passive approach, waiting for the hiring company or recruiter to contact you. This is *not* our recommended strategy.

- **Assertive:** An assertive letter ends with a statement such as "I look forward to interviewing with you and will follow up next week to schedule a convenient appointment." In this sentence, you are asserting yourself, telling the recipient that you will follow up, and asking for the interview!

We strongly recommend that you end your cover letters with an assertive closing paragraph. Remember, the only real objective of your cover letter is to get an interview, so *ask for it!* Furthermore, we also advise that you outline an agenda that communicates you will be expecting their call and that if you don't hear from them, you will follow up. This puts you in the driver's seat and in control of your job search. It also demonstrates to a prospective employer that once you've initiated something, you follow it through to completion. This is a valuable trait for any professional.

Inevitably, there will be instances in your job search when you will not be able to follow up:

- If you are responding to a blind advertisement with a P.O. box, you won't know who to call.

- If you are responding to an advertisement that states "No Phone Calls," don't call.

- If you are sending out 1,000 letters to recruiters across the nation, don't waste your time calling them. If they're interested or have an opportunity for which you are suited, they'll call you.

- If you know that you'll never get the individual you want to speak with on the phone, don't waste your time or money.

The closing paragraph of your cover letter is also the preferred placement for any personal or salary information you will include. There are generally only two times you will want to include this type of information:

- **When it has been asked for in an advertisement:** Common requests include such things as salary history (what you have made in the past and are currently earning if you are employed), salary requirements (what your current salary objectives are), citizenship status, or geographic preference.

- **When you are writing "cold-call" letters to recruiters:** When contacting recruiters, we recommend that you at least minimally address your salary requirements (a range—$65,000 to $75,000 annually—is fine) and any geographic preferences in the closing paragraph of your cover letter.

STEP 6: POLISH, PROOFREAD, AND FINALIZE

The process we recommend for writing your cover letters suggests that you first craft the opening, then the middle, and then the closing of each letter. Although the step-by-step process makes the task fairly quick and easy, you will probably find that your letters need final polishing, wordsmithing, and tweaking to ensure that each section flows into the next and that you have a cohesive-sounding whole.

Take the time to proofread each letter thoroughly and carefully. Read it for sense and flow; then read it again to check for spelling errors, punctuation mistakes, and grammatical inconsistencies. We cannot emphasize this point enough. The people who receive your cover letter and resume *do* judge your professionalism based on the quality and accuracy of these documents.

In fact, in a survey of hiring authorities we conducted for a prior book, *90 percent of respondents* mentioned quality and appearance factors (such as typos, misspellings, smudged print, and low-quality paper) as reasons for *immediately discarding a resume*. Don't take a chance that your carefully written letter and resume will end up in the circular file before your qualifications are even considered.

Here are a few things to look out for during the polishing phase:

- **Spelling:** Use your computer's spell-checker, but don't rely on it totally. The spell-checker won't flag an "it's" that should be "its" or a "there" that should be "their." Make triple-certain you've correctly spelled all names: people, organizations, and so on.

- **Grammar and punctuation:** If you're not confident about your grammar and punctuation skills, purchase an all-purpose reference guide and use it as often as you need to. Don't let your cover letter be discarded because of basic grammar and punctuation errors.

- **Interesting language:** As much as possible, avoid cliches and outdated language (such as "Enclosed please find my resume"). It's difficult to find new ways to express familiar sentiments (such as "I would appreciate the opportunity for an interview"), and it's certainly not necessary to come up with unique language for every phrase. But make sure that your cover letter doesn't sound like a cookie-cutter, one-size-fits-all letter that could have been written by any job seeker.

Best Tips for Writing Winning Cover Letters

Here's our most important cover-letter advice for career changers, gleaned from our experience writing thousands of cover letters, thank-you letters, and other job-search communications.

DON'T REINVENT THE WHEEL

Much of our discussion has focused on the fact that your cover letters should be written individually based on the specific situation. And that is quite true. The more focused your letters, the greater the impact and the more likely you are to get a response and an opportunity to interview. However, you *do not* have to reinvent the wheel with each and every cover letter you write. If you're transitioning into a teaching career and are writing in response to numerous teaching advertisements, you can very often use the same letter with just a few minor editorial changes to match each opportunity. Remember to use your word-processing program's copy and paste function. It's a great, labor-saving tool!

SELL IT TO ME; DON'T TELL IT TO ME

Just like resume writing, cover letter writing is sales—pure and simple. You have a commodity to sell—yourself—and your challenge is to write a marketing communication (AKA, a cover letter) that is powerful and pushes the reader to action. (You want him to call you for an interview!) Therefore, it is essential that when writing your letters you *sell* your achievements and don't just *tell* your responsibilities.

Here's a quick example. If you've been a computer programmer and now want to transition into a career in technology sales, you could tell your reader that you developed new computer programs for inventory management and warehousing. Or, you could sell the fact that your new inventory programs generated more than $2 million in annual cost savings for your company's clients in the logistics and transportation industries. Which letter would capture your interest?

DON'T ALWAYS MENTION THAT YOU'RE A CAREER CHANGER

In certain instances you'll want to mention in your cover letter that you're a career changer; in other instances you will not. If you've just completed a training program, certification course, or college degree to facilitate your career transition, you'll always want to highlight that in your cover letter. In fact, in many situations, it will be your most prominent selling point. Conversely, in most other circumstances, you won't want to wave a red flag that states you're changing careers. Rather, focus on the skills, accomplishments, talents, experiences, and more that you bring to a new employer that support your new career objectives. In essence, showcase the items that are of most interest to a new employer's needs. The fact that you have those qualifications and talents is what matters the most, and not the fact that you have to transition them from one career path into another.

GET OVER WRITER'S BLOCK

Very often, the most difficult part of writing a cover letter is getting started. You can sit and look at that blank piece of paper or computer screen for hours, frustrated and wondering whether the whole world has such a hard time writing cover letters. If writing is part of your daily work responsibilities, the process might not be too arduous. However, if you do not have to write on a regular basis, cover letters can be an especially formidable task. That's why it is so important to follow the step-by-step process we have created. It is guaranteed to make cover letter writing faster, easier, and much less painful!

If you're still having trouble, consider this simple thought:

You do not have to start at the beginning.

Even after writing thousands and thousands of cover letters, we'll sit stumped, unable to come up with just the right opening paragraph. Instead of wasting time and brain power, and getting frustrated, we'll just leave it alone and move on to another section in the letter that we feel more confident writing. You'll find that once you get going, new ideas will pop into your head and the more difficult sections will come much more easily and confidently.

ANSWER THE EMPLOYER'S MOST IMPORTANT QUESTION: "WHAT CAN YOU DO FOR ME?"

A powerful cover letter can help you get what you want: a new, perhaps more advanced, and more satisfying position in the new career of your choice. It is certainly important that you understand what you want to do, the kind of organization you'd like to work for, and the environment in which you'll be most productive. Yet you must remember that employers aren't really interested in you. They're interested in *what you can do for them*. If you do not keep this thought in the forefront of your mind when writing your cover letters, you're likely to produce a self-centered-sounding "here I am" letter that probably won't do much to advance your job search.

When writing your cover letters, consider the employer's needs and make sure that you communicate that you can add value, solve problems, and deliver benefits for that employer. You can do this through a strong focus on accomplishments ("Ah, she did that for IBM's technology center so I'm confident she can transfer those skills and do the same for me") and through careful attention to the wording and tone of your letter so that you appear to be more interested in contributing to the organization than satisfying your own personal needs.

Then, be sure to review the Cover Letter Checklist on the next page to be certain that your letters meet all of our requirements for style, appropriateness, quality of text, quality of presentation, and effectiveness. Follow our rules and we guarantee that your letters will open doors, generate interviews, and help you land your next great professional opportunity.

FORMAT APPROPRIATELY

Most of the cover letters that appear in chapter 14 are formatted for printing and mailing. If you look at three of the cover letters that have companion resumes (letters 2, 6, and 7), you will see that they have the same headings, typestyles, and overall appearance as the resume. Whenever you have the occasion to print and mail or hand-deliver a cover letter, be certain that its format matches your resume to create a consistent and professional image.

Of course, we realize that most of the time you will be sending your cover letter as an e-mail message and not as a printed and mailed letter. We recommend that you paste or type your letter into the body of the e-mail and attach your resume as a Word document. Do not include the heading and contact information that normally appear at the top of your cover letter. Simply begin with the salutation, followed by your cover letter, followed by an e-mail signature line that includes all of your key contact information. Letter #8 in chapter 14 is formatted as an e-mail message. You can see that it is clean and professional, and includes all pertinent contact information at the bottom.

As a final note, be certain to write a clear explanatory subject line when sending your resume and cover letter by e-mail.

Cover Letter Checklist

Before mailing, faxing, or e-mailing each cover letter you prepare, complete the following checklist to be sure that you have met all the rules for cover letter writing. If you cannot answer "yes" to *all* of the questions, go back and edit your letter as necessary before mailing it. The only questions for which a "no" answer is acceptable are questions 5 and 6, which relate specifically to the organization to which you are writing. As we have stated previously, there will be instances when you can find this information, but there will also be instances (for example, when writing to a P.O. box) when you cannot.

		YES	NO
1.	Do I convey an immediate understanding of who I am in the first two sentences of my cover letter?	❑	❑
2.	Is my cover letter format unique, and does my letter stand out?	❑	❑
3.	Have I highlighted my most relevant qualifications?	❑	❑
4.	Have I highlighted my most relevant achievements?	❑	❑
5.	Have I included information I know about the company or the specific position for which I am applying?	❑	❑
6.	Have I highlighted why I want to work for this company?	❑	❑
7.	Is my letter neat, clean, and well-presented without being over-designed?	❑	❑
8.	Is my letter error-free?	❑	❑
9.	Is my cover letter short and succinct, preferably no longer than one page?	❑	❑

	YES	NO
10. Do I ask for an interview in the letter?	❑	❑
11. Have I formatted my cover letter appropriately for mailing or e-mailing?	❑	❑

CHAPTER 14

Sample Cover Letters for Career Changers

Following are eight more sample cover letters for your review. Look at them closely. Select opening paragraphs, closing paragraphs, formats, and styles that you like, and then model your own cover letters accordingly. You'll find that by using these sample letters for hints, your letter-writing process will be much easier and faster. To see even more samples and get more help with writing your cover letters, see our book *Cover Letter Magic* (JIST Publishing), the industry's leading book on cover letter writing, now in its fourth edition.

HILMON C. HEARD

5875 Northcrest Manor
Covington, GA 30012

hcheard@gmail.com

770.666.8988

March 15, 2010

Brian M. Phillips
Director of Human Resources
WCK Enterprises
2607 Valley Ridge Blvd.
Atlanta, GA 30305

Dear Mr. Phillips:

I have been waiting for an opportunity like this to write to you. Please take into consideration my application for the position of Network Operations Area Manager—an excellent match for my qualifications. Your organization will benefit from my strong process-improvement orientation, expert problem-solving skills, and ability to communicate persuasively and openly.

Highlights of my professional career include the following:

➢ Demonstrated client value-add through all client interactions at all levels.
➢ Integrated technological, procedural, and organizational changes into business.
➢ Continuous development and implementation of process improvements.
➢ History of reliably exceeding quality, productivity, and capacity targets.
➢ Focus on proactive, predictive management.

For the past 10 years, I served overseas as a contractor with the military as a Project Manager, and I'm confident my skills will translate well into this position. You will find me to be decisive, articulate, energetic, and confident—the type of person on whom your team will rely.

I would appreciate the opportunity to further discuss my experience and qualifications with you. Please feel free to call me at (770) 666-8988. Thank you for your consideration.

Sincerely,

Hilmon Heard

Enclosure: Resume

Wonderful example of a quasi military-to-civilian career transition cover letter where focus is on skills, qualifications, and successes, with only very brief mention of military experience.

COVER LETTER 2: BY CAROL ALTOMARE, MRW, ACRW, CPRW, CCMC, CJSS

ROBERT EVANS, D.C.

18 Lee Boulevard ◆ Woodbridge, VA 22192 ◆ 703-884-2060 ◆ evansdc@gmail.com

March 15, 2010

Human Resources Director
P.O. Box 10998
Columbia, MD 21046

RE: Mid-Atlantic Pharmaceutical Sales Executive

Dear Sir/Madam:

As a respected chiropractic doctor with a demonstrated skill in marketing and promoting medical services to clients, I believe I am someone who will be an asset to your sales organization. With extensive medical knowledge, strong client management skills, and a proven record of success in building and growing a thriving business, I would like to explore the opportunity of putting my talents to work for you.

Key to my success, I am highly effective in leveraging relationship-building skills and a solution-oriented approach to identify need, communicate value, and gain client buy-in. Further, I have a wealth of knowledge about pharmaceuticals, medical devices, anatomy and physiology, and all of the other disciplines you would expect of a practicing doctor.

Among my accomplishments, I have

- Effectively marketed and promoted my chiropractic practice, as well as individual client services, building a successful business in a short period.

- Cultivated productive business relationships within the medical profession to build a pipeline for referrals and open new opportunities for growth.

- Excelled in managing client relationships, providing exceptional service while maintaining client accounts long term.

In short, I am a driven professional who gets results. I am confident I have what it takes to be an outstanding contributor in your organization and welcome your call to discuss this opportunity further. As requested, my salary history has averaged $150,000 over the past several years.

Sincerely,

Robert Evans, D.C.

Enclosure

Sent in response to a posted opening, this cover letter emphasizes a combination of business success and medical, pharmaceutical, and patient management experience. The closing paragraph responds to a request for salary information. (Companion resume on page 122.)

COVER LETTER 3: BY JULIANNE S. FRANKE, MS, CCMC, CPRW, MRW

LYNNE SUTHERLAND
2229 Pond Hollow Drive
Lawrenceville, GA 30043
(770) 922-7744
lsutherland29@aol.com

March 15, 2010

P.O. Box 12908
Atlanta, GA 30908

RE: Human Resources Manager Job Posting #HR-3728

As an innovative and resourceful management professional with a proven record as a strategic thinker and *change agent,* I am seeking a leadership position in human resources management. My broad-based background includes 15 years of experience in volunteer administration, program development, advocacy, fund-raising, and human resources, and I am confident that I can make an immediate and long-term contribution to your organization.

Having excelled in challenging environments involving diverse responsibilities and the ability to multi-task, several strengths have emerged:

- As a *strategic thinker* with strong tactical execution skills, I can turn a fledgling organization into a smooth-running operation by creating policies, procedures, and systems to improve customer service and ensure compliance with regulatory guidelines.

- As a *dynamic leader* with excellent communication skills, I can effectively manage transitions and empower staff and volunteers to facilitate synergy and *esprit de corps*.

- As a *self-starter* who takes the initiative to make things happen, I can put programs in place to drive strategic initiatives, recruit and motivate staff, and champion the cause through development programs to secure funding.

- As a *relationship-oriented* individual, I have cultivated alliances with individuals at all levels and segments of society—in the corporate world, with Boards of Directors, and with key people in government and social services. My negotiation skills and subtle power of persuasion have been instrumental in making things happen through mutual cooperation and by leveraging win-win solutions.

These examples are just a sampling of what I can offer your organization. The attached resume documents my career accomplishments in more detail. I do believe it would be beneficial to both of us to meet, explore your challenges, and allow me to expand on how I can be of service. Thank you.

Sincerely,

Lynne Sutherland

Resume enclosed

Great example of well-targeted cover letter supporting job seeker's transition from the not-for-profit sector into a human resources management position with a for-profit company. Note the bulleted items that focus on the core talents detailed in the online job posting.

CARTER DANIELS
2901 Hickory Wind Drive, Montgomery, AL 33772
Cell: 303.555.2837   Email: cdan24@aol.com

March 15, 2010

Mr. Trent Todd, CFP
Franklin & Associates Investments
1703 Bradford Boulevard
St. Louis, MO 63123

Dear Mr. Todd:

It is with great anticipation and enthusiasm that I submit my resume and cover letter for the position of Financial Adviser with Franklin & Associates Investments. After speaking with you on the phone earlier today, I fully appreciate the opportunity your company presents. Please allow me to detail my background as a high school educator and coach and explain how those experiences will serve FAI.

You are looking for a performance-driven individual. With 17 years of experience in teaching and coaching, I possess a results-oriented focus that emphasizes goal attainment in the classroom and on the football field. As you are aware, Clayton High School has reached the state football finals in 4 of the past 6 years, with 2 state championships to its credit. As important to me as our wins are, I am perhaps even more proud of the fact that CHS football players have collectively earned one of the highest team GPAs in Missouri high school football.

FAI offers career autonomy through independent franchise ownership. This opportunity is the perfect use of my business acumen, leadership skills, outgoing personality, and results-focused coaching style. I have managed the financial aspects of all my teams and have proven to be a savvy businessperson with tremendous attention to detail. When I began as head coach at Clayton High School in 2000, I inherited a team with poor financial records, unnecessary spending, and ill-executed fund-raising projects. Since that time, my team has operated solely in the black, and I have cut spending by more than $20K annually.

Financial advisers at FAI have unlimited earnings potential. As we discussed on the phone, one of the drawbacks of my current position is the lack of financial incentives for excellence. I welcome the opportunity for a commission-based earnings structure that would translate my hard work into financial success.

In summary, I am **exactly** the kind of person FAI is looking for. I am driven to excellence in all that I do, have a high profile and excellent reputation in our community, possess the requisite business and financial management skills, and desire the financial rewards that come with hard work. I will call you on Thursday, March 18, between 3:30–5:00 to answer any questions you may have about my qualifications and motivation and to schedule an interview time. Until then, I hope to see you in the stands Friday as we make another run for the state championship!

Sincerely,

Carter Daniels

Enclosure: resume

Outstanding example of letter supporting major transition from high school coach to financial advisor, focusing on the commonality of skills, qualifications, and performance across both professions. Note the nicely worded, yet assertive, closing paragraph.

Kim Stiler

5118 Sapphire Park Vista, Cherry Hill, NJ 07392
765-222-9223 H • 765-222-3627 C • stiler@aol.com

March 15, 2010

Mr. Hank Givenchy
Worldwide Recruiters
2134 Elm Street
Rochester, NY 14605

Dear Mr. Givenchy:

Do you have a client in need of an innovative business development professional with an impressive record of driving revenue and market-share growth through innovative sales, marketing, and public relations initiatives? My experience embraces 14 years in **health care**, my preferred field of interest, as well as 6 years of success in real estate.

My professional portfolio of qualifications includes:

- Conceptualization, strategic development, design, and execution of hundreds of **marketing, communications, advertising, and PR campaigns** that generate new opportunities and expand existing business.
- Strong **relationship-building** skills and an acute ability to turn around lackluster performance, boost morale, and ignite change.
- Outstanding success in creating **press releases** that reduce the cost of advertising as well as corporate-wide communications that promote cross-functional interactions.
- Solid **market research, analysis, and strategic planning** skills, the foundation for every one of my successful business development campaigns.

In today's highly competitive health-care arena, companies need business development professionals who can make things happen. This is what I do. I have the passion, drive, and experience to help your client achieve its goals.

I will call your office on Friday, March 19, to schedule an appointment, and I look forward to what I anticipate will be the first of many positive communications. You can, of course, feel free to contact me sooner if you'd like. Thank you for your consideration.

Sincerely,

Kim Stiler

enclosure

Unique, well-targeted cover letter that explains this job seeker's transition from health care to real estate and now back to health care, her true career passion. The closing paragraph is assertive, giving a specific date for follow-up with the recruiter who is managing this search for the client company.

COVER LETTER 6: BY ROBYN L. FELDBERG, NCRW, ACRW, CJSS, CCMC

KATHRYN LAWRENCE

8827 Buchanan Drive • Lewisville, Texas 75027 • KathrynLawrence@gmail.com • (214) 555-9628

March 15, 2010

Ms. Sally Morrison
Director of Hiring
Montview Hospital Center
1000 Montview Drive
Dallas, TX 78723

Dear Ms. Morrison:

Throughout my career, the one constant has been my sincere desire to help people.

Having worked for 6 years as an initial responder to serious, multiple-trauma traffic accidents, I gained extensive experience providing first aid and assisting with triage. In this capacity, I also found my true calling and passion—caring for people who require emergency medical attention and using strengths from my previous career to make quick and accurate assessments, ensure prompt and conscientious decisions, and provide calm and attentive customer service.

When you review my enclosed resume, you'll note that I'll graduate from nursing school at the end of this month, when I'll also test for my RN license. At this time, I'm eager to explore opportunities to work in Montview's emergency department. I feel certain that my background, while slightly unusual, uniquely qualifies me to succeed in the fast-paced world of emergency medicine. Your organization will benefit from my professionalism, dedication to excellence, and willingness to work hard every day to do whatever it takes to become a world-class nurse.

Some notable performance highlights related to my education and student nursing experience include the following:

- **Maintained a 3.47 GPA out of 4.0,** and made the Dean's List 2 out of 3 semesters.
- **Won a coveted position in Baylor Grapevine's Emergency Department,** 1 of only 3 students accepted.
- **Earned Lifesaving (BLS) for Healthcare Providers Certification** in 2008.
- **Attained Advanced Cardiac Life Support Certification** in 2009.
- **Chaired the first Bone Marrow Donation Drive** in conjunction with Cook Children's Hospital and North Central Texas College.
- **Served as an Executive Board Member and Class Representative** for the National Student Nurses' Association.

I would welcome an opportunity to meet with you to discuss Montview's needs and the results you could expect from me, and I will follow up with you in the next two weeks. Regarding salary requirements, I would prefer to discuss that during our interview when I have a better understanding of the position and hours. Thank you for your time and consideration.

Sincerely,

Kathryn Lawrence

Enclosure: Resume

This cover letter clearly communicates this job seeker's specific educational and professional qualifications for her transition from a police officer to a nurse. Note language for responding to a request for salary requirements. (Companion resume on page 160.)

KATHERINE ESPERIAN

191 South Main Street ▶ Manchester, CT 06042 ▶ (860) 685-9148 ▶ Kathy@SBCGlobal.net

WEB DESIGNER

Strategic Design ▶ Interactive Media ▶ Consultation
View my portfolio at www.StrategicWebDesign.com

March 15, 2010

Cheri Stevens, Senior Recruiter
Olympic Staffing, Inc.
43 South Main Street
Glastonbury, CT 06033

Dear Ms. Stevens:

With a focused commitment on business strategy, organization, web design, and adherence to project deadlines, I am confident my background and skills will interest you in regards to a web designer or project manager position.

I bring to an organization strong qualifications in various areas of marketing and project management that include client relations, web and graphic design, production operations, and SEO/SEM management.

Having executed consistent results over the last several years, I am eager to hear back from you regarding how I can apply my strengths to help your client. I have enclosed my resume to provide more information on my career strengths and skills.

I appreciate your consideration.

Sincerely,

Katherine Esperian

enclosure

Brevity is often the best strategy, as is clearly demonstrated in this cover letter supporting this job seeker's transition from self-employment to a company position in Web design and management. (Companion resume on page 110.)

COVER LETTER 8: BY ANN BOYER, M.ED., CCMC, ACRW

Subject: **Corporate & Onboard Employment: Commitment to Excellence**

As a courteous and outgoing **Travel Industry Professional** with domestic onboard cruise line experience and a proven track record for creating and promoting profitable tour endeavors and services, I am confident my background will enhance Meridian Cruises' corporate values and standards of excellence.

Over the course of my 20-year career, I have developed strong competencies in the following areas:

Customer Service: Diverse, well-rounded hospitality industry experience and training with a solid record of formulating creative, cost-effective solutions that exceed customers' expectations and promote company goodwill.

Development/Planning/Promotion: Demonstrated ability to create and implement educational, recreational, and promotional travel programs utilizing my research, writing, marketing, photographic, and display abilities. Accomplishments include tour development, tour arrangement and planning, event planning, sales, and outdoor and portrait photography.

Operational Knowledge: Practical experience in cruise line operations and procedures. Shipboard certifications include Merchant Mariners Document (MMD), Occupational Safety & Health Administration (OSHA) Certification, and United States Public Health (USPH) Certification.

I am interested in both corporate and onboard employment opportunities. In addition, I understand the ramifications of working onboard and am willing to relocate.

Creativity, commitment to excellence, and ability to successfully manage myriad diverse challenges serve as the basis for my career achievements. I believe these qualities, along with my cruise line and hospitality experience, bring value to Meridian Cruises.

Sincerely,

Thomas M. Williams
901-321-4900 (Home)
910-916-5432 (Cell)
tmwilliams25@att.net

Perfect example of an e-mail cover letter used to help this Transportation Security Officer transition back into a corporate or onboard position in the travel industry. (Companion resume on page 128.)

APPENDIX

Internet Career Resources

The Internet has changed job search forever. Information that used to take days or even weeks to find can now be accessed in just minutes. It truly is a revolution.

However, the pace of development and the number of new Internet sites that emerge every day make it impossible to provide a comprehensive list of *all* Web sites related to employment, careers, and job search. The following list includes some of our favorite sites, some of the largest sites, and some of the best sites.

This list is by no means comprehensive. We strongly suggest that you devote the time necessary to conduct your own independent Web-based research as applicable to your specific job search campaign and career path.

Dictionaries and Glossaries

These sites provide outstanding information on keywords and acronyms.

Acronym Finder	www.acronymfinder.com
ComputerUser Dictionary	www.computeruser.com/resources/dictionary
Dave VE7CNV's Truly Canadian Dictionary of Canadian Spelling	www.luther.ca/~dave7cnv/cdnspelling/cdnspelling.html
Duhaime's Legal Dictionary	www.duhaime.org
High-Tech Dictionary Chat Symbols	www.computeruser.com/resources/dictionary/chat.html
InvestorWords.com	www.investorwords.com
Law.com Legal Dictionary	www.dictionary.law.com
Legal Dictionary	www.nolo.com/lawcenter/dictionary/wordindex.cfm
Merriam-Webster Collegiate Dictionary & Thesaurus	www.m-w.com/home.htm

TechWeb TechEncyclopedia	www.techweb.com/encyclopedia/
Verizon Glossary of Telecom Terms	http://www22.verizon.com/wholesale/ glossary/0,2624,P_Q,00.html
Washington Post Business Glossary	www.washingtonpost.com/wp-srv/ business/longterm/glossary/index.htm
Webopedia: Online Dictionary for Computer and Internet Terms	www.webopedia.com
Whatis?com Technology Terms	http://whatis.techtarget.com
Wordsmyth: The Educational Dictionary/Thesaurus	www.wordsmyth.net
Yahoo! Babel Fish Text Translation	http://babelfish.yahoo.com/

Job Search Sites

You'll find thousands of current professional employment opportunities on these sites.

GENERAL SITES

6FigureJobs	www.6figurejobs.com
AllStar Jobs	www.allstarjobs.com
America's CareerInfoNet	www.acinet.org/acinet
BlackWorld Careers	www.blackworld.com/careers.htm
BlueCollar.com (Australia)	www.bluecollar.com.au
Canada WorkInfo Net	www.workinfonet.ca
CareerBuilder	www.careerbuilder.com
Career.com	www.career.com
CareerExposure	www.careerexposure.com
CareerJournal	www.careerjournal.com
Careermag.com	www.careermag.com
Career Services (New Zealand)	www.careers.govt.nz/
Contract Employment Weekly	www.ceweekly.com
EmploymentGuide.com	www.employmentguide.com
Excite	http://careers.excite.com
Futurestep	www.futurestep.com
Help Wanted	www.helpwanted.com

The Internet Job Locator	www.joblocator.com
JobBankUSA	www.jobbankusa.com
JobCircle	www.jobcircle.com
Job.com	www.job.com
JobHuntersBible.com	www.jobhuntersbible.com
Job-Hunt.org	www.job-hunt.org
Jobserve	www.jobserve.us
Monster.com	www.monster.com
NationJob Network	www.nationjob.com
Net Temps	www.net-temps.com
NowHiring.com	www.nowhiring.com
Online-Jobs.Com	www.online-jobs.com
The Riley Guide	www.rileyguide.com
Saludos Hispanos	www.saludos.com
Spherion	www.spherion.com
The Ladders	www.theladders.com
TrueCareers	www.truecareers.com
Vault	www.vault.com
Yahoo! HotJobs.com	http://hotjobs.yahoo.com
WorkTree	www.worktree.com

MILITARY TRANSITION SITES

About.com: Military Separation	http://usmilitary.about.com/library/weekly/aa082001a.htm
Absolute Portal	http://abportal.50megs.com/careers/military.html
Air Force Times	www.airforcetimes.com/careers/
Army Times	www.armytimes.com
Career Command Post	www.careercommandpost.com/
Corporate Gray	www.corporategray.com/
G.I. Jobs Magazine	www.gijobs.net
Hire Vets First	www.hirevetsfirst.gov
Key to Career Success	www.careeronestop.org/militarytransition/
Military.com	www.military.com/Careers/Home
Military Exits	www.militaryexits.com/

Military Hire.com	www.militaryhire.com
Military Money	www.militarymoney.com/resources/careers/
Military Resumes	www.militaryresumes.org/
Military-to-Civilian Interview Questions	www.job-interview.net/Bank/QMilitary.htm
Military Transition Links	www.militarytransitionlinks.com/
Navy Times	www.navytimes.com/careers/
The Riley Guide	www.rileyguide.com/vets.html
Transition Assistance Online	www.taonline.com/
USAJOBS	www.usajobs.gov/veteranscenter/
Washington Post: How to Switch from a Military to a Civilian Career	www.washingtonpost.com/ac2/wp-dyn?pagename=article&node=&contentId=A60971-2003Feb24&notFound=true

CAREER-SPECIFIC SITES

Accounting Careers

American Association of Finance and Accounting	www.aafa.com
Career Bank	www.careerbank.com
CFO.com	www.cfonet.com
CPAnet	www.CPAnet.com
SmartPros Accounting	www.accountingnet.com

Arts and Media Careers

Fashion Career Center	www.fashioncareercenter.com
Playbill (Theatre Jobs)	www.playbill.com/jobs/find/
TVJobs.com	www.tvjobs.com

Education Careers

Chronicle of Higher Education Career Network	www.chronicle.com/jobs
Council for Advancement and Support of Education	www.case.org
Educationjobs.com	www.educationjobs.com
Teaching Jobs	www.teaching-jobs.org
TopSchoolJobs.org	www.topschooljobs.org
UniversityJobs.com	www.universityjobs.com

Food Service Careers

Chefs Job Network	www.chefsjobnetwork.com
Escoffier On Line	http://escoffier.com
Foodservice.com	www.foodservice.com

Government Careers

Federal Jobs Net	www.federaljobs.net
FRS Federal Jobs Central	www.fedjobs.com
GetaGovJob.com	www.getagovjob.com
GovExec.com	www.govexec.com
HRS Federal Job Search	www.hrsjobs.com
USAJOBS	www.usajobs.gov

Health Care/Medical/Pharmaceutical Careers

Alliance of Medical Recruiters	www.physicianrecruiters.com
AlliedHealthCareers.com	www.alliedhealthcareers.com
HealthJobSite.com	www.healthjobsite.com
MedHunters.com	www.medhunters.com
Medzilla	www.medzilla.com
Monster Healthcare	http://healthcare.monster.com
Nurse.com	www.nurse.com
Pharmaceutical Company Database	www.coreynahman.com/ pharmaceutical_company_ database.html
RehabJobsOnline	www.rehabjobs.com
Rx Career Center	www.rxcareercenter.com

Human Resources Careers

HR Hub	www.hrhub.com
HRJobs.com	www.hrjobs.com
Human Resources and Skills Development Canada	http://www.hrsdc.gc.ca/en/ home.shtml
Jobs4HR	www.jobs4hr.com
Society for Human Resource Management	www.shrm.org/jobs

International Careers

EscapeArtist.com	www.escapeartist.com
International Jobs Center	www.internationaljobs.org

LatPro	www.latpro.com
OverseasJobs.com	www.overseasjobs.com

Legal Careers

AttorneyJobs.com	www.attorneyjobs.com
Greedy Associates	www.greedyassociates.com

Sales and Marketing Careers

American Marketing Association	www.marketingpower.com/careers/
MarketingJobs.com	www.marketingjobs.com
NationJob	www.nationjob.com/marketing
SalesJobs.com	www.salesjobs.com
Sales Ladder	http://sales.theladders.com

Technology/Engineering Careers

American Institute of Architects	www.aia.org
American Society for Quality	www.asq.org
Chancellor & Chancellor Resources for Careers	www.chancellor.com/fr_careers.html
ComputerWork.com	www.computerwork.com
Computerworld Careers Knowledge Center	www.computerworld.com/careertopics/careers?from=left
Dice	www.dice.com
IEEE-USA Job Service	www.ieeeusa.org
National Society of Professional Engineers	www.nspe.org
National Technical Employment Services	www.ntes.com

Sites for Miscellaneous Specific Fields

AG Careers/Farms.com	www.agcareers.com
American Public Works Association	www.apwa.net/WorkZone/
AutoCareers.com	www.autocareers.com
CEOExpress	www.ceoexpress.com
Environmentalcareer.com	www.environmental-jobs.com
Environmental Career Opportunities	www.ecojobs.com

Find a Pilot	www.findapilot.com
Logistics Jobs	www.jobsinlogistics.com
MBACareers.com	www.mbacareers.com
Social Work Jobs	www.socialservice.com

Company Information

These outstanding resources can be a great help when you are researching specific companies.

555-1212.com	www.555-1212.com
Brint.com	www.brint.com
EDGAR Online	www.edgar-online.com
Fortune Magazine	www.fortune.com
Hoover's Business Profiles	www.hoovers.com
infoUSA (small business information)	www.infousa.com
OneSource CorpTech	www.corptech.com
SuperPages.com	www.bigbook.com
U.S. Chamber of Commerce	www.uschamber.com/
Vault	www.vault.com

Interviewing Tips and Techniques

The expert guidance at these sites will help you sharpen and strengthen your interviewing skills.

About.com Interviewing	http://jobsearch.about.com/od/interviewsnetworking/
Bradley CVs Introduction to Job Interviews	www.bradleycvs.demon.co.uk/interview/index.htm
Job-Interview.net	www.job-interview.net
Northeastern University Career Services	http://careerservices.neu.edu/job_search/interviewing.php
Wendy Enelow	www.wendyenelow.com/articles/?page_id=11

Salary and Compensation Information

Learn from the experts to strengthen your negotiating skills and increase your salary.

Abbott, Langer & Associates	www.abbott-langer.com
Bureau of Labor Statistics	www.bls.gov/bls/wages.htm
CareerOneStop	www.careeronestop.org/SalariesBenefits/
Clayton Wallis Co.	www.ictcw.com/
Economic Research Institute	www.erieri.com
Janco Associates MIS Salary Survey	www.psrinc.com/salary.htm
JobStar	www.jobstar.org/tools/salary/
Monster.com Salary Info	salary.monster.com/
Salary.com	www.salary.com
Salary Expert	www.salaryexpert.com
WorldatWork: The Total Rewards Association	www.worldatwork.org

INDEX OF CONTRIBUTORS

The sample resumes and cover letters in chapters 4 through 14 were written by professional resume and cover letter writers. If you need help with your resume and job search correspondence, you can use the following list to locate a career professional. Many, if not all, of these resume professionals work with clients long-distance as well as in their local areas.

You will notice that most of the writers have one or more credentials listed after their names. In fact, some have half a dozen or more! The careers industry offers extensive opportunities for ongoing training, and most career professionals take advantage of these opportunities to build their skills and keep their knowledge current. If you are curious about what any one of these credentials means, we suggest that you contact the resume writer directly. He or she will be glad to discuss certifications and other qualifications as well as information about services that can help you in your career transition.

Catherine A. Alfandre, CCMC, MRW, ACRW
P.O. Box 453
Easton, CT 06612
Phone/fax: (203) 445-7906
E-mail: cathy@cathyalfandre.com
www.cathyalfandre.com

Carol Altomare, MRW, ACRW, CPRW, CCMC, CJSS
World Class Resumes
P.O. Box 483
Three Bridges, NJ 08887
Phone: (908) 237-1883
E-mail: carol@worldclassresumes.com
www.worldclassresumes.com

Ann Baehr, CPRW
Best Resumes of New York
49 Fern Ave.
East Islip, NY 11730
Phone: (631) 224-9300
E-mail: resumesbest@earthlink.net
www.e-bestresumes.com

Mark Bartz, ACRW
3198 Bellflower Way
Lakeland, FL 33811
Phone: (863) 248-6105
E-mail: mark@hiringleaders.com
www.WhatTheHeckDoIDo.com

Janet Beckstrom, ACRW, CPRW
Word Crafter
1717 Montclair Ave.
Flint, MI 48503
Phone: (810) 232-9257
E-mail: janet@wordcrafter.com

Ann Boyer, M.Ed., CCMC, ACRW
P.O. Box 1143
Fair Oaks, CA 95628
Phone: (916) 942-9207
E-mail: aboyerconsult@aol.com

Diane Hudson Burns, CPRW, CCMC, CCM, CEIP, JCTC, CLTMC, CPCC, CFJST
Career Marketing Techniques
Phone: (208) 323-9636
E-mail: diane@polishedresumes.com
www.polishedresumes.com

Romona Camarata, M.S.Ed., ADM, GCDF, CPRW, CCC, CCMC, MBTI
R.C. Consulting LLC
571 Holliday Lane, Ste. 100
Indianapolis, IN 46260
Phone: (317) 258-2761
E-mail: camarata@iquest.net
www.romonacamarata.com

Annemarie Cross, CPRW, CEIP, CRW, CCM, CERW, CEIC, CMRW
Advanced Employment Concepts
P.O. Box 91
Hallam, Victoria 3803 Australia
Phone: +613 9708 6930
E-mail: success@aresumewriter.com.au
www.aresumewriter.com.au

Jean Cummings, MAT, CPBS, CPRW, CEIP
A Resume For Today
123 Minot Road
Concord, MA 01742
Phone: (978) 254-5492
Toll-free: (800) 324-1699
E-mail: jc@YesResumes.com
www.AResumeForToday.com

Norine Dagliano, CPRW
ekm Inspirations
616 Highland Way
Hagerstown, MD 21740
Phone: (310) 766-2032
E-mail: ndagliano@yahoo.com
www.ekminspirations.com

Michael Davis, ACRW, CPRW, GCDF
Davis Resume Service
940 Ashcreek Dr.
Centerville, OH 45458
E-mail: mdavis49@hotmail.com

Kirsten Dixson, CPBS
Online Identity Expert, Kirsten Dixson LLC
Exeter, NH 03833
Phone: (603) 686-0330
E-mail: kirsten@kirstendixson.com
www.kirstendixson.com

George Dutch, BA, CMF, CCM, JCTC
JOBJOY
275 Slater St., Ste. 900
Ottawa, ON Canada K1P 5H9
Toll-free: (800) 798-2696
E-mail: george@jobjoy.com
www.jobjoy.com

Debbie Ellis, MRW, CPRW
Phoenix Career Group
Toll-free: (800) 876-5506
E-mail: debbie@phoenixcareergroup.com
www.phoenixcareergroup.com

Wendy S. Enelow, CCM, MRW, JCTC, CPRW
2265 Walker Rd.
Coleman Falls, VA 24536
Phone: (434) 299-5600
wendyenelow@wendyenelow.com
www.wendyenelow.com

Dayna Feist, CPRW, CEIP, JCTC
Gatehouse Business Services
265 Charlotte St.
Asheville, NC 28801
Phone: (828) 254-7893
E-mail: gatehous@aol.com
www.BestJobEver.com

Robyn L. Feldberg, ACRW, NCRW, CJSS, CCMC
Abundant Success Coach
1287 Blue Lake Dr.
Frisco, TX 75034
Phone: (972) 464-1144
Toll-free: (866) WIN-AJOB
Toll-free fax: (866) 923-7632
E-mail: Robyn@AbundantSuccessCoach.com
www.AbundantSuccessCoach.com

Louise Fletcher, CPRW
Blue Sky Resumes
15 Merriam Ave.
Bronxville, NY 10708
Phone: (914) 337-5742
E-mail: lfletcher@blueskyresumes.com
www.blueskyresumes.com

Julianne Franke, MS, CCMC, CPRW, MRW, Certified Life & Career Transition Coach, Certified NOW WHAT Facilitator
Breakthrough Connections
258 Shire Way
Lawrenceville, GA 30044
Phone: (770) 381-0876
Fax: (770) 381-0877
E-mail: jfranke1@bellsouth.net
www.breakthroughconnections.com

Louise Garver, CPRW, CMP, JCTC, CEIP, MCDP, CJSS, CPBS, CCMC, CLBF
Career Directions, LLC
P.O. Box 587
Broad Brook, CT 06016
Phone: (860) 623-9476
E-mail: louise@careerdirectionsllc.com
www.careerdirectionsllc.com

Sharon Green, CPRW, MA, LPC
Ace Resume
3040 E. Shea
Phoenix, AZ 85028
Phone: (602) 494-1688
E-mail: resource56@cox.net

Susan Guarneri, NCC, NCCC, CERW, CPRW, CCMC, CEIP, MCC, CPBS, CMBS, COIMS
Guarneri Associates
6670 Crystal Lake Rd.
Three Lakes, WI 54562
Toll-free: (866) 881-4055
E-mail: Susan@AssessmentGoddess.com
www.assessmentgoddess.com

Cheryl Ann Harland, CPRW, JCTC
Career Source, Inc./Resumes by Design
25227 Grogan's Mill Rd., Ste. 125
The Woodlands, TX 77380
Phone: (281) 296-1659
Toll-free: (888) 213-1650
E-mail: cah@ResumesByDesign.com
www.ResumesByDesign.com

Beverly Harvey, CPRW, JCTC, CCM, CCMC, MRW, CPBS, CLTMC, CJSS
Beverly Harvey Resume and Career Services
P.O. Box 750
Pierson, FL 32180
Phone: (386) 749-3111
Toll-free: (888) 775-0916
E-mail: beverly@harveycareers.com
www.harveycareers.com

Gayle Howard, CERW, CCM, CPRW, CRW
Top Margin Career Marketing
P.O. Box 74
Chirnside Park (Melbourne), VIC 3116
Australia
International phone: 613 9726 6694
E-mail: getinterviews@topmargin.com
www.topmargin.com

Lesa Kerlin, CPRW, MBTI Master Practitioner
LEK Consulants
1703 Meadow View Dr.
Kirksville, MO 63501
Phone: (660) 626-4748
Email: lesaeke@hotmail.com

Bill Kinser, MRW, CPRW, JCTC, CEIP, CCM
To The Point Resumes
4117 Kentmere Sq.
Fairfax, VA 22030
Phone: (571) 276-8342
E-mail: bkinser@tothepointresumes.com
www.tothepointresumes.com

Wanda Kiser, MBA, CPRW, CEIP, ACRW, CPCC
Advantage Career Services, Inc.
3525 Piedmont Rd.
7 Piedmont Center, Ste. 300
Atlanta, GA 30305
Toll-free: (877) 314-8872
Toll-free fax: (877) 314-8873
E-mail:
resumeinfo@advantagecareerservices.net
www.advantagecareerservices.net

Myriam-Rose Kohn, CPRW, CEIP, JCTC, CCM, CCMC
JEDA Enterprises
27201 Tourney Rd., Ste. 201
Valencia, CA 91355
Phone: (661) 253-0801
E-mail: myriam-rose@jedaenterprises.com
www.jedaenterprises.com

Cindy Kraft, CPBS, COIS, CCMC, CCM, JCTC, CPRW
Executive Essentials
P.O. Box 336
Valrico, FL 33595
Phone: (813) 655-0658
E-mail: cindy@cfo-coach.com
www.cfo-coach.com

Bonnie Kurka, CPRW, JCTC, FJST
Resume Suite
Tulsa, OK
Phone: (918) 494-4630
E-mail: bonnie@ResumeSuite.com
www.resumesuite.com

Louise Kursmark, MRW, CPRW, JCTC, CEIP, CCM
Best Impression Career Services, Inc.
Reading, MA 01867
Phone: (781) 944-2471
E-mail: LK@yourbestimpression.com
www.yourbestimpression.com

Lori Lebert, CPRW, IJCTC, CCMC
The Loriel Group/Resumes For Results
P.O. Box 267
Novi, MI 48376
Phone: (248) 380-6100
Toll-free: (800) 870-9059
E-mail: Lorie@DoMyResume.com and
Info@CoachingROI.com
www.DoMyResume.com and
www.CoachingROI.com

John Leggatt, MBA, M.Ed., ACRW, CPRW
Resume Architects
4152 Meridian St. #105-401
Bellingham, WA 98226
Phone/fax: (360) 733-9422
E-mail: John@ResumeArchitects.com
www.ResumeArchitects.com

Peter S. Marx, JCTC
Phone: (813) 832-5133
E-mail: marxps@aol.com

Sharon McCormick, MS, MCC, NCC, NCCC, CPRW
Sharon McCormick Expert Career & HR
Consulting, LLC
2530 Meridian Parkway
Durham, NC 27713
Phone: (919) 424-1244
E-mail: careertreasure@gmail.com
www.careertreasure.com

Eva Mullen, CPRW
A+ Resumes & Career Services
3000 Pearl St., Ste. G-1
Boulder, CO 80301
Phone: (303) 444-3438
E-mail: info@aplusres.com
www.aplusres.com

Carol Nason, CPRW
Career Advantage
95 Flavell Rd.
Groton, MA 01450
Phone: (978) 448-3319
E-mail: nason1046@aol.com
www.acareeradvantageresume.com

Kris Niklawski, ACRW
A-Professional Resume Service
3317 144th Court
Cumming, IA 50061
Phone: (515) 240-2950
E-mail: krisnik@L2speed.net

John O'Connor, MFA, CRW, CPRW, CCM, CECC, CFJST, CFRW
Career Pro Inc.
3700 National Dr., Ste. 215
Raleigh, NC 27612
Phone: (919) 787-2400
E-mail: john@careerproinc.com
www.CareerProResumes.com

Debra O'Reilly, CPRW, CEIP, JCTC, FRWC
A First Impression/www.resumewriter.com
Brandon, FL
Phone: (813) 651-0408
E-mail: debra@resumewriter.com
www.resumewriter.com

Don Orlando, MBA, CPRW, JCTC, CCM, CCMC
The McLean Group
640 S. McDonough
Montgomery, AL 36104
Phone: (334) 264-2020
E-mail: yourcareercoach@charterinternet.com

Tracy M. Parish, CPRW
Career*Plan,* Inc.
P.O. Box 957
Kewanee, IL 61443
Toll-free: (888) 449-2200
E-mail: resume@CareerPlan.org
www.CareerPlan.org
www.ExecutiveCareerSolutions.com
www.ResumesForSuccess.com

Loretta Peters, ACRW, MRW
Enterprising Careers
86 Tumblebrook Dr.
Vernon, CT 06066
Phone: (860) 463-1165
E-mail: lpeters@enterprisingcareers.com
www.enterprisingcareers.com

Sharon Pierce-Williams, M.Ed., CPRW
The Resume Doc
609 Lincolnshire Lane
Findlay, OH 45840
Phone: (419) 422-0228
E-mail: Sharon@TheResumeDoc.com
www.TheResumeDoc.com

Barb Poole, CCMC, CLTMC, CERW, CPRW, CPHR
Hire Imaging
St. Cloud, MN area
www.hireimaging.com

Judit Price, MS, CCM, IJCTC, CDFI, CPRW
Berke & Price Associates
6 Newtowne Way
Chelmsford, MA 01824
Phone: (978) 256-0482
E-mail: Judit.Price@comcast.net
www.careercampaign.com

Michelle Mastruserio Reitz, CPRW
Printed Pages
3985 Race Rd., Ste. 6
Cincinnati, OH 45211
Phone: (513) 598-9100
E-mail: michelle@printedpages.com
www.printedpages.com

Jane Roqueplot, CPBA, CWDP
JaneCo's Sensible Solutions
194 N. Oakland Ave.
Sharon, PA 16146
Phone: (724) 342-0100
E-mail: jane@janecos.com
www.janecos.com

Jennifer Rushton, CERW, CARW, CEIC, CWPP
Keraijen
Level 14, 309 Kent St.
Sydney, NSW 2000 Australia
Phone: 612 9994 8050
E-mail: info@keraijen.com.au
www.keraijen.com.au

Mary Schumacher, ACRW, CPRW, CEIP, CPCC
TheLadders Resume Services
resume.theladders.com

Debbie Shalom, MRW, ACRW, CCMC, MAT
Amazing Resumes & Coaching Services
2840 Quarry Heights Way
Baltimore, MD 21209
Phone: (410) 653-7679
E-mail: amazingresumes@comcast.net
www.amazingresumesmd.com

Janice M. Shepherd, CPRW, JCTC, CEIP
Write On Career Keys
Bellingham, WA 98226
Phone: (360) 738-7958
E-mail: janice@writeoncareerkeys.com
www.writeoncareerkeys.com

Igor Shpudejko, BSIE, MBA, CPRW, JCTC
Career Focus
23 Parsons Ct.
Mahwah, NJ 07430
Phone: (201) 825-2865
E-mail: Ishpudejko@aol.com

Marjorie Sussman, ACRW, MRW, CPRW
Dover Productions
148 Undercliff Ave. #3
Edgewater, NJ 07020
Phone: (201) 941-8237
E-mail: marjorie1130@aol.com

Ilona Vanderwoude, MRW, ACRW, CPRW, CCMC, CEIP, CJST
Career Branches
P.O. Box 330
Riverdale, NY 10471
Phone: (718) 971-6356
E-mail: ilona@careerbranches.com
www.careerbranches.com

Vivian VanLier, CPRW, JCTC, CEIP, CCMC
Advantage Resume and Career Services
6701 Murietta Ave.
Valley Glen (Los Angeles), CA 91405
Phone: (818) 994-6655
E-mail: vvanlier@aol.com
www.CuttingEdgeResumes.com

Rosa Vargas, MRW, NCRW, ACRW
Creating Prints
5301 Yosemite St.
Greenwood Village, CO 80111
Phone: (303) 600-8603
Toll-free fax: (888) 448-1675
E-mail: rvargas@creatingprints.com
www.creatingprints.com

Jitka Vesela, M.Ed., ACRW
Resume Architects
4152 Meridian St. #105-401
Bellingham, WA 98226
Phone/fax: (360) 733-9422
E-mail: Jitka@ResumeArchitects.com
www.ResumeArchitects.com

James Walker, MS
ACAP Center
Bldg. 210, Rm. 006, Custer Ave.
Ft. Riley, KS 66442
Phone: (785) 239-2278
E-mail: jwalker8199@yahoo.com

Pearl White, CPRW, JCTC, CEIP
A 1st Impression Resume & Career Coaching
Services
41 Tangerine
Irvine, CA 92618
Phone: (949) 651-1068
E-mail: pearlwhite1@cox.net
www.a1stimpression.com

LOCATION UNKNOWN

Trish Allen

Diana Holdsworth

Jan Holliday

Marcy Johnson

Michael Levy

Kim Little

Carol Rossi

Gail Taylor

IN MEMORIAM

Ellen Mulqueen

INDEX